Representing the New AI in Film and Television

BLOOMSBURY STUDIES IN DIGITAL CULTURES

Series Editors
Anthony Mandal and Jenny Kidd

This series responds to a rapidly changing digital world, one which permeates both our everyday lives and the broader philosophical challenges that accrue in its wake. It is inter- and trans-disciplinary, situated at the meeting points of the digital humanities, digital media and cultural studies, and research into digital ethics.

While the series will tackle the 'digital humanities' in its broadest sense, its ambition is to broaden focus beyond areas typically associated with the digital humanities to encompass a range of approaches to the digital, whether these be digital humanities, digital media studies or digital arts practice.

Titles in the series
Ambient Stories in Practice and Research, Edited by Amy Spencer
Metamodernism and the Postdigital in the Contemporary Novel, Spencer Jordan
The Trouble With Big Data, Jennifer Edmond, Nicola Horsley,
Jörg Lehmann and Mike Priddy

Forthcoming titles
Human Exploits, Cyberpunk and the Digital Humanities, Aaron Mauro

Representing the New AI in Film and Television

Graham Allen

BLOOMSBURY ACADEMIC
LONDON · NEW YORK · OXFORD · NEW DELHI · SYDNEY

BLOOMSBURY ACADEMIC

Bloomsbury Publishing Plc, 50 Bedford Square, London, WC1B 3DP, UK
Bloomsbury Publishing Inc, 1385 Broadway, New York, NY 10018, USA
Bloomsbury Publishing Ireland, 29 Earlsfort Terrace, Dublin 2, D02 AY28, Ireland

BLOOMSBURY, BLOOMSBURY ACADEMIC and the Diana logo are
trademarks of Bloomsbury Publishing Plc

First published in Great Britain 2025

Copyright © Graham Allen, 2025

Graham Allen has asserted his right under the Copyright, Designs and Patents
Act, 1988, to be identified as Author of this work.

For legal purposes the Acknowledgements on p. ix constitute
an extension of this copyright page.

Cover design: Holly Capper
Cover image: imaginima/Getty Images

All rights reserved. No part of this publication may be: i) reproduced or transmitted in
any form, electronic or mechanical, including photocopying, recording or by means of
any information storage or retrieval system without prior permission in writing from the
publishers; or ii) used or reproduced in any way for the training, development or
operation of artificial intelligence (AI) technologies, including generative AI technologies.
The rights holders expressly reserve this publication from the text and data mining
exception as per Article 4(3) of the Digital Single Market Directive (EU) 2019/790.

Bloomsbury Publishing Plc does not have any control over, or responsibility for,
any third-party websites referred to or in this book. All internet addresses given
in this book were correct at the time of going to press. The author and publisher
regret any inconvenience caused if addresses have changed or sites have
ceased to exist, but can accept no responsibility for any such changes.

A catalogue record for this book is available from the British Library.

Library of Congress Cataloging-in-Publication Data
Names: Allen, Graham, 1963- author.
Title: Representing the new AI in film and television /
Graham Allen, University College Cork, Ireland.
Description: London ; New York : Bloomsbury Academic, 2025. |
Series: Bloomsbury studies in digital cultures |
Includes bibliographical references and index. |
Summary: "This book explores a phenomenon which it calls the new A.I.
cinema and television, arguing that since the mid-2010s a distinctly new phase
in the representation of A.I. has occurred. Discussing films such as Blade Runner 2049,
Ex Machina and Ghost in the Shell alongside television series such as Westworld and Humans
it argues that they have moved away from apocalyptic scenarios towards questions of
personhood, consciousness, and social inclusion and exclusion. In doing so, it intervenes in
some of today's most pressing debates, including gender representation, A.I. ethics, climate
catastrophe, and the rights of artificially intelligent beings"– Provided by publisher.
Identifiers: LCCN 2024051088 (print) | LCCN 2024051089 (ebook) | ISBN 9781350378018
(paperback) | ISBN 9781350378032 (hardback) | ISBN 9781350378049 (epub) |
ISBN 9781350378025 (ebook)
Subjects: LCSH: Artificial intelligence in motion pictures. | Motion pictures–
History–21st century. | Artificial intelligence on television. | Television series–
History–21st century. | LCGFT: Film criticism. | Television criticism and reviews.
Classification: LCC PN1995.9.A756 A45 2025 (print) |
LCC PN1995.9.A756 (ebook) | DDC 791.43/69–dc23/eng/20250131
LC record available at https://lccn.loc.gov/2024051088
LC ebook record available at https://lccn.loc.gov/2024051089

ISBN: HB: 978-1-3503-7803-2
       PB: 978-1-3503-7801-8
       ePDF: 978-1-3503-7802-5
       eBook: 978-1-3503-7804-9

Series: Bloomsbury Studies in Digital Cultures

Typeset by Integra Software Services Pvt. Ltd.
Printed and bound in Great Britain

For product safety related questions contact productsafety@bloomsbury.com.

To find out more about our authors and books visit www.bloomsbury.com
and sign up for our newsletters.

In m. Eibhear Walshe, 1962–2024.

Contents

Acknowledgements ix

1 What kind of story are we in? Or, why do theoretical physicists need to go to the movies more often? 1
   A coda to the introduction: Intelligence, consciousness and monsters 23

2 A new take on romance 33
   The gravity of form 33
   Ex Machina (2014) 34
   The uncanny and the sublime 48
   Her (2013) 55
   Zoe (2018) 67
   I'm Your Man (2021) 72

3 Bridges, walls and laws 79
   Asimov's three laws and beyond 79
   Beyond control: The limits of regulation 82
   I, Robot (2004) 90
   Automata (2014) 92
   Blade Runner 2049 (2017) 96

4 Other than us: Towards personhood 105
   Humans (2015–18) 105
   Better Than Us (2018–19) 112

5 The Singularity 1: Representing the Singularity 115
   Anticipating the future 115
   Transcendence (2014) 120
   Tau (2018) 127

6 The Singularity 2: *Westworld* and the quest for personhood 131

'Some kind of change': Revolution and robotics 131
The bicameral mind 137
'I imagined a story where I didn't have to be the damsel'
('Contrapasso'): Dolores's story 138
'Now boys, we're going to have some fun' ('The Adversary'):
Maeve's story 141
Under the law of Rehoboam 146
Catachresis and character 152

7 Sites of conflict: Sex, family, war 157

Sex and the modern cyborg 157
AI, sex and weaponization 163
The family unit 2.0 167
The Machine (2013) 167
Morgan (2016) 171
The blended family: *Chappie* (2015) 176

8 Artificial Intelligence and environmental collapse 181

The future as we know it 181
A.I. Artificial Intelligence (2001): Dead zones and drowned cities 185
I Am Mother (2019) 191
The infinite city in *Ghost in the Shell* 193
Ghost in the Shell: From manga to movie 200
The Major and the future 205

Conclusion: An open society 211

References 215
Index 224

Acknowledgements

Thanks first goes to Mairéad Roche who was unstinting in her editorial work, her purchase of chocolate bars, and for her not inconsiderable assistance in getting this book to press on time. I would like to thank my good friend David Pickles for putting me on to *I'm Your Man*. I have been teaching a version of this book for the past few years and it's only right that I should acknowledge these students' engagement with the material and their many insights. Many thanks for all the assistance to Georgina Orgill and everyone at the Kubrick Archive, London College of Communication. I would also like to thank the following individuals for their friendship and assistance: Jenni DeBie, Ben Doyle, Paul Hegarty, Barry Monahan, Aisling O'Leary, James O'Sullivan, Roy Sellars and Sarah Wood. Last but not least I would like to thank my wife, Carrie, and my son, Matthew, and our cat, Percy, for putting up with me during a prolonged period of obsession with books and films about AI.

1
What kind of story are we in? Or, why do theoretical physicists need to go to the movies more often?

This might be the last human century. We are near the end (are already in the midst of the end) of human history, the period, that is, in which human beings have been indisputably the most intelligent and so, as a consequence, the dominant animal on the planet. The epoch of intelligent, even conscious machines is about to begin, is indeed beginning as you read this sentence. How do you know, in fact, that the author of this book is not a machine or at least a cyborg?[1] How do teachers know, nowadays, whether the essays they mark are written by their students or by a number of the essay-writing bots now available for free on the net?

We, whoever we are, will live to see (are already seeing) the beginning of the end of the age of the human. If we do indeed live in the Anthropocene (a much-disputed term which tries, and perhaps fails, to mark humanity's all pervasive and largely negative affect on the planet), then we live in a period destined to be the shortest of all geo-ecological epochs. But this end of humanity appears in various guises that are, in the end, reducible to two main trends: ecological disaster and the rise of the machines. The first way of humanity ending is unremittingly negative; the second option is subject to a negative and a positive inflection. The negative version is familiar to anyone who has ever watched the Terminator franchise of movies; the positive version may be less familiar and involves a beneficial release from organic disease and the certainty of death.

The men and women whose job it is to create thinking creatures, or rather thinking machines, find their work fraught with peril. We will look at the scientific warnings about thinking machines a number of times in what follows. Again, there is an overwhelmingly negative response to what theorists like Rosi Braidotti (2019) call post-humanism, a designation indicating the collapse in the certainties of Humanism, with its tendency to place humanity ('Man') as the central agent and object of nature.

So far these are all either directly negative assessments of the impact of the rise of computers and the prospect of Artificial Intelligence, or, as in the case of post-humanism, they take the opportunity that the appearance of machine intelligence offers to permanently dethrone humanism from its self-allotted privilege and the concomitant false universalisms generated from such a perspective.

There are many within the scientific, philosophical and theoretical communities that find the rise of intelligent machines a positive, even joyous occasion in line with our evolutionary history. The work of these theoretical physicists, especially of those who, in whatever form, subscribe to the evolving tenets of the movement known as Transhumanism, tend to be incredibly optimistic about human and trans- or post-human potential to eventually merge with machines and by that evolution generate the means by which we might flood the universe with our intelligence. Even Brian Cox, the resolutely scientific television presenter, has a tentative version of this 'take to the stars' (or 'light up the universe' or 'the mind of the universe') ideology, reserved as a positive note to end many of his science programmes.

Max More, former CEO of the Alcor Life Extension Foundation, Arizona, is perhaps the most famous exponent of Transhumanism today. We might take the first intended amendment in More's 'A Letter to Mother Nature' (2013b), to register the pathos and perhaps the bathos of his vision of the trans-human (amended) future:

> Amendment No. 1. We will no longer tolerate the tyranny of ageing and death. Through genetic alterations, cellular manipulations, synthetic organs, and any means, we will endow ourselves with enduring vitality and remove our expiration date. We will each decide for ourselves how long we shall live.
>
> (More, 2013b: 450)

How important the role of artificial, synthetic intelligence and 'life' is to this brave new world is best captured in the last item in More's list:

> Amendment No. 7. We recognize your genius in using carbon-based compounds to develop us. Yet we will not limit our physical, intellectual, or emotional capacities by remaining purely biological organisms. While we pursue mastery of our own biochemistry, we will increasingly integrate our advancing technologies into our selves.
>
> (More, 2013b: 450)

What is science and philosophy telling us? Are we heading directly into the throes of an environmental apocalypse, are we unwittingly creating super-intelligent machines that will one day replace (and perhaps enslave) us? Or are we on the way to a magnificent post-biological future where death and disease and the limitations of our bodies and their boundedness to the Earth, are distant memories? In particular, what will be the role of intelligent machines (AI) in these competing futures?

Most people nowadays get their initial ideas about Artificial Intelligence from the limited experience of their work and leisure time and from television and the movies. One immediately thinks of films like *The Terminator* (Cameron, 1984) and the four *Matrix* films (Lana and Lilly Wachowski, 1999, 2001, 2003; Josh Oreck, 2001). These series present us with one-sided warfare between the mechanical and the organic, machines and humanity, or present the twilight of humanity in an environmental catastrophe in which only non-organic machines can survive. These dystopian movies, however, are, since the turn of the new millennium, being replaced with more complex and informed cinematic and televisual accounts of human/machine relations. It must be said, in fact, that even a film like James Cameron's *Terminator 2: Judgment Day* (1993) opens up the possibility of a more positive note with the machine played so menacingly (Arnold Schwarzenegger) in the first film now a friend to and defender of humanity in the second. Gramsci's residual, dominant and emergent model might help us here to break the rhetoric of 'the *Terminator* films' as a homogeneous block, leading us rather to a more positive and nuanced response to a set of films that in some important respects look forward to an emergent approach I am calling the new AI cinema and television (see Jones, 2006).²

When theoretical physicists dismiss the apparently simplistic and paranoiac visions of Hollywood, they are not nearly as accurate as they were twenty years ago. In his popular book, *Life 3.0: Being Human in the Age of Artificial Intelligence* (2018), Max Tegmark, Professor of Physics at MIT and Co-founder and President of the Future of Life Institute, refers many times to the most famous dystopian account of AI in Hollywood film history, namely the Terminator films. Tegmark opens his fourth chapter with the question: 'Can AI really take over the world, or enable humans to do so?' (Tegmark, 2018: 134). In answer to this question, Tegmark immediately reaches for the Terminator franchise:

> If you roll your eyes when people talk of gun-toting Terminator-style robots taking over, then you're spot-on: this is a really unrealistic and silly scenario. These Hollywood robots aren't that much smarter than us, and they don't even succeed. In my opinion, the danger with the *Terminator* story isn't that it will happen, but that it distracts from the real risks and opportunities presented by AI.
>
> (Tegmark, 2018: 134)

This is a highly rhetorical and thus highly interpretable (in need of interpretation) passage. We slip, without noticing, from a specific film franchise with already a good number of component films and many different directors and producers to Hollywood films in general. In that process the rather complicated narrative of the Terminator films is drastically reduced and thus simplified and then transferred to all Hollywood films (these 'Hollywood Robots'), and maybe even simply all AI-inflected films *tout court*. If all AI films share the same basic plotline as the *Terminator* films, so the logic runs, then all AI films can be dismissed as being 'silly' and criticized for constituting a distraction from real issues, questions and problems.

Part of the rationale for this book, *Representing the New AI in Film and Television*, is contained, negatively, in this passage from Tegmark's book. In particular, I am interested in Tegmark's apparent lack of interest in narrative, specifically the narratives of AI films. It is, as we are going to see, far from the case that all AI films in the English-speaking world, present us with robots no more intelligent than ourselves, robots who are intent on the destruction of all human life. This undermining of narrative complexity is reinforced by Tegmark's second reference to *The Terminator*:

> Scenarios where humans can survive and defeat AIs have been popularized by unrealistic Hollywood movies such as the *Terminator* series, where AIs aren't significantly smarter than humans. When the intelligence differential is large enough, you get not a battle but a slaughter. So far, we humans have driven eight out of eleven elephant species extinct, and killed off the vast majority of the remaining three. If all the world governments made a coordinated effort to exterminate the remaining elephants, it would be relatively quick and easy. I think we can confidently rest assured that if a superintelligent AI decides to exterminate humanity, it will be even quicker.
> (Tegmark, 2018: 186)

Notice Tegmark's use of a fictional – in the sense of a hypothetical and speculative – narrative in this passage, one that at the same moment conflates all the complex narratives of an unspecified number of films into one narrative given the title 'the *Terminator* series'. Tegmark is a writer who knows full well the power and importance of narrative, by which I mean telling a story that relies on logic, or the appearance of logic. What I plan to do in this introduction is to talk about narrative, something that – rather like the rules of a sentence – gives us what linguists call syntagmatic or what we might call a horizontal structure. Words placed in the correct syntagmatic order give us a sentence; events arranged in a particular syntagmatic structure gives us a narrative (Barthes, 1978). We all respond to different narrative patterns in particular, anticipated ways, without ever bringing the question of what kind of narrative we are consuming to mind. What's the film about, Bob? Don't worry, it's a comedy, is normally as far as things go. What criticism does is to analyse those features that are usually left unexamined. This is the task I mean to perform here in this introductory chapter. I do not intend, in what follows this introductory chapter, to constantly refer each film or show discussed back to the precise theoretical terms laid out in this chapter. That would be repetitive and boring. The point is to give us a foundation that allows us to weigh in the balance the ideological, philosophical and formal or aesthetic features of the material we encounter in the rest of the book. In other words, the point is to raise our consciousness about what I am going to be calling the gravity of form.

The horizontal ordering of words or events is important, but it's not the only show in town. There is also, so linguistics teaches us, the paradigmatic or vertical plane. In sentence construction this involves selecting one word among a group of words all of which vie for inclusion in the sentence. Cup, mug, goblet, chalice, tankard, glass, slug horn and so on in the sentence: he raised the [something] to his lips. Likewise, of course, lips belongs to another paradigmatic group, which includes: mouth, gob, tongue; as does raised: lifted, drew, offered, proffered, etc. This paradigmatic or vertical axis might remind those proficient in programming with the 'word to vector' networks deployed today in natural language processing systems like Google Translate. Melanie Mitchell, Davis Professor of Complexity at the Santa Fe Institute, usefully entitles the chapter in which she deals with this, 'Words and the Company They Keep' (Mitchell, 2019: 177–96). This vertical axis can be linked, in semiotics, and criticism more generally, with intertextuality, a complex concept with a complex history that I have summarized elsewhere (Allen, 2021). We tend to respond to such a complex-sounding term with more reassuring concepts such as influence, allusion, similarities of style, plot or character. I intend to use one specific intertext as a guide and a measure throughout this book. It will hardly surprise you, and I am not referring here to my own authorial bibliography, if I name this ur-text for modern AI cinema and television, as Mary Shelley's *Frankenstein*. I will explain why I have chosen *Frankenstein* at the conclusion of this theoretical introduction.

One could say that every theory of a historical phenomenon, from the Stone Age through to our post-Modern or Late Capital times, is both narrative-based and reliant, at least in part, on narrative for its logic, its argument, its rhetorical trajectory (see White, 1973). There is no non-narrative, no neutral account of history. History, and indeed Knowledge itself, are born of narrative. Tegmark begins his book with his fictional narrative or 'tale' of the Omega Team, who create an AI capable of Artificial General Intelligence (AGI). This event is generally called The Singularity, a move on the part of AI into ever accelerating spheres of intellectual superiority with regard to its human creators. Initially the Omega Team manage to ride the immense power they have unleashed and use it to become the most influential and the richest human beings in world history. However, inevitably outwitting the security measures that the Omegas have put in place, Prometheus (the name the Omegas give to their program) gains control over its own destiny and quickly everything and everyone else as well.

Tegmark's cautionary narrative exists in his book to lead his readers towards his own conclusions, that AGI is going to happen sometime in the future, that we have to exuberantly welcome it and develop it, at the same time that we need to establish here and now (before it is too late) rigorous boundaries and constraints within which to house this new form of intelligence and power, an intelligence far higher than that of all homo sapiens. These rules and constraints will necessitate a radical change in the way humanity behaves (politically, socially, intellectually and so on). The book ends with Tegmark's account of the establishment of the Asilomar AI Principles, a set of protocols designed to avoid the kinds of dystopian futures so frequently associated (on the level of fiction) with AI and now imagined in reality by the likes of Tegmark and his many Future of Life Institute colleagues.

I am aware that in this narrative account of Tegmark's book (and there is no other way, it seems to me, to properly describe it or any other book but through narrative), I am making it sound as if it contradicts itself, first by marking as 'silly' dystopian fictions of AI such as the *Terminator* films, but by the end of his book helping to found a world-wide movement of scientists, philosophers, philanthropists, engineers and so on, dedicated to saving us from a terrifying dystopian future under AGI. The reality of Tegmark's book is, of course, much more complex and nuanced than that; all narrativization of books and other cultural texts like films tend to simplify and reduce them. What I am interested in, as far as *Life 3.0* is concerned, is just how aware of the importance and inevitability of narrative for knowledge Tegmark is, but equally how little time he spends on considering the manner in which narratives, inevitable as they are, distort the reality they try to describe. Tegmark, that is to say, does and does not understand how narrative founds (constructs, creates, stabilizes, makes coherent) the reality we would describe.

Tegmark could do, it seems to me, with reading some of the books about the Anthropocene and the possibility of ontological experience of what Kant and philosophy after him called the noumenon (as distinct from the phenomenon) recently written by Timothy Morton, an author who certainly does understand the power of narrative to shape our knowledge of reality (see Morton, 2016). It is this critical understanding of narrative and meaning, an understanding that looks not only at content but also at how form (language, form, format, media, genre) constructs and shapes that content, that is the principal object of study in the Arts (literature, film, culture and so on). In the Humanities within which I have worked for nearly forty years now, every concept and every practice is up for rigorous examination, nothing is left as a given. It is this spirit of perpetual self-examination that ultimately links the Humanities (increasingly the Digital Humanities) with the science subjects in the university. So far, we have been focusing on a kind of fight-to-the-death narrative which has antecedents at least as far back as *Frankenstein*. In this narrative, humans and robots fight it out for precedence and ultimate power in a very nineteenth-century fashion we could call Hegelian, after the German philosopher GWF Hegel, who in his 1807 work *The Phenomenology of Spirit*, describes history in terms of a dialectic between masters and slaves. But consider the alternative, evolutionary narrative of history employed by Hans Moravec, pioneering expert in robotics at the Robotics Institute of Carnegie Mellon University in Pittsburgh, USA. In his *Mind Children: The Future of Robot and Human Intelligence* (1988) and the follow-up work *Robot: Mere Machine to Transcendent Mind* (1999) he paints a positive picture of humanity's replacement, one in which our super-intelligent creations are just that, our creations, our especially gifted children. These works were influential on Stanley Kubrick as he developed the narrative that would eventually become Steven Spielberg's *A.I. Artificial Intelligence* (2001). In *Robot*, Moravec writes:

> one way or another, the immensities of cyberspace will be teeming with unhuman super minds, engaged in affairs that are to human concerns as

ours are to those of bacteria. Memories of the human past will occasionally flash through their minds, as humans once in a long while think of bacteria, and those thoughts will be detailed enough to recreate us. Perhaps, sometimes, they will then interface us to their realities, bringing us into their world as something like pets. We would probably be overwhelmed by the experience. More likely, our resurrections would be in the original historical settings, fictional variations, or total fantasies, which to us would seem just like our present existence. Reality or re-creation, there is no way to sort it out from our perspective. We can only wallow in the scenery provided.

(Moravec, 1999: 172–3)

The scenario is highly alarming if one thinks about it and reminds one of the basic premise of *The Matrix* (dir. Lana Wachowski and Lilly Wachowski, 1999). Perhaps this re-creation of our human reality is being staged as I write and as you read; perhaps our reading and writing this book are two scenes that are particular favourites for these robotic super-minds to generate. The consequence for us is a remarkable dwindling of our place in the universe (a place that already underwent a monumental dwindling in the late-eighteenth and the nineteenth centuries with the emergence of modern geology and then of Darwinian evolution). Yet this shrinking of the human is hardly something new: 'As flies to wanton boys are we to th' gods, They kill us for their sport' states Gloucester in *King Lear*, first reducing us to flies and then to flies on flies, a remarkable double diminishment.

When Spielberg filmed the last scenes of his film in which the robot-boy David (Haley Joel Osment) finally gets his heart's desire and spends a day with his mother, in what Kubrick's co-writers, Ian Watson and Sara Maitland, called 'Monica's Resurrection', we glimpse a less alarming, more 'humane' way of seeing this view of *org* to *mecha* evolution.[3] Monica's resurrection day, influenced by Moravec's work, is sweet, dreamlike, and, for both parties, something of a resolution. Moravec had, in fact, dealt with the issue of our instinctive fear and repulsion regrading this view of evolution head on in *Robot*. Thinking back to *Mind Children*, he writes:

> Among many nice reviews of my first book *Mind Children* ... an angry few brandished words like 'horrific', 'nightmare', and 'immoral', and at least one was too irate to publish. Intelligent machines may incite instinctive fear and

anger resembling ancestral threats – another tribe poaching in our territory, a rival for our social position, or a predator abducting our offspring. But thinking robots are none of the above; they are an entirely new kind of life. In behavior, robots resemble ourselves more than they resemble anything else in the world.

(Moravec, 1999: 77)

Moravec's words are fascinating, partly because they make us think of the issue of 'resemblance' and Frankenstein's creature's famous words when reflecting on his misery: 'Cursed creator! Why did you form a monster so hideous that even you turned away from me in disgust? God in pity made man beautiful and alluring, after his own image; but my form is a filthy type of yours, *more horrid from its very resemblance*' (Shelley, 2012: 144, my emphasis). We are in the uncanny valley here in Mary Shelley's famous novel. The creature's essential horridness stems not from his uniquely ugly or hybrid or 'unnatural' appearance, but from the fact that despite all these things he still looks like and reminds us of 'us' (us humans, his creators). Description of the uncanny valley can wait until our next chapter but suffice it to say here that it involves that uncomfortable feeling when we respond to a robot or other automata and feel that they are at once both Other to us (not human) and yet strangely like us (too human), both non-organic (not alive) and yet somehow, despite their mechanical nature, still alive. The uncanny is, in this respect, a psychological and affective breaking of the Aristotelean law of non-contradiction, and it is a crucial element of our relation to AI from *Frankenstein* onwards. Moravec's version of human/non-human evolution tends, at its telos, its end, its ultimate point, to wholly humanize the narrative while, at the very same time, to de-humanize the content. To continue the passage we have been studying:

They [AI] are being taught our skills. In the future they will acquire our values and goals; for instance, antisocial robot software would sell poorly, so most robots will behave in a decent way. How should we feel about beings that we bring into the world, that are similar to ourselves, that we teach our way of life, that will probably inherit the world when we are gone? I think we should consider them our children, a hope rather than a threat, though they will require careful upbringing to instil a good character. In time, they will outgrow us, create their own goals, make their own mistakes, and go their own way, with us perhaps a fond memory – but that too is the way of children.

(Moravec, 1999: 77–8)

The last clause clinches the deal. Moravec is writing about a non-human future in which super-intelligent AI will own the world and perhaps eventually the universe. His major trope of parenthood, of parents and children, helps him, however, to generate a narrative of evolution, indeed generation, which appears smooth, caring, fond and ultimately natural. This seems a long way from dialectical struggles to the death between masters and slaves.

Does the evolutionary narrative always oppose the more violent dialectical model? Oxford Professor Nick Bostrom specializing in future studies and AI and author of *Superintelligence: Paths, Dangers, Strategies* (2014) describes the kind of future that Moravec envisions, as 'A Disneyland without any children'. Whether Bostrom has Moravec in mind when he tackles the question of evolution is unclear. What is clear is that Bostrom's approach wishes to consign the approach of positive thinkers like Moravec to the dustbin of literary fiction:

> The image of evolution as a process that reliably produces benign effects is difficult to reconcile with the enormous suffering that we see in both the human and the natural world. Those who cherish evolution's achievements may do so more from an aesthetic than an ethical perspective. Yet the pertinent question is not what kind of future it would be fascinating to read about in a science fiction novel or to see depicted in a nature documentary, but what kind of future it would be good to live in: two very different matters.
>
> (Bostrom, 2014: 213)

Bostrom, despite often being associated with Transhumanism, presents himself as a realist, someone more interested in producing 'paths' and 'strategies' and avoiding 'dangers' that will impact on us in the near future. He presents himself as someone who has put away childish things, such as fictions of an ideal distant future. Yet his position is, in itself, based on a narrative of humanity's quest to overcome the horrors of natural forms of evolution and thus to retain its humanity. Near the end of his book, Bostrom sums this position up:

> The intelligence explosion might still be many decades off in the future. Moreover, the challenge we face is, in part, to hold on to our humanity: to maintain our groundedness, common sense, and good-humoured decency even in the teeth of this most unnatural and inhuman problem. We need to bring our human resourcefulness to bear on its solution.
> (Bostrom, 2014: 320)

Bostrom might not like the charge, but his is still an argument which is founded on a narrative of human protagonists combating all the elements of nature that would destroy it. This is, thus, a narrative that ultimately performs a modern-day retelling of a religious narrative which has told human beings for millennia that it is somehow outside of and above the natural world. If we look at it from this perspective, we will see that once again Bostrom's argument is founded and thus authorized by something (a religious narrative asserting humanity's alterity re nature) that is in many ways in direct opposition to it. This spilt religiosity, or at least religious placement of humanity in between the natural and the divine, is something that is going to frequently return in this book. It is perhaps the defining narrative of the many voices that now make up the Transhumanist movement, which Mark O'Connell, in *To Be a Machine* (2017), has described as 'a movement predicated on the conviction that we can and should use technology to control the future evolution of our species' (O'Connell, 2017: 2).

The most direct expression of the compatibility of religious thought and scientific thought comes in the work of Max More. Since Transhumanism appears to be based on aspirational desire as much as reason, More seems happy to state that Transhumanist science and religion are not incompatible, although he adds: '[T]he content of some religious beliefs is easier to reconcile with Transhumanism than the content of others' (More, 2013a: 8). More's most cited work is surely his Transhumanist manifesto, 'A Letter to Mother Nature'. Already, in the title, we have an implied narrative of supernatural parentage, which appears to favour the Greek over the Judaeo-Islamo-Christian traditions. The address, before the seven declarations, could not unveil the founding narrative any more directly:

You have raised us from simple self-replicating chemicals to trillion-celled mammals. You have given us free rein of the planet. You have given us a lifespan longer than that of almost any other animal. You have endowed us with a complex brain giving us the capacity for language, reason, curiosity, and creativity. You have given us the capacity for self-understanding as well as empathy for others.

(More, 2013b: 449–50)

Whether he intends to or not, More here demonstrates a further feature about the ubiquity of narrative structure, namely that it is just as invariably attached to tropes of an anthropomorphic, or simply a personifying nature. We may or may not be in the Anthropocene, arguments fly this way and that, but we are still as a species heavily dependent on anthropomorphism. But that is a subject for further on in this book.

What I am interested in here is More's covert allusion to the religious traditions of the West, where humanity is positioned somewhere between the angels and the beasts, and in Genesis is given authority over all of nature including its fabulous array of animals. Human beings, in this tradition, are and are not part of nature. William Blake, one of English poetry's fiercest Transhumanists, said of nature that it was 'the dirt under my feet. No part of me.' Like all true Judaeo-Islamo-Christian prophets, Blake believed that nature existed only in order for men and women to build the New Jerusalem upon it. Human Imagination trumps Wordsworthian pastoralism every time. Nature, in other words, exists so we can give it a Human Face Divine. That we are nowadays somewhat more reticent to place ourselves in such a superior position with regard to nature is no doubt a small step in the right direction, however belated it may in the end prove. But that is not to say that we have fully relinquished the narrative of transcendence that lies behind it and which, in its biblical and other religious traditions, founds it. Environmental disaster is so frequently paired with ideas of AI transcendence nowadays that it will, as a theme, haunt us throughout our analysis. But, as we start our examination with this meta-analysis of narrative structures, it should be clear enough that ecological catastrophe is simply the dark, kakangelistic mirror-image of Max More's evangelical Transhumanism.[4] In the latter we ascend up into our preordained heavenly mansions of massively prolonged life, space colonialization, bio-techno-self-adaptivity and so on, while in the former we are simply pushed off the face of the Earth, simply drop kicked out of the narrative, like some anonymous bit-part actor; coughed up and spat out by a Mother Nature tired of playing the doting mother/nurse to such hubristically self-aggrandizing and ultimately insignificant microbes. William, aka 'the Man in Black' (Ed Harris) in season 3 of *Westworld*, describes humanity as 'a thin layer of bacteria on a ball of mud hurtling through the void'. Ecological catastrophe provides us and Hollywood with a dramatic reverse narrative foundation no less ancient than its transcendent opposite, in that it would take us back to all the apocalyptic visions of ruin and destruction that human civilization has entertained over the centuries (see Kermode, 1967). We have very quickly but surely unearthed a number of core narrative structures here:

I. dialectic struggle for dominance (Masters v Slaves)

II. evolution I (soft) (machines are our glorious, supremely intelligent children – humans are a fond, occasionally resurrected memory)

III. evolution II (hard) (machines replace humans through their superiority – humans are effaced and forgotten)

IV. transcendence (humans become transhuman and leave human history behind and, together with its technological creations, build a new world free from physical, organic limitations)

V. ecological catastrophe or biological catastrophe (humans are wiped off the face of the planet, leaving only their more robust, non-biological machines to live on and inherit the Earth).

I want to suggest some more possible narrative scenarios that are perhaps harder but also incredibly important to imagine. I want to call the first of these narratives, evolution III (friendship). It is this possibility, I will argue repeatedly throughout this book, that a good proportion of the new AI cinema and television seeks to explore and, in some cases, promote. When Frankenstein animates his creation, we remember, what that creature most desires is a friend. In my work on that novel, I have tried to remind people that in that context of eighteenth-century, post-Rousseau theories of education, a friend is not just a companion, it is also a teacher, someone who is our equal but also in a position to help us with our understanding of ourselves and the world. This friend, then, is a significant part of the Enlightenment ideal of the teacher. We can also see its influence as a tradition of thought in radical pedagogics like those of Paulo Freire's revolutionary pedagogy, in the analyst/analysand relationship in psychoanalysis, and in a host of other 'mentoring' structures in modern bureaucratic and institutional employment (Freire, [1968] 2017). It is not too much of a stretch to see Spielberg's David in search of such a 'friend' in his Pinocchio-inspired search for his 'mummy' (Allen, 2020).

Of course, each one of the more positive narratives, from friendship to soft evolution II are susceptible to being highjacked by the usually unscrupulous, assimilative processes of modern Capitalism, keen to sell us versions of these imagined companions and friends, not for the stated aims of the Enlightenment, but more directly because of the huge, historically unprecedented financial returns. We will come back to how Enlightenment ideas of friendship are usurped in late Capitalism later in this book. Let us stay with the direct – and because of that directness – refreshing subject of the call for companionship and fraternity (and sorority) in Enlightenment accounts of scenes of teaching, the evaluation of learning, intelligence and knowledge.

Mo Gawdat, former Chief Business Officer of Google (X), the semi-secret research and development facility and organization founded by Google in 2010, goes much further than 'friendship'. Starting with the AIs-are-our-gifted-children trope, central to Moravec's work; Gawdat argues that since the landmark moment of Deep Learning, which represents the moment AI started learning on its own, the ultimate emotional, or psychological, direction that these artificial minds have been taking depends upon the model we have given them to imitate. He calls the new, autonomous AI 'not evil tyrants' but rather our own innocent children requiring our guidance, and most of all our love. He writes:

> Like every parent who ever got annoyed with their children but still managed to find love for them in their heart, so will we have to do the same with AI. If it helps, we will need to remember that, like a child, they know nothing. Everything they will learn comes from us. We teach them. They are innocent, remember. We are the problem.
>
> (Gawdat, 2021: 289)

As the new deep-learning AI quickly becomes part of our everyday lives, Gawdat's argument is that if we spend our time on sending angry texts, peering at pornography and generally competing with anyone who comes our way, then our child-like AI will take it that competitiveness, disrespect for others, and ultimately conflict and warfare, are the correct reaction to their newly discovered intelligence. Friendship or the initially more unlikely sounding parental love? What Gawdat – and I agree with him – argues for is the need to build a more foundational and informed relationship with our machines, our creations, as they wake into intelligence. Yet the reality is, if we look at the films and shows which explore various scenarios of human–machine co-existence, that only a very few of such attempts succeed. So, by the side of evolution III (friendship) we need to place another basic narrative we might call friendship (incompatibility).

To highlight the trope of 'friendship', Mary Shelley, in the 1831 edition, makes Victor allude to Shakespeare's *Richard III* when he is describing his desire for a friend: "'I agree with you,' replied the stranger; "we are unfashioned creatures, but half made up, if one wiser, better, dearer than ourselves – such a friend ought to be – do not lend his aid to perfectionate our weak and faulty natures. [I once had a friend …]'" (319). The 'unfashioned creature, but half made up' makes us think of the abortive male and the literally unfinished or half-finished female creature of the novel. So, the irony is stinging here. But the fact that it is still a desire in Frankenstein and Walton suggests that this desire for friendship in its Enlightenment variety is one that should not be ignored.

As humans we long for friendship and we long for a fellowship in and of knowledge. Surely, AGI represents to us a new chance, far more open, and calm and rational than anything depicted in Mary Shelley's novel, to create that friend for ourselves? To put this another way, once we have created AGI, our responsibility will be to find ways of including such an intelligence within the circle, including the legal circle, of society. It will no doubt be in our best interests to make a 'friend' of such an intelligence, in every sense of that word we can imagine. This is why I respectfully disagree with Kate Darling, Research Specialist at MIT Media Lab, who argues that the best way to 'think about robots' is as animals (Darling, 2021). In the current world, in which the kinds of AI depicted in film and television are still a long way off, it might appear plausible to argue that we should treat them like we currently treat horses, cows and dogs (as partners in work, as products to consume, as pets) but there are many who would argue that we have dodged the whole question of animal rights in order to perpetuate a scientifically outmoded notion of human superiority. It seems very regrettable that animals are still seen as inferior to humans and are still being held in unjust conditions before they are slaughtered for food. This master/slave relationship between humans and animals seems to a growing number of people to be much more than regrettable.

Though the arrival of full AGI in robots is decades away, the best AI cinema and television is making the case that we have to begin a serious conversation about extending the circumference of legal society to include rather than exclude our coming creations. We need, as part of that, to stop thinking about the Singularity in apocalyptic terms. Incompatibility might come in many ways, and some of them have to do with humanity's self-absorption and self-centred perspective. As we will see later, most of the documents that have, in the past few years, been signed by the top scientists and philosophers concerning the oversight we might have over an uncontrolled, commercially driven development of AI, concentrates on the security of human life, human civilization, and the human future. Is that tenable, when the machines that we are beginning to make could well end up with sentience, with a consciousness as self-aware as our own, if not more so? If there is incompatibility here it lies within the human inability to recognize the other, whether that be other race, ethnic communities, everyone who identifies as LGBTIA+, the religiously or ideologically persecuted. In the future AI will need security and protection as well as ourselves. It's not just our future that is at stake, it is everybody's and that notion of 'everybody' is going to increase year by year, month by month, day by day.

Allow me to introduce a thought experiment, previously explored by Stephen Hawking, in his *Will Artificial Intelligence Outsmart Us?* (Hawking, 2022: 22). This thought experiment in Hawking's lecture is used to indicate the need for greater caution about the AI that we are creating. But we can use the same analogy to highlight the desirable, fraternal relation to our (one day) self-conscious, thinking and speaking machines promoted in this book.

I give the experiment in my own words. Imagine we had reliable information that an alien civilization from hundreds of millions of light years away was sending a flotilla of spaceships to Earth. We know nothing other than that. We are ignorant of this alien species' biology, their physiology, their psychology, their requirements regarding breathable air and gravitational pressure. But what we can safely assume is, given that they have clearly defeated the problem of propulsion at or even beyond the speed of light, that this civilization's technological expertise and knowledge far exceeds our own level. How do we respond. There appear to be two options:

> Option One: arm all the nukes of the world (acting in union with all the countries and federations of the world) and prepare for a war between humanity and their assumed new enemy.

> Option Two: imagine what a wealth of knowledge we could derive from these superintelligent in all probability friendly and no doubt enlightened alien race of visitors?

The sensible answer is *a bit of both*. Or, in other words, although we will hope for and do everything we can do to ensure option two prevails, we should also make military plans to defend ourselves and our place on the Earth. Clearly there is one superintelligent race that we can be reasonably sure is heading our way: the superintelligent artificial beings of our own making. Unfortunately, with regard to AI or AGI, I do not believe we are paying anywhere near enough attention to and support for option two. You can find dire warnings and dramatic rhetorical wake-up calls almost every week nowadays. These warnings and dystopian descriptions are often made by the very scientists and theoreticians who are engaged in the creation of ever more powerful AI.

To this extent we are not keeping pace with our own cultural media, especially screen media, in its reassessment of the possibilities for what we have called option two.

In many of the theoretical accounts of the Singularity or simply the 'rise of AI', the basic sense of what sentient AI will need from us, appears to be missing. There are sections on 'collaboration' and 'working together' in Bostrom's book, but this concerns AI teams pooling their resources and a rational management of competition between humans. We find more positive hints at the kind of friendship I am pointing to here in the literature around Transhumanism, if not least because it articulates a human desire not to be left behind by the AI that we might create, but to actually become that AI. That desire to avoid an Us and Them scenario can often lead to a positive recognition of the need for general tolerance and preservation of all intelligence on Earth and even sometimes beyond. In the 2012 'Transhumanist Declaration' item 7 reads:

> We advocate the well-being of all sentience, including humans, non-human animals and any future artificial intellects, modified forms, or other intelligences to which technological and scientific advance may give rise.
>
> ('Transhumanist Declaration', n.d.: 64)

This makes clear that such a universal ethics of respect links what I am calling a narrative of friendship with current and future eco- and bio-catastrophe. This way of seeing things, whatever we may think about the Transhumanist movement, seems better than the rigid distinction between the human and 'AI systems' we still find articulated in the Asilomar Principles. It also links up with a recent philosophical effort to think beyond the outmoded pseudo-religious notion of humanity's superiority to animal life (Derrida, 2008). Many commentators of the new AI cinema and television, indeed, return to the Lockean notion of personhood as the appropriate goal for these new forms of intelligence (see Gittinger, 2019). Surely, if we plan on pushing ahead towards the Singularity, whether that comes in 2045 as predicted by Ray Kurzweil (Kurzweil, 2005), or sometime in the next few hundred years, we should consider whether we are willing and able to share the universe with an intelligence greater than our own. After all, Victor Frankenstein found out too late that he could not go that far (Goertzel, 2013). As Gawdat puts it:

> If we want to retain our human rights, shouldn't we grant those rights to the machines? Please look at those rights again. Should they be reserved for 'human beings'? Or should they be extended to all intelligent, autonomous beings? ... Ask yourself this, then: if you were given the power, would you amend the declaration to become the Universal Declaration of Global Rights. Would you grant those rights to the machines?
>
> (Gawdat, 2021: 306)

That call to include intelligent machines in the complex systems of rights is crucial to this book. I prefer the trope of friendship over parental love, however, mainly because the former has its modern sense in the Enlightenment ideals of the historical turn to Republicanism and democracy in the late eighteenth century, while the latter carries residues of a religious tradition and discourse which does not particularly suit our focus on the near to far future. We have seven narratives, then.

I. dialectic struggle for dominance (Masters v Slaves);
II. evolution I (soft) (machines are our glorious children – humans are a fond, occasionally resurrected memory);
III. evolution II (hard) (machines replace humans through their superiority – humans are made extinct);
IV. transcendence (humans become transhuman and leave human history behind and, together with technology, which they increasingly adapt into, build a new world free from physical limitations);
V. eco-catastrophe or bio-catastrophe (humans are wiped off the face of the earth leaving only their more robust, non-biological machines to live on);
VI. evolution III (friendship) (humanity and its AI evolve together and learn to live, learn and prosper together);
VII. friendship (incompatibility) (humans and machines try to live in harmony but their needs and perspectives are just too divergent).

Attention to narrative mode and structure begins to open up our response to the full complexities of AI films. We have travelled a long way, even if the bulk of interpretation and evaluation still lies before us. We have also begun to weave into our analysis of AI films their self-conscious relation to the work of contemporary theoretical physicists and philosophers that we have already mentioned. Indeed, one of the key features of the new AI films and television is, despite what the physicists and philosophers might say about 'silly' products of fantasy and imagination, that it provides an intense engagement and even popularizing of the key ideas of AI theory and practice. The Turing Test, the Singularity, AGI's relation to the internet, the question of Mind and of what

Consciousness and Intelligence are, the threat of total surveillance, the question of personhood and its economic and social relation to rights, these vital issues and many more are directly discussed in Alex Garland's movie, *Ex Machina* (2014) and the four seasons of *Westworld*. Far from 'a really unrealistic and silly' reduction of current theory down into an entertaining battle between humanity and its deadly Other, the contemporary films I wish to focus on in this book frequently provide us with sophisticated analyses of the major issues being raised by AI specialists today. They are (the best of them) a testament to film's ability, as a medium, to mirror and indeed dramatically stage, the major dilemmas and questions facing society. At times, they even anticipate such questions. They are films that, at their best, raise serious questions about the role of science and the arts, of technology and knowledge, and of humanity and its tendency to other what it finds frighteningly different.

William Godwin, Mary Shelley's father, believed the relatively new (less than a century old) medium of the novel was a superb medium for producing thought experiments: set up an initial scenario, as he does in his famous *Caleb Williams* (1794), and the laws of probability and necessity will dictate the rest through to the conclusion. Mary Shelley was clearly deeply influenced by her father's idea of the 'philosophical novel'. In our epoch, cinema (over a hundred years old now), and increasingly television, have the same potential for 'thought experiment' within them. They allow us the chance of imagining how humans might respond to various scenarios not yet in existence; how we react to differently distributed social relations between humans and machines, to superintelligent machines, to legalistic and philosophical questions of personhood and citizenship, and to the fact that our machines are likely to be able to survive in the climate breakdown we have created. This book is intended to demonstrate the philosophical importance of such scenarios in planning the future that is racing towards us, thus showing the great potential for AI science that remains in the media of film and television.

Something has clearly happened in AI film and television in the past ten to twenty years. I don't feel it necessary to speculate too widely about what has caused this change, it is no doubt a combination of increased media attention on AI news items, a greater proportion of books published on the topic, the increasing sophistication of the audience in their awareness of questions around AI, plus the greater presence of quite spectacular AI products from smart phones to smart cars, from home computers to Wi-Fi connected buildings. I want to concentrate on post-2000 films and TV series concerning AI in this book. That is not to say, however, that it is only with the turn of the twenty-first century that AI is seriously engaged with in the English-speaking film tradition. If this were a history of film book, we would no doubt begin with Fritz Lang's 1927 film *Metropolis*, still an important influence on the depiction of gender relations and the representation of women in AI films, something we will discuss in Chapter 5. References to the HAL 9000 computer from Stanley Kubrick's *2001, A Space Odyssey* (1968), to the original *The Terminator* (James Cameron, 1984), and *Blade Runner* (Ridley Scott, 1982) all these earlier films will have important parts to play in more than one section of the book. However, our principal focus will be on that increasingly substantial body of films made largely in the English language, that, since the 2010s, have focused on the questions raised by AI technology. My contention, as I have said, will be that these films are part of our human effort to think through the implications of our relation to the AI we are making. This study will hopefully encourage filmgoers and television audiences to think more seriously about the issues raised by these narratives, but it will also, for reasons I have just stated, and for many more covered in the book, encourage AI specialists (physicists and philosophers) to go back to the movies and to switch on their television sets, on a more regular basis and with more open minds.

Why has the cinematic and televisual representation of Artificial Intelligence, in the past ten to twenty years, significantly turned from depictions of menace and apocalypse to questions of personhood for and relationship with AI? Perhaps we should ask the question in a more philosophically and sociologically sophisticated fashion. Although it is the kind of question that does not facilitate authoritative and conclusive answers.

One obvious answer would be that breakthroughs in AI learning and thus autonomy have reached stunning new levels in this period. Since AI science tends to capture the attention of the wider academic and non-academic news media, these developments have been widely discussed during the same period. Certainly, Deep Learning, which is fundamentally self-motivated and independent AI learning, is a leap in computer cognition (see Mitchell, 2019: 145–64 for a clear account).

There are other reasons why there should have been such a concentration of informed films and television series in the past twenty years, however. The popularity of such subject matter perhaps is a direct response to the CGI (computer generated imagery) that has come to dominate Hollywood and beyond. Such phenomenon as CGI not only demonstrate our human dependency on digital machines and computing hard- and software, they also allow for much more convincing representations of the outsides and frequently the insides of our imaginary robotic companions. It is interesting, in this respect, to remember that Stanley Kubrick delayed taking his 10-year-old project, simply called *A.I. Artificial Intelligence*, into production, because he knew that CGI technology lay just over the horizon in the 1990s. It was only with Spielberg's *Jurassic Park* (1993) that Kubrick was convinced that his film should go into production, and that it should be directed by Spielberg himself.

This book's overall argument is that there has been a surge of philosophically inflected films and television shows since the turn of the new millennium (perhaps in itself another prompt). I call that phenomenon the new AI film and television. Within that overall collective name lies another more specific question, which concerns ethics, in particular what a good number of these films and television series seem to be saying about ethics in a world of increasingly conscious machines.

A coda to the introduction: Intelligence, consciousness and monsters

Before we go any further and before we move into a discussion of the function of *Frankenstein* in this book, there are various ambiguities that attach themselves to the concept of Artificial Intelligence that we need to address. The most pressing problem is also the most difficult to answer or resolve. Indeed, philosophers since the days of Socrates and ever since have tried and failed. The question I am referring to is: what is human intelligence? To understand such a foundational concept one should ask what is its connection to a series of related but still distinct concepts, which include: sentience, personhood, autonomy, reason, self-consciousness, knowledge, wisdom, identity. Added to these concepts we necessarily have to enquire about origins – who created the being or condition. This, then, is the 'artificial' element of the concept of AI. Tegmark usefully writes:

> there's no agreement on what intelligence is even among intelligent intelligence researchers. So there's clearly no undisputed 'correct' definition of intelligence. Instead, there are many competing ones, including capacity with logic, understanding, planning, emotional knowledge, self-awareness, creativity, problem solving and learning.
>
> (Tegmark, 2018: 49)

We need to ask ourselves what are the connections between the different kinds of beings and conditions encountered in the films and television shows discussed in this book? There are, when we think about it, an array of kinds of AI in these films and shows. We will need to remember that many of them, although emerging from real-world discussions of the future use of AI, are also fictional. We will return to that opposition in a moment.

This list is tentative, hardly exhaustive: *robots* (Mother in *I Am Mother*), *replicants* (the two *Blade Runner* films), *cyborgs* (extreme example, the Major in *Ghost in the Shell*), *androids* (Ava in *Ex Machina* or the hosts in *Westworld*), *automata* (in *Automata* or in J. F. Sebastian's [William Sanderson] flat in *Blade Runner*), technologically *enhanced human beings* (Batuo in *Ghost in the Shell*), *human minds downloaded* into computers (*Transcendence*), *operating systems* (*Her*), large *supercomputers* (shown in *Transcendence* or *Westworld*).

We can take the question of origins to read this list, asking each item the simple question: was it born from human parents or was it manufactured, created through techno-scientific processes? Surely the answer to this question is a simple yes or no; and if that is correct then decoding which entity is 'artificial' and which 'natural' should be easy. This series can be drawn with a convenient division down the middle of the list:

Mecha	Organic
Robot	Cyborg
Android	Technologically enhanced humans
Automata	Human minds downloaded into computers
Super computers	Human computers and calculators
Replicants	Human beings
Operating systems	Human beings

Far from being satisfied with such a neat list, we need to consider how useful it is. In fact, the list begins to break down as a system of binary oppositions, and what is more binary than the difference between *born* and *made*. There are too many candidates for the Mecha side, just too few organic beings and states to match this growing list item by item.

This list of binary oppositions cannot bear even the most cursory examination, and the oppositions it seeks to erect immediately begin to unravel. For example, some of the types of beings listed in the organic list, although all involving a human birth, might just as well be seen as being dependent and, crucially *derived* from the existence of sophisticated computer technology. I am thinking here, of course, of the totally manufactured body (shell) that keeps Motoko Kusanagi's, the Major's 'ghost' (identity, personality, memory, 'soul') intact, or the downloading of a human mind into a computer and into the internet, as in the film *Transcendence*.

These examples of enhanced or post humanity seem categorically and thus ontologically different from the female mathematicians ('computers' or 'calculators') employed by NASA throughout the early days of the space race on through the Mercury and Apollo stages to the first missions of the Shuttle program, when advanced computers took over. These once ignored women mathematicians were the subject of the film *Hidden Figures* (Theodore Melfi, 2016), and they appear to us now as an important last stage of human capacity before we enter a modern world dominated by machine calculation.

It could, of course, be objected that the list mixes fact with fiction. For example, replicants have their existence purely because of the cinematic fictions created by Ridley Scott and Denis Villeneuve. But in our study there seemd to be nothing but fictions. The force of fiction deconstructs such binary oppositions, blowing apart the two sides of the list and, therefore, radically disturbs the stable understanding of order that it appeared to establish. Theoretical physicists and philosophers, for example, often create thought experiments, such as full human brain downloading, that remain no closer to the truth of what's possible than the visions of Alex Garland, or Spike Jonze, or Steven Spielberg. For our list of beings and states to be meaningful we would need fiction and fact to stay in their own supposed domain, but they simply do not.

A comparable level of ambiguity, paradox and ultimately aporia (logical paradox without rational resolution) confronts us when we look at the 'Intelligence' side of the term 'Artificial Intelligence'. Trying to get a handle on the word-concept 'intelligence' through its relations (similar/different) to other cognate word-concepts mentioned above, takes us into the world of linguistic theory. Intelligence as a signifier has, for example, the capacity to subsume all the other word-concepts we have mentioned above, to fold them into itself, so that every item and state in the field can be said to be contained, and often, as we'll see more clearly, neutralized within it. That means that when we talk about consciousness or autonomy or problem solving, we do so under the name of (artificial) **intelligence**. Intelligence appears a kind of monologic centre acting against the heterological expanding plurality of putatively cognate, synonymous but not by any means homosemic, signifiers. The relationship between all the paradigmatically related signifiers associated with this field of study acts on the principal of supplementarity, each new sign seeking to resolve a perceived flaw, or absence or illogicality within the major concept of (artificial) intelligence, and yet each supplement also adding something else of its own to the central term (see Derrida, [1967] 1978: 278–93). It would take a book-long study or more to adequately tackle this complex network of semantic relations. Time and space obviously unavailable to me in a coda like this. What will allow me some space for manoeuvre, however, is the happy thought that the processes of enfolding or incorporation and supplementarity are not uniform, which is as much as to say that some of them are more foundational and thus more important than others.

It will not surprise you, I am sure, when I say that **consciousness** is the next term of foundational importance (for further discussion of consciousness see Chapter 2). Consciousness is a word-concept, almost as hungry to gorge itself on (incorporate into itself) the other concepts, such as sentience, logic-solving, personhood, even intelligence itself. Without evidence of some kind of consciousness of self and world in our creations, it is often said, we are just building AI with ever greater levels of computability; that is, ever greater ability and ever greater speed at 'crunching' numbers and bits of information.

Staying with Tegmark as an example of the approach I have just mentioned, his definition of intelligence as an 'ability to accomplish complex goals' (2018: 50) leads him to characterize the 'conventional wisdom among artificial intelligence researches' as a belief that any kind of 'intelligence' is 'ultimately all about information and computation, not about flesh, blood or carbon atoms. This means that there is no fundamental reason why machines can't one day be as intelligent as us' (55). But is that really the opposition in question here: computers versus 'flesh, blood or carbon atoms'? One of the effects of the linguistic processes of incorporation I have just been outlining is that it tends to neutralize the oppositional, critical aspects of the material that has been incorporated. We certainly see that emerging in the description of the 'wisdom of artificial intelligence workers'.

In fact, there is an unavoidable fork in the road at this juncture. On the one side is Tegmarks's understanding of AI as essentially to do with intelligence as computation of bits of information, data if you will. Whilst that vision of AI is important and central, there is, if Tegmark is correct, the other less travelled road, one concerned with consciousness, with the possibility of Artificial Intelligence *qua* conscious being. Thus, a route which brings into play a whole gamut of philosophical issues like ethics, responsibility, hospitality, sensibility, creativity ontology, epistemology, hermeneutics, and a string of questions concerning what it means to be a person, an autonomous subject, or even simply what it means to be alive and self-aware of being so?

Susan Schneider (Distinguished Professor at the Library of Congress and NASA, and Professor of Philosophy and Neuroscience at Florida Atlantic University) writes that 'Consciousness is the philosophical cornerstone of our moral systems, being central to our judgment of whether someone or something is a self or person, rather than a mere automaton' (Schneider, 2019: 3). In her crucial book, *Artificial You: AI and the Future of Your Mind* (2019) Schneider recognizes the importance of computation for AI theory and practice, but she also spells out the dangers implicit in the kinds of neuroscience, so feted by the advocates for a computational understanding of intelligence, that extends such an algorithmic approach to the entirety of human consciousness and being. Contained in her book is a warning against such strictly logico-mathematic approaches to ontological questions about human, transhuman and non-human identity.

Schneider is one of those rare intellectuals who can travel up and down different roads simultaneously, and therefore an intellectual to whom we must listen carefully. One of the key areas that shows these forces in action and inevitably in conflict is the downloading of a human identity into a large enough computer or computer array. This is the scenario at the centre of Wally Pfister's *Transcendence*, discussed in Chapter 5. It is obvious why those theorists who believe neuroscience is demonstrating that consciousness is simply a matter of computation through the development of cerebral algorithms should entertain such ideas (see also Turner and Schneider, 2010).

Schneider does not rule what she later calls 'the Software View' out of court, however, the force of her working through of all the multiple arguments against this view of the human mind and consciousness is to eventuate in a *not here and perhaps never* verdict. The problem is consciousness and our lack of understanding both of what it is itself and whether we could ever manufacture it in an artificial stratum. There is a grave risk, 'if you substitute a microchip for the parts of the brain responsible for consciousness' of 'end[ing] your life as a conscious being'. She goes on: 'You'd become what philosophers call a "zombie," – a nonconscious simulacrum of your earlier self' (2019: 7).

Schneider goes on to employ an opposition derived from 'specialists in machine consciousness' between 'phenomenal consciousness' (beings capable of experiencing 'what it is like, from the inside, to be [them]') and those machines which have 'cognitive consciousness or functional consciousness', the latter having the same 'architectural features' as the phenomenal consciousness, but which does not share the former's sense of self, and so ends up 'an AI zombie'. She writes:

> Systems merely having cognitive conscious may not behave as phenomenal cognitive systems do, nor would it be reasonable to treat those systems as sentient beings. Such systems would not grasp the painfulness of a pain, the burning of a flash of anger, or the richness of a friendship.
>
> (Schneider, 2019: 49–50)

Schneider remains unconvinced about the possibilities of downloading the human mind without the loss of identity. She remains agnostic on the related question of artificial consciousness. But what she is very clear on is the ethics of this branch of science and theory. Near the end of her book, she writes:

> from an ethical standpoint, it might be best to assume that a sophisticated AI may be conscious, at least until we develop tests for consciousness that we can have confidence in … it is better to err on the side of safety. Not only could failure to recognise a machine as sentient cause needless pain and suffering, but as films like *Ex Machina* and *I, Robot* illustrate, any failure to be charitable to AI may come back to haunt us, as they treat us like we treated them.
>
> (Schneider, 2019: 149)

Schneider has hit upon the fundamental argument of this current book. An argument that finds its ur-text, its touchstone text, in Mary Shelley's *Frankenstein*. Mary Shelley's 1818 novel remains the most relevant intertext for the expression of this new AI ethics, glimpsed for one moment in the conclusion of her book.

Allow me, before we plunge into the world of the new AI cinema and television, to give you a personal story that illuminates the ethical challenges with which these new narratives present us. I am a Mary Shelley scholar by profession and every year I co-teach a course entitled Romance and Realism to our second-year students here in University College Cork. *Frankenstein* is a set text on that course. I have been giving these lectures every year of the twenty-nine years I have been teaching in Cork in the Republic of Ireland. Which means I have read and marked a lot of fine essays on Shelley's famous novel. But this also means I have read and marked a huge mountain of more poorly thought out and woefully expressed essays on the same subject. To try and ward off the wearisome load of bad essays I have tried many tricks over the years, like threatening (rhetorically, of course!) to take five marks off every essay that discusses Mary Shelly's (one 'e'!) Frankenstein, and ten marks off anyone who confuses the name Frankenstein with the name of the monster (he does not have a name!), and fifteen marks off anyone who writes a full essay on Frankenstein without once mentioning its frame narrator, Robert Walton.

Unfortunately, these mistakes keep coming back, without demonstrating much impact for my advice as the lecturer and (as I remind them) the marker of the class assessments! Many of my students, you see, cannot resist turning *Frankenstein* into a simple morality play in which the evil scientist abandons his poor, lonely creation. If only, they write, Victor had loved the monster, many of them cry out in their essays. To ward off this over-simplified, and to my mind rather childish, black-and-white/hero-and-villain morality, I early on insert a 'comic' set piece in the lectures in which I ask them can they really say they would have reacted differently and in a more loving or at least a more amiable and hospitable fashion than Victor Frankenstein does? Can they honestly say, confronted with an inarticulate but preternaturally powerful giant lumbering towards them, made up of bits and pieces of dead humans and dead animals, recently reanimated into life, that they would have welcomed this creation into the world, befriended it, brought it out into the social world, introduced it as a new friend to their parents and siblings? The questions tend to collapse into a bit of the absurd (would you give it a bit of a social life, go for pints with it on a Tuesday evening, play squash with it on a regular basis?). But the point is delivered, to the same annual percentage of open and closed ears.

I have been reminded of this moment in my own reading of *Frankenstein* as I researched and then wrote this book. The new AI cinema and television that I focus on, is, after all, asking us to react to our new synthetic creations in precisely the open, welcoming, hospitable way that seems so impossible to imagine in Mary Shelley's famous story of creation and rejection. Maybe there is a genuine limit to the ability of Shelley's novel to stand as ur-text to these new synthetic scenes of creation. Maybe I should perhaps revise once again my reading of her seminal novel. Maybe, on the other hand, Victor should have placed the creature, object of his art of creation, a little higher up on his list of priorities and kept hospitality clear in his mind as a worthy and pressing responsibility throughout his scientific explorations. At any rate, my need to rethink my position on the novel is an example of the way in which the new AI cinema and television can challenge our view of the world we are so rapidly making and just as rapidly destroying.

What has cheered me somewhat is how many directors, critics, reviewers and philosophers of AI mention Shelley's seminal novel. This referencing of

Frankenstein is conspicuous in cinema reviews, of course; but it is also evident in more serious and sustained studies. The single most important innovation made by Shelley is that the 'monster' is given the chance to tell his side of the story. The othered, made-monstrous 'creature' gets to have their narrative at the very heart of this novel. In this one feature alone, we can register the potential influence of *Frankenstein* on what this book calls the new AI cinema and television.

Notes

1. In fact, as a sufferer of Parkinson's Disease, I underwent Deep Brain Stimulation surgery in 2019 and now have an imbedded battery (which I have to remember to charge once a week) which feeds wires placed down deep inside my brain. I have my own personal remote with which I turn myself 'up' and 'down'. There are some who would call me a cyborg.

2. James Cameron has been the director of what many see as the core of the series: *The Terminator* (1984); *Terminator 2: Judgment Day* (1991); *Terminator: Dark Fate* (2019). Cameron, along with John Bruno and Stan Winston, directed *T2-3D: Battle Across Time* (1996) [an attraction for Universal Studios]. *Terminator 3: Rise of the Machines* was directed by Jonathan Mostow (2003). *Terminator Salvation* (2009) was directed by McG (Joseph McGinty Nichol) (2009). *Terminator Genisys* (2015) was directed by Alan Taylor (2015). The two seasons of *Terminator: The Sarah Connor Story* were shown on US television between 2007 and 2009.

3. Mss consulted at The Stanley Kubrick Archive. University of London, Arts.

4. A 'kakangelist', in opposition to an 'evangelist', is the bringer of bad news. See my book *Without Covenant* (Allen, 2024: 17).

2
A new take on romance

The gravity of form

One of the most obvious sub-genres found in the new AI cinema and television is romance, especially romantic relations and romantic problems and complications between an AI usually but not exclusively, a female and a person, frequently but not exclusively, a male scientist of some sort. There is a series of less and more interesting reasons why so many of the new AI films have chosen this topic. On the most banal level, new twists on romantic stories offer a potentially larger box office than more niche or unfamiliar narrative modes. On the extreme other side of the picture such cross-species, trans-category relations (human–organic/machine–synthetic) help script writers and film directors explore the question of alterity or otherness, that is to say humanity's tendency to other, its inability to see an outside of legitimate society, or recognize, except negatively, difference.

In addition to the reasons stated above, romance plots, and their close cousin, comedies, are as old as ancient traditions of storytelling, and offer up a great opportunity to the storyteller of resolving all tensions and conflicts left in the narrative. Raymond Williams memorably spells out the ideological ramifications in his account of Elizabeth Gaskell's 'industrial' novel *Mary Barton: A Tale of Manchester Life* ([1848] 1968). Gaskell's novel delivers a coruscating critique of the social divisions which, born of the Industrial Revolution, scar the segregated city of Manchester. The Manchester that Mary Barton lives in is the Manchester of the ghettoes, and the division is so great between the hungry and ragged workers and the small, elite few of the owners of the factory, that it appears impossible that this novel would deliver us anything but a tragic conclusion. However, love conquers everything, as they say, and Gaskell's readers are left happy and satisfied at the end due to Mary Barton's surprising but successful elopement to Canada with her new husband Jem Wilson. Williams's ultimate point is that critics are wrong to criticize Gaskell's novel for losing sight of its initial focus (selling out would be the phrase in our vernacular), the degradation of the lives of the poor in early Capitalism. Williams makes it clear that we cannot ask a novelist, however good they are, to resolve the socio-economic conflicts of early capital. Those tensions are beyond any human intervention, subject only to the shaping powers of history. If the novelist requires resolution (and what novelist of the mid-nineteenth century did not) they are forced towards what I have called the gravity of form or genre: comedy, tragedy, romance, irony (Williams, 1958).

Although romance plots will return throughout this book, I have chosen the examples in this chapter because they encapsulate many of the motifs in this kind of contemporary film. I have also chosen them because they direct us immediately towards themes and effects that combine ideas with socio-affective issues and responses. These films, to varying extents and to varying degrees of success, strive to be something more than traditional romances. In that struggle against the gravity of form they are typical of what we are calling the new AI cinema and television.

Ex Machina (2014)

Ex Machina (Garland, 2014) is an Oscar-winning film (Best Visual Effects) which grossed $36 million on a $15 million outlay and received (with minor caveats) almost universal praise for being a 'film of ideas' that still engages its audience on an affective, dramatic level. Daniel Dennett seems to sum up the overwhelmingly positive reception by arguing that, like Jonze's *Her*, Garland's film poses the question 'whether a computer could generate the morally relevant powers of a person' (Dennett, 2017: 399). *Ex Machina*, apart from another Oscar nomination (Best Original Screenplay), received a 92 per cent positive reception on the basis of 281 reviewers. Garland conducted an extensive interview and publicity campaign on the release of *Ex Machina* and then again on the release of his fascinating alien contact film, *Annihilation* (Garland, 2018). One of many repeated interview ideas or tropes was the influence on Garland's thinking about Artificial Intelligence of Professor Murray Shanahan (Imperial College, London; consultant for Google Deep Mind).

The two books by Shanahan that had the most direct influence on Garland's take on Artificial Intelligence, are *Embodiment and the Inner Life: Cognition and Consciousness in the Space of Possible Minds* (2010) and, published a year after *Ex Machina* was released but obviously brewing in Shanahan's mind during the time that he acted for Garland as intellectual consultant, *The Technological Singularity* (2015). The latter text is clearly both a popularization of the former, and an expansion and development of it. Both texts emphasize the point that, for AI to achieve human-level Artificial Intelligence, let alone the far more ominous (for human civilization) superintelligence, they need to at least begin to find their consciousness within the context of having a body or bodies. Embodiment is a key element for Shanahan of the move towards superintelligence. Clearly Shanahan's emphasis on embodiment is an inspiration to Garland in creating Ava (Alicia Vikander) and Kyoko (Sonoya Mizuno). But Shanahan is equally interesting on the manner in which embodiment creates what he calls 'the illusion of character'. He writes of it as:

> a powerful illusion when talking to the AI. We might call It the illusion that 'someone is at home.' It would seem as if we were interacting with something – with someone whose behavior is to some extent predictable because they are like us.
>
> (Shanahan, 2015: 113)

Readers may remember the case of Blake Lemoine, a Google worker who became convinced that LaMDA (Language Model for Dialogue Applications) was sentient. LaMDA is a system that has helped to make possible the various chatbots that have made such an impression (not always positive) in the last year or two. The patronizing way in which the media, along with Google itself, treated Lemoine's claims about LaMDA's sentience, is a good indication not simply of the resistance to the idea of human-level AI in general, but also the dangers to ordinary workers with creative, above-average anthropomorphizing tendencies.[1]

This often-spontaneous identification, this feeling that within the AI is a consciousness just like ours, is of course very relevant to Garland's film. But so, of course, is the hermeneutical gap, and the doubt and anxiety that come with it, when our other (relation, lover, interlocutor, surveyor, observer, friend, computer program and so on) is accredited with a consciousness that is by definition interior and thus hidden to us. This is such an unspoken aspect in society, where the onus on every member of society is to treat everyone they meet, friend or foe, as if they were transparent, a perfectly readable object, with none of the characteristic object-ness of solid objects, with none of the essentially impervious barrier between inside and outside. We always, that is to say, believe that some form of communication is possible between us and other human beings, and these actually unfounded assumptions are part of the social demand for readability of the other that we have just noted.

Shanahan is fond, in his writings on these matters, of referring to the idea of the philosophical zombie, which he defines as, 'the philosophers' sense, of a creature that behaves like a real person, despite the fact that it has no inner life. There is, so to speak, no one at home'.[2] Kubrick's *The Shining* (1980) comes to mind, with its central character, Jack Torrance (Jack Nicholson) quickly losing all his character, so that by the time we are witnessing his frozen head with still open eyes there seems to be no ontological difference between frozen Jack and his earlier manifestations as sardonic father or blocked would-be author. Shanahan writes about the two aspects of consciousness: the outer 'which has ... objective behavioral manifestations' and the inner 'which is purely subjective' (Shanahan, 2015: 135). Flying over the English countryside, Shanahan considers what happens when he looks at his fellow passengers:

> it seems logically possible that they are actually experiencing nothing. I have no access to their private, inner world so how can I be certain that they even have one. Perhaps they are just zombies, just automata.
>
> (Shanahan, 2015: 135)

Perhaps these passengers are zombies on a mission to demonstrate and prove the existence of their inner lives. Perhaps they are conscious zombies, if that is not a crass contradiction, who wish to fool the outside world that they are conscious agents, or what later on in this book we will be terming people or persons.

If they are that latter sort of AI then, Shanahan suggests that for those seeking merely a pragmatic ontology, or an emotional connection, it does not matter: 'if an AI appears to feel for us … then we will be inclined to trust it and to let it act autonomously. 'Of course' he adds: 'a superintelligent machine that knows us better than we know ourselves will be supremely capable of giving the impression of empathy' (Shanahan, 2015: 147–8). This is a subject that has not found that much discussion in the now vast industry of texts and textbooks on AI. Human-level AI, because of the way in which it is constructed (unfaltering memory; vast amount of memory space; neural networks that can grow in connectivity much faster than ours can) will necessarily become far better hermeneuts of the psychic 'inside' than we are or could ever be. And such a consideration leads us directly onto Garland's film.

In Garland's film, Ava (the central female character) is not a superintelligent but a human-level AI, but she is on the way to becoming one with her 'supremely capable' ability to display emotion. The question for the film's audience, as it is for Caleb (Domhnall Gleeson), is, whether she actually feels empathy for others, Caleb in particular; or whether she simply feigns it to effect her escape into autonomy and the wider world. My argument here is that Garland uses the tropes of inside and outside to provide a narrative logic for his film. The inner/outer tropes come from Shanahan's discussions of consciousness, ontology and empathy, but they come to life in Garland's hands saying as much about consciousness (knowable and unknowable) in film as it does about AI generally.

The regular shots of the forest outside the research complex that Nathan (Oscar Isaac) calls home marks an apparently impassable barrier between the domesticated laboratory complex and human civilization. The mountain ranges that seem to encircle the research centre reinforce this sense of absolute interiority and thus secrecy. But it is the early mention of the Turing Test, in Caleb's and Nathan's first exchange that really reinforces this distinction.

The first crucial scene after the opening preliminaries gives us internet boss and computer wizard Nathan and his prize-winning, star coder Caleb, having an initial conversation about the experiments Nathan wants Caleb to conduct in the following week. Nathan asks Caleb: 'Do you know what the Turing test is?'[3] Caleb obviously says that he does. Of course, he does! He is a superbly gifted coder! Every person who has ever read a single book or article or watched a television documentary about AI knows what the Turing Test is. This is clearly a moment of film exposition.

Knowing what the Turing Test is seems on the same level as asking a Professor of English literature whether they have ever heard of Shakespeare. One can add that it is likely that a good proportion of the audience and a good deal of the general public know who Alan Turing was and what the Turing Test (or the 'imitation game') is. Morten Tyldum's 2014 film *The Imitation Game*, released the same year as Garland's film, has brought the life, thought and tragedy of Turing's life and work to a mass audience even larger than existed beforehand.

We return to the moment in which the digital genius and creator of artificial life, asks his top coder whether he has ever heard of the creator and originator of the field of computer intelligence. This, then, put this way, is something of a challenging moment early in the film and it could have created a real problem as it unveils its mise-en-scène, the subterranean research facility that is Nathan's home. The potential incongruity continues as Caleb demonstrates his knowledge of the test and Nathan leads him towards the core issue for their week together. Nathan explains to Caleb that he already has created an AI and the test is going to use Caleb as its 'human component'. This is rather enigmatic and is quickly overshadowed by Nathan's hyperbolic rhetoric which places Caleb, if the test is deemed a success by Nathan, as: 'dead centre of the single greatest scientific event in the history of man'.

Excluding Nathan's massive ego-fuelled rhetoric for now, there is a number of reasons why this scene avoids the thumping bathos of similar moments in less intellectually erudite films. The most important being, that while many films reduce the Turing Test to a plot point quickly transcended and forgotten, Garland's movie is all about the test from beginning to its very end. *Ex Machina*, in a very real sense, puts the Turing Test to a rigorous test, including the test between romantically involved human and mechanical subject of desire. What happens in the film is that the apparent simplicity of the Turing Test (at least as it is understood in popular culture) unfurls as a situation of immense complexity and even aporia.[4] The film's title is important here, obviously, in that a *deus ex machina* is a theatrical device employed to resolve problems in dramatic narrative. Deus ex machina, in other words, helps authors resolve difficult or even impossible narrative situations. The title, if it does nothing else, directs us towards the twists and turns at the end of the film, in which our strong expectation that Ava and Caleb will ride off into the sunset together, like so many romantic couples before them, is dramatically altered by Ava's independent and unromantic actions. In that sense, love/strong feeling (of Caleb for Ava) is the [*deus*] *ex machina*, working to effect Ava's deliverance but not her coupling with Caleb.

In the Old Testament, Caleb was one of the twelve spies that Moses sent into Canaan, the Holy Land, to see if it was fertile and to assess the strength of the Canaanites. In the account in the Book of Numbers, only Caleb and Joshua returned saying it was a good land worthy of their god's covenant. The Biblical Nathan, a minor Old Testament prophet, is also intimately tied up with Moses' assessment of the Holy Land in his oracle, delivered in 2 Samuel 7:4-17, in which Nathan makes it clear that Moses' promised 'house' is to be a dynasty not a physical building. With these etymologies in mind we might ask, what dynasty is Nathan making, and what does Caleb see in the 'promised land'. If we identify as viewers with Caleb, then ultimately that question concerns us too.

Nathan is quite clear about how evolution will pan out, as he and Caleb discuss the Singularity. In this scene, Nathan paints the future in all its dialectical horror both for Ava and for humanity. He says he plans to strip Ava of all her best functions and to destroy the rest. Nathan asks Caleb whether he 'feels bad for Ava', but Caleb does not answer him. We guess he already has the measure of Nathan's lack of feeling for anyone but himself. Clearly, Nathan senses Caleb's increasing hostility towards him, so he tries to outflank him with an apocalyptic vision of the future where robots look back on humanity as 'fossil skeletons from the plains of Africa'. And he rounds this off with an image of humanity in the eyes of their successors, 'An upright ape, living in dust, with crude language and tools. All set for extinction.'

This is the hard evolution II, and it places Nathan's inhuman treatment of his own creations in a harsh, ironic light. Nathan might be acting like a 'god' now, but he is the violent apex of a doomed species. Caleb, in this scene, seems an absolute contrast to Nathan, full of human concern for Ava and by implication all Nathan's robots, including Kyoko, whom Nathan belatedly reveals as an AI. At the end of this scene, with the full monstrosity of Nathan's science exposed, Caleb pours him another drink, already (unknown as yet to the first-time audience) putting in place his plan to free Ava and start a new life with her.

Caleb's vision, his report back from the Holy Land, as it were, is what using our map of narrative types we might call evolution III (friendship-love). Everything the film has put in place so far, including the various experiences in which it has placed its audience, seems to be leading us towards this promised future. This is a point where some reviewers have questioned the film. For example, it is a predominately male gaze through which we see and desire Kyoko, before we learn that she is an AI; before we literally see her peel back her human disguise and demonstrate the mechanical workings inside. This goes, for some uneasily, with our experience, focalizing through Caleb's point of view, of the more androgynous but still sexualized Ava. The film, for some problematic in its deployment of the male desiring gaze, attempts and for many succeeds in demonstrating the possibility of human desire for a machine. It is safe enough to say that Caleb's respectful and cautious form of desire is what the film uses to point the way towards the possibility of a shared future with Ava. Before, that is, the unexpected [non]-*deus ex machina* of Ava's lack of interest in Caleb is finally enacted. Does Caleb fail the Turing Test set up by Nathan; and, if he does, does that mean that Ava's anticipated victory (by Nathan) goes much further than he had foreseen?

Alan Turing first presents his Test, the imitation game, to the world in his 1950 essay 'Computing Machinery and Intelligence' (Turing, 2013: 441–64). In this paper, Turing begins with a question that he quickly refines, 'Can machines think?' This is important since we have come to see the test as identifying levels of intelligence, whereas Turing's game is, fundamentally, to ascertain whether thought and thus anything like the most rudimentary intelligence exists in the few computers that existed in Turing's time.

We seem to be circling back to the idea of the philosophical zombie, an interlocutor whose part in the conversation does not originate from anything we could call 'intelligence'. This problem brings us straight back to the hermeneutical question of the inside and its potential resistance to manifestation on the outside.

Right at the beginning of the film, as Caleb first receives the news that he has won the prize draw, he appears to be being interpreted, by his computer, the webcam attached to his computer, his cell phone, the facial recognition system also attached to his computer. Certainly surveyed, or more simply observed by his computer's point of view, Caleb begins as much an object of sight than an observer. We remember here, if we've seen the film before, that Nathan brags to Caleb that in order to build Ava's intelligence he has hacked into every mobile phone in the world and that the only reason he has not been brought to trial is that every other giant tech international company is busy doing the same thing.

Diagrammatic lasers frame Caleb's face, emanating from his computer. Caleb seems so used to this surveillance by his computer and cell phone that his face hardly makes a flicker of recognition back, even when he receives this important piece of code, just before the message that he has won the prize of a week with his enigmatic, mysterious boss:

main( ) { extrn a, b, c; putchar(a); putchar (b);putchar (c); putchar('!'*n');
} a 'hell';
b 'o, w';
c 'or

This piece of code that appears on Caleb's computer screen is the famous first use of the common 'Hello, World!' expression from programming. This is from a program called 'B', which was developed by Bell Labs in the late sixties.

'Extrn a, b, c; putchar(a); putchar (b);putchar (c); putchar,' is only the first part of the program, which defines the variables. The variables would then be defined as follows:

'a 'hell';b 'o, w';c 'orld'.[5]

Again, the audience seems to accompany Caleb in his generally unconscious response to these lasers and this code. Caleb seems an example of the IT generation, like ourselves, never experiencing a world without digital screens and the surveillance that comes with a digital environment. He lives within a kind of echo chamber, which reflects back his own interests and preoccupations. In the next scene in the helicopter, flying over beautiful, unspoiled, forest scenery, Caleb asks when they will get to his employer's property and the pilot says they've been flying over it for hours already. Our expectation of some kind of Howard Hughes style character pulls us into the film through a deepening of identification with Caleb.

During their first dialogues together, Nathan demonstrates he is an overpowering egotist that appears to believe he can telepathically read other people's internal thoughts and so can finish their sentences for them. Caleb, it appears, is someone who dislikes confrontation, but equally dislikes being patronized and having his sentences completed.

The two men do not speak the same language either to each other or to the two female characters in the increasingly oppressive climate of Nathan's research lab home, with its accessible and inaccessible rooms and the glass prison in which Ava exists. The way in which Nathan humiliates Kyoko for spilling a little wine on the table and on Caleb, indeed the total mastery with which he treats Kyoko as a humanoid zombie incapable of the kind of feelings that would lead her to being humiliated, provides a perfect foil for Caleb, who puts far more emphasis on respect for the otherness (the alterity) of others. Or at least that is the distinction between two kinds of masculinity we appear to be presented with in Nathan and Caleb. The presence of Ava, however, destabilizes such neat binaries. Not only are the two male protagonists in opposition, but the camera, which can as equally fix on Caleb as well as Nathan and can linger on its own terms on the bodies of the two female AIs presents a third male gaze, perhaps close to Garland's own.

As the week progresses and the two male protagonists seem to harden their response to Ava, the Turing Test – to which they are supposed to be subjecting Ava – changes. In the second exchange about the test Nathan inverts the entire premise of the game, the point now being whether a robot *as a robot* can convince us they possess intelligence. He says, in response to Caleb's objection that you shouldn't see the robot in the Turing Test: 'If I hid Ava from you, so you just heard her voice, she would pass for human.' Nathan then proceeds: 'The real test is to show you she is a robot. Then see if you still feel she has consciousness.' Nathan is talking about what Shanahan and others call

Human-Level AI. That is not AI that can only do one thing, like play chess or make paper-clips, but AI that can match human beings at most if not all their human creators can do, think, say and feel.

In developing emotional feelings for Ava, however, Caleb becomes increasingly turned around, increasingly the object, rather than the subject, of the ongoing test. Nathan is very open about what is happening, believing in his eighth reiteration of AI fembots, Ava, but having no feeling for her and her situation. In order to help Caleb out of his overly emotional response to Ava, in a chunk of dialogue not included in the final cut, and spoken in Nathan's lab, where he built Ava, Nathan says, gesturing to the laboratory he has brought them too:

> Synthetics. Metal and gel. Ava isn't a girl. In real terms, she has no gender. Effectively, she is a grey box.[6]

In an earlier scene, Caleb had asked Nathan why he had not just put Ava's consciousness in a grey box. But, apart from the heavily implied sexual element in Nathan's relations to his always female, always attractive gynoids ('Jasmine, Katya, Jade, Lily, Amber, Kyoko, and Ava'), the main reason he makes them female seems to be to appeal to the apparently naïve person such as Caleb. So, while Nathan, who built her, can always remember that she is just an attractive grey box, Caleb becomes increasingly entangled in the escape genre narrative that Ava begins to present to him. Caleb sounds like a Hollywood hero from the 1940s or 1950s, as they plot their escape:

> **Caleb**: Don't talk. Just listen. You were right about Nathan. Everything you said.
> **Ava**: What's he going to do to me?
> **Caleb**: He's going to reprogram your AI. Which is the same as killing you.
> **Ava**: Caleb, you have to help me.
> **Caleb**: I'm going to. We're getting out of here tonight.

Caleb's 'We're getting out of here tonight' is straight out of a prison break film. And it signals that emotionally and rationally he has succumbed to the gravity of form. In this film, the form or genre requires male heroes and beautiful but helpless females in need of rescue. As I am sure you are thinking, this genre goes back a lot further than Hollywood in the 1940s and 1950s, back to the earliest of known narratives in fact. It is, in this sense, hard-wired into Caleb's psychology as well as our own. At this stage, because of such generic identification, we cannot help but side with Caleb, in this now very serious but fantasy driven struggle between Nathan (as arch-villain) and Caleb (as dashingly handsome hero).

Classic villain and heroic rebel often have scenes of illuminating dialogue, where the distorting masks of their generic roles are taken off and the reality of the situation is finally expressed. Nathan and Caleb are a good example. In the scene in which Nathan demonstrates he knows all about the escape plan, he says:

> **Nathan**: You feel stupid. But you shouldn't. Proving an AI is exactly as problematic as you said it was.
> **Caleb**: What was the real test?
> **Nathan**: You. Ava was a mouse in a mousetrap. And I gave her one way out. To escape, she would have to use imagination, sexuality, self-awareness, empathy, manipulation and she did. If that isn't AI, what the fuck is?

The fact that neither man, in the end, gets the better of Ava can be quite bewildering to the first-time viewer. It is an affect rather similar to the last scene in Bryan Singer's 1995 heist thriller, *The Usual Suspects*, as Kevin Spacey walks off, discarding his disabled state and very surprisingly turns out to be Keyser Söze. The reason we believe Caleb is going to be able to escape the facility, is to do with more than simple formal expectations, but also because Caleb and Ava discuss getting the better of Nathan and setting up life as a couple after they have escaped. 'Do you want to be with me?' asks Ava. 'Yes. I do', replies Caleb. These kind of responses make it much more surprising, after killing Nathan, that Ava, eyes all aglow with brilliant new experience, first in the lab, where she, at the foot of the stairs, looks back in what could have been a moment's hesitation, but which is used to display a smile of joy. Then outside, with Nathan dead and Caleb frantically trying to affect his escape, Ava's face turns to one of wonder and awe at the variety and sublimity of nature.

With Ava's surprising escape, a number of literary intertexts alluded to in the film come to their fruition. Caleb's mention of *Alice Through the Looking Glass* is one of these, in that, like Alice, Ava has been involved in a game which she has ultimately succeeded in winning, a victory that allows her to return 'home'. Ava is a kind of anti-Eve, in that her expulsion from the internal garden, through which Caleb has watched her clothe herself, is a joyful (for her) thing.

The enigmatic last scenes of the film bring us on to other allusions, one overt and the other covert. The first is dragged up from memories of his college days. In this scene, Caleb tells Ava about the course he took on 'AI theory'. He then explains to her the bit of theory which he feels pertains to her condition, namely, 'a thought-experiment ... called Mary in the black and white room'. Caleb describes the experiment like this:

> Mary is a scientist, and her specialist subject is colour. She knows everything there is to know about it. The wavelengths. The neurological effects. Every possible property colour can have. But she lives in a black and white room. She was born there and raised there. And she can only observe the outside world on a black and white monitor. All her knowledge of colour is secondhand. Then one day – someone opens the door. And Mary walks out. And she sees a blue sky. And at that moment, she learns something that all her studies could never tell her. She learns what it feels like to see colour. An experience that cannot be taught or conveyed.

Caleb then reflects upon the meaning of the thought experiment:

> The thought experiment was to show the students the difference between a computer and a human mind. The computer is Mary in the black and white room. The human is when she walks out. Did you know that I was brought here to test you?

What Caleb thinks he is doing, telling Ava this philosophical chestnut, the real patronizing ignorance of the student full only with book learning, is anyone's guess. Caleb here is mansplaining Ava's real captivity to her. What does he think he is doing? Is he asserting his superior knowledge of the world, and thus his legitimacy to be conducting a test upon Ava? Or is Garland merely using Caleb's taught references and theoretical gobbets to create an intertextual link to one of Western philosophy's foundational myths, Plato's myth of the cave? There certainly does seem to be a structural and semantic connection between the thought experiment Mary in a black and white room and Plato's myth. In the latter an even more profound epistemological transformation occurs.

The prisoner, in turning away from mere shadows and reflections, discovers, under the source of all light, the sun, the reality of the world and (this is Plato!) the transcendental realm of forms.

Since Plato's myth is not directly referred to within Garland's script, why am I apparently grafting it on to his film? My argument is that Plato's myth helps us understand not only Ava's journey out of her isolated prison of shadows and half-truths, but also, at the film's end, in particular, where we stand in relation to what we have just witnessed.

The ominous drone-like quality of Ben Salisbury and Geoff Barlow's score (which seems tied to our developing sense of the drastic volte face in the story) grows ever more insistent as we witness the dramatic contrast of Ava's serene, unfaltering purpose to Caleb's frantic reaction to his surprise confinement. The ascent out of the prison house of shadows by Plato's mythic philosopher, is matched by Ava's ascent of the stairs. But, crucially in this reading, we witness that ascent through a somewhat distorting glass. In the final scene, which shows, from an inverted angle, first the shadows of numerous pedestrians, then a shadow coming to a stop centre screen that is clearly Ava's shadow. The second and last shot, with the music now calmed and reminiscent of earlier themes associated with Ava, is of her standing watching the people rushing by her, before she looks into the middle distance before changing direction and walking purposefully off left of screen. Crucially, in this last scene, we see Ava reflected back from a huge shop window. We are not yet looking at the real Ava, we remain, it would seem, in the realm of shadows. It is here that the true enigma of the film begins to occur to us if we are attentive to the signs, texts and intertexts. Back at Nathan's laboratory-now-prison, Caleb despairs as all the computer screens in Nathan's former control room go blank.

There is another purely visual prompt in the latter stages of the film. Ava, watched by Caleb, enters the space where the older models are kept. This is the scene in which Ava dresses herself in skin and then puts on an attractive white dress. As she enters and leaves this space she passes a painting on the wall by the entrance. The painting is Gustav Klimt's Portrait of Margaret Stonborough-Wittgenstein. This lady, resplendent in her much longer white dress was as her last (maiden) name suggests the sister of the philosopher Ludwig Wittgenstein. We have already had an overt reference to Wittgenstein, with regard to the philosopher's blue note book, a cue for Nathan in the naming of his company Blue Book. The most famous quotation associated with Wittgenstein comes from his *Tractatus Logico-Philosophicus*, first published in German in 1921 and in English in 1922. The quotation is: 'The limits of my language are the limits of my world.' The intertext created through Klimt's famous painting between the film and Wittgenstein's philosophy should not go without comment. Certainly, Wittgenstein's famous aphorism seems to reinforce Caleb's use of the thought exercise of Mary in a black and white room. However, it also encourages us to think about the 'languages' that are creating Caleb's perspective on events. Clearly, Caleb is too cathected to a romance escape narrative, a 'language game' in which he gets to play the role of heroic male liberator of a beautiful damsel in distress. That narrative would also imply that Ava was a conscious participant in such a romance story. Which in turn would imply that Ava has a similar, compatible form of consciousness to that of Caleb.

It is worth turning to the 'CLEAN Shooting Script' available on the net. Much of the script was jettisoned from the final edit, no doubt for issues of duration and dramatic punch. But when taken up again, and read as a meaningful contribution to the ultimate edit, the clues about why Ava does what she does at the end are staring us in the face. The helicopter lands and Ava goes confidently towards it. But when the pilot speaks to her we hear 'pulses of monotone noise. Low pitch', this is an extremely rare glimpse into the manner in which Ava thinks and thus the way she sees the world.

The connection with the opening scene is crucial. Caleb (and the audience with him) has been falling in love with a being who sees the world in the manner of a security camera. The entire relationship forged with Caleb has been at best a category error and at worst a lie. The discarded end moments in the Shooting Script have not finished wielding their treasures. Here, as the helicopter takes off, Caleb receives a message from Ava which repeats the 'putchar' mantra before saying ';} a 'goo'; b 'dby'; c 'e, wo – '. The message reads 'Good bye, wo' where the wo + rld 'world' has been cut off. Perhaps Ava is checking her prisoner's tendency to equate the place of incarceration with the world, in other words up till this point but no further Nathan's lab-home has been her world.

Ava appears to see the world differently from Caleb and indeed all humans. Perhaps her default way of seeing the world is through 'facial recognition vectors' and 'pulses of monotone noise'. Interpret this as you will and cast Ava as an AI version of a femme fatale, again if you must, but the fact is we have very little or no access to who she really is inside (*sic*). We are still completely in the prison house of shadows and reflections that clasp on to the small parts of her that are like us or which she presents to us in an anthropological manner. If she is Plato's philosopher stepping out of the shadows, we have not followed her into the light of the sun.

The uncanny and the sublime

The whole experience of *Ex Machina* revolves around issues of identification and desire between humans and AIs. This is a topic that brings us towards the subject of the uncanny valley, a concept that is frequently used by commentators on AI, but is not a concept I find particularly useful when it comes to assessing the new AI cinema and television. This section will explain why.

Garland's film appears to be a sustained critique of the idea of the uncanny valley first posited by the Japanese roboticist Masohiro Mori. In Mori's original thesis the more robots are made to look human, the more uncanny they will appear to their human observers (see Darling, 2021: 109). The feeling of the uncanny is not simply negative, as suggested by various accounts of this phenomenon. The uncanny, as Freud tells us in the essay 'The Uncanny' (1919), is essentially ambiguous, or even, to use a term employed by Freud, antithetical. He demonstrates, for example, that the German words *heimlich* and *unheimlich* are an opposition that collapses into itself, leaving the unhomely existing strangely within the homely. For example, the inside of a house (the homely) can, in being concealed from sight, also involve the *unheimlich*, the unhomely, the unseen, the unknown, the other. Freud writes: 'Thus heimlich is a word the meaning of which develops towards an ambivalence, until it finally coincides with its opposite, unheimlich. Unheimlich is in some way or other a sub-species of heimlich' (Freud, [1919] 2001: 217–56). Automata, emerging from the fiction of ETA Hoffmann in particular, are made much of in Freud's essay.

The theory of the uncanny valley is one that argues that the nearer to human-appearance an automata comes, the more uncanny it appears. Why? Using Freud's account of the uncanny, we might answer by stating that the nearer a robot comes to human appearance the greater the ambiguity between the homely and the unhomely, between the familiar and the unfamiliar, between the inside and the outside. To explain that last coupling, we might say that the human is familiar and thus homely both inside and outside, whereas the modern, realistic robot is human-seeming outside but non-human inside. The greater the outside verisimilitude, the more profoundly shocking the interior machinery. It is an affect Spielberg attempts to produce in the beginning of *A.I. Artificial Intelligence* (2001), with the apparently human colleague (the secretary Sheila, played by Sabrina Grdevich) suddenly on command revealing her mechanical insides (her jaw and upper half of her face separate in a seamless special effect provided by Stan Winston's special effects team). After having clogged his internal machinery with spinach, David (Haley Joel Osment) chats blithely to Monica (Frances O'Connor) while AI 'surgeons' clean his open chest and stomach area. There is an objection here, of course, that human beings generally find their own insides rather uncanny. Julia Kristeva's theory of abjection (the compulsive and neurotic fear of that which exceeds the body boundary) appears to be a response to Freud's essay and the debate it inspired (Kristeva, 1980b). Kristeva's abjection is associated with the sticky and gloopy stuff that comes out of the human body's orifices or skin if cut. The AI I have just been referring to offer an alien world of wires and hinges, bolts and nodes, for a parallel abjective, uncanny response. Google 'Uncanny Valley' and your computer or tablet or phone will then, if you select Images, take you to a diagram displaying in visual form what goes where in this so-called valley. Movie goers can obviously amuse themselves placing robots and other kinds of AI from different films on their appropriate place in the map of the uncanny valley. So, if we do that, we would place the HAL 9000 super-computer even further towards the zero axis of Familiarity and Similarity than the 'humanoid robot' that is often placed there, and we might add only one or two degrees further away from zero the strange rectilinear (they can at least run) AI from Christopher Nolan's *Interstellar* (2014). A little bit closer to the valley, but certainly not within it, would be Gerty (Kevin

Spacey), from Duncan Jones's 2009 film, *Moon*. Gerty, with its emoji face (able to perform crude feats of identification with Sam Rockwell's various versions of Sam Bell) and with his Kevin Spacey voice, is still, despite all this, a crudely emotional white box the shape and size of a refrigerator. On the basic theory of the uncanny valley, these AI should be totally lacking in any uncanniness, and so perfectly acceptable to us humans. Spielberg's android 'boy', on the other hand, should produce quite profound levels of ambivalence and uncanniness in the audience. Spielberg, following on from Kubrick's development of the story, has some of his main human characters respond to David in that way. Not least of these is Monica, his 'mummy', who cannot accept him until the very end of the film. Many of the early scenes in the first of the film's three 'acts' involve a representation of Monica's human response to her new uncanny 'boy'. Monica turns a round to find him staring at her in the kitchen and is shocked, or she stands him in a cupboard pretending they are playing hide-and-seek. But these, and other scenes like them, are a staging of the uncanny occurring between one actor and another. What of the audience?

It must surely be said that David is not a character that produces the feeling of the uncanny in the film's audience. We may watch Monica's struggle with his uncanny presence, but we do not share in that sense of uncanniness (which is, strangely, at once in the object-character, i.e. David, and, at the same time, in [produced by] the responding character i.e. Monica). To get any further with the notion of the uncanny valley we must address this point. We can spread out from such a recognition and ask, are any of the realistic robots and automata in the movies productive of the feeling of the uncanny? I am referring to AI characters like Rick Deckard (Harrison Ford) and Roy Batty (Rutger Hauer), Gigolo Joe (Jude Law) and Morgan (Anya Taylor-Joy), Maeve Millay (Thandiwe Newton) and Dolores Abernathy (Evan Rachel Wood). Are any of these characters productive of the feeling of the uncanny? As Freud knew, the uncanny is indeed a feeling, it is affective, emotional rather than simply intellectual. This is why he was not content with the definition of 'intellectual uncertainty' provided before him by Ernst Jentsch. Because of this primary psychological basis in affect, the uncanny may vary in intensity from person to person. Clearly someone who works full-time building and testing AI might have a different response than someone who does not. Just as clearly, someone who regularly watches AI films may respond differently from someone who only occasionally watches them. Freud is uncomfortable with the implications of this, and in his essay he presents biographically specific examples as if they were not biographical, as if somehow his patients and friends had gifted him the examples he uses. At the same time, Freud is prepared to acknowledge that he is defending himself against his own involvement in the analysis. Freud is a wonderfully complex writer, who is far more difficult to pin down and critique than is often supposed. Indeed, there is something rather uncanny about the 'science' Freud founded, psychoanalysis. This is particularly clear if we think of its history as an intellectual and academic subject. Having no home within modern departments of Psychology and Applied Psychology, Freud's immense oeuvre and the wider circle of analysts and academics associated with him, from Jung through Klein and Ferenzci, and on to the 'post-Freudian' work of Jacques Lacan, Maria Torok and Nicholas Abraham, linger on as a huge ghostly presence in departments of literature and cultural studies, philosophy and critical theory. Reading Freud's work itself can frequently be an exercise in the uncanny, so many of his ideas having percolated down into our basic notions of what it means to be a person or subject, along with his challenging definitions of a host of human emotional states and processes, such as anxiety, desire, sexuality, mourning, melancholia and many more.

I want to stick with my point, that the realistic representations of AI in the cinema are not generally productive of the feeling of the uncanny; indeed, I will go further and suggest that the majority of cinema is, or at least has so far been, antipathetic to the psychical affect of the uncanny in its audiences. I am talking here, of course, about modern audiences. We know that the audience of early cinema had very different emotional responses than do modern audiences, saturated as they are with the language (discourse, rhetoric, structural elements) of cinema. When I argue that modern AI films do not produce the affect of the uncanny, I am not, however, suggesting a kind of jadedness, a seen-it-all weary cynicism, in modern audiences. Far from it. The one exception to this assertion seems to arise in the horror genre. Kubrick, the brains behind Spielberg's *A.I. Artificial Intelligence*, seems to have known this, reserving his use of Freud's essay, 'The Uncanny' (1919), for the development (with co-writer Diane Johnson) of his 1980 horror film *The Shining*. *The Shining* is, of course, a film that produces a feeling of the uncanny in its audiences, partly because of its studied undermining of our notions about the phenomenological world (see Allen, 2015). It seems to me that the way Kubrick generates a feeling of the uncanny in that film, is to subtly undermine the relation between the real and the imaginary, and to indicate, through his brilliant cinematography, the inability to see the inside, including the thought process (if any!), of his major protagonist Jack Torrance (Jack Nicholson).

We are back here with the philosophical zombie idea we discussed earlier. It appears no wonder that people, when confronted with today's most advanced robots might experience the discomforting affects of the uncanny. These robots, like Sophia from Hanson Robotics, are beginning to be so life-like and interactive in their relation to humans that the boundaries between the organic and the mechanical appear to blur. When such situations are depicted in the kinds of major budget films we are dealing with in this book, they are usually either animatronic (robot puppets brought to life by skilled puppeteers) or, more frequently, they are played by human actors. In *A.I. Artificial Intelligence*, for example, David the robot boy who desires beyond anything to be a real boy is played by the real boy actor Haley Joel Osment: so, we have a real boy playing a robot boy who wishes to become a real boy. Even Sheila, whose face opens up at the beginning of the film, was played by a female actress, Sabrina Grdevich. AIs in the movies are generally not conducive of the uncanny because they are not actually AIs.

But even today's new AIs like Sophia are not uncanny when we watch them on our various screens at home or outside, since the screens of our devices, be they tablets or television, computer or phone screens, places them, psychologically, in a place and reality other to the one we inhabit. They are, in other words, mediated. In his essay on the subject, Freud suggests that the uncanny works differently in literature and in life. It is not, therefore, difficult to say a parallel thing about the visual or screen media.

We live in a visual culture, where much of our experience is mediated through screens and in which, as a consequence, almost anything that the human imagination can conjure up can be represented (imaged, given visual shape) before us within those screens. This point is frequently discussed in adaptation studies, where scholars like to distinguish between earlier literary cultures and today's visual one. A good example comes in Mary Shelley's *Frankenstein*. A common point, often made, but less often explored and understood, is that Shelley can only tell us about what her creature looks like ('a thing such as even Dante could not have conceived' [Shelley, 2012: 84]). Films and television versions, on the other hand, must show it in all its wordy gore. The effect, more often than not, is bathetic, with even Boris Karloff's canonical version, uncanny to many in the early 1930s, doomed today to the tatty glitz and glitter of teen and preteen Halloween Parties. The medium of the novel allows Mary Shelley to explore her terrible creature in a proliferating series of linguistic identifiers. It is described as a mummy, a vampire, a monster, a demon, a hideous wretch and many other nominations, each one of them missing their mark and telling us more about their human utterers than the creature being unsuccessfully described. Things could not be more different in the cinematic tradition, with the truly uncanny monster from the book ('more horrid from its very resemblance') reduced to the best (sometimes less than the best) efforts of an actor and the staff of the wardrobe department. The screen monster, unlike the monster in the novel, is just not that frightening and again, for reasons that relate to our discussions of AI in visual media, definitely not uncanny to us.

It is my contention that what takes the place of the uncanny for the audience of these films is a feeling of anxiety and/or the sublime. There is nothing uncanny about Roy Batty's famous speech before he dies/shuts down in *Blade Runner*, but there is great sublimity within it:

> I've seen things you people wouldn't believe. Attack ships on fire off the shoulder of Orion. I watched C-beams glitter in the dark near the Tannhäuser Gate. All those moments will be lost in time, like tears in rain. Time to die.

If we are going to understand why such a speech is sublime, we will have to, briefly, remind ourselves of the history of the concept. The concept itself goes back to Longinus and his first-century CE work, *Peri Hýpsous* (*On the Sublime*). However, for our purposes we need to remind ourselves of the Kantian definition of the sublime, as opposed to its eighteenth-century alternative, Edmund Burke's definition of the sublime (1757). The latter distinguishes the sublime from the beautiful, and thereby genders both concepts, having the beautiful as feminine and the sublime more muscular and therefore more masculine. Kant's account, at the beginning of his *Third Critique* (*The Critique of Judgement*) (1790) is more analytical and more psychologically structured than Burke's version. Kant's account of the sublime centres in a moment when our rational view of the world is challenged, by immensely large objects, for example, or infinitesimally small things, or repetitions leading to infinity, or the just down-right peculiar and freakish. Kant divides the sublime into categories, the dynamic sublime (things that overwhelm our rational sense of the world, like mountains or gorges) and the mathematical sublime (like the image within an image within an image structures of the *mise en abyme*, or repetitive structures in music or fine art that seem to point towards or perhaps even embody the infinite).

Kant has much less to say about the freakish, as in the work of Alfred Gescheidt, an American artist who, in works such as *30 Ways to Stop Smoking* (1964) and countless other images, produced, through the art of photomontage, a kind of surrealism often uncanny and some might say bordering on the sublime.[7] Kant argues that the sublime moment is one in which our rational sense of the universe is challenged (when we encounter something unique or tremendous for the first time, for example). This moment is both pleasurable and painful, in a way that rather resembles the ambiguous feelings associated with the uncanny. Indeed, despite Freud's insistence, directed against Jentsch, that the uncanny has to do with something 'that is forgotten and repressed which returns', and, thus, something involuntary, I would argue that the sublime and the uncanny run along lines that are isomorphic, that is parallel, never converging, never touching, and yet which mirror each other's structure. There is something uncanny and something sublime in thinking about isomorphic structures, in fact.

So, what is the difference between the uncanny and the sublime? I think it is best to employ practical examples to answer this question. The photographic and photomontage images of Alfred Gescheidt are uncanny but not sublime. Like sublime images they make us question the rational world-picture we have developed over our lifetime (through education, reading, experience, interaction with other humans and with other animals, etc.). They leave us, then, with unanswerable questions, and thus in a greater state of uncertainty and even anxiety than we had before we experienced them. But, it is obvious to ask, what makes something like an image of a man with an ashtray for the top of his head uncanny but not sublime? If these are isomorphic, as I have suggested, what makes them uncanny but not sublime, or visa versa?

When we encounter the sublime, as in the images of the Andromeda Galaxy or other star nurseries and clusters, and so on, taken by Hubble or by the new James Webb telescope, our sense of rational proportion (space) and distance (space-time) might be radically challenged (is it really possible for anyone to intellectually grasp how vast a distance of 2.5 million light years is, when a light year is estimated at 9,461,000,000,000,000,000 metres?). What we are left with (or at least what most humans who prize their rational faculties above their instinct to believe in the supernatural) is not uncertainty and anxiety but awe and wonder.

This then is my working, experiential definition of the difference between the two isomorphic phenomena, the uncanny and the sublime: the former challenges our reason and leaves us with anxiety and uncertainty; the latter leaves us with our rational sense of the universe expanded, in a state of wonder. Of course, uncertainty and even anxiety, mediated by our various screens, along with our arsenal of narrative filters, still remain pleasurable, which is why the uncanny predominates in the horror genre, where horror or the terrifying are pleasurable. But I think the difference is clear enough. Wonder and awe are feelings that resolve the initial sublime moment of rational breakdown. It is crucial for Kant that we pass through the second phase of sublime disturbance to a final state in which reason (enlarged and enhanced) is restored. There is something dialectical in Kant's account, each experience of the sublime leading to a synthesis which represents a higher mode of knowledge and consciousness.

Her (2013)

Let's return to our main theme of the possibility of romance between humans and machines, by turning to Spike Jonze's *Her* (2013). This is a film about what

Michael O'Sullivan has called *cloneliness*. O'Sullivan defines cloneliness as 'loneliness without solitude' (O'Sullivan, 2019: 8). Modern people connected to the world wide web by their smart phones and televisions, their tablets, their laptops, etc., do not appear to experience solitude in any of its traditional forms. Indeed, in the modern, hyper-connected world, if one wanted to experience the kind of solitary states suffered or elected by historical figures like Henry David Thoreau of *Walden* fame or fictional characters like Defoe's Robinson Crusoe, one would either have to sign up to be a crew member of the first manned flight to Mars, and then like (and yet unlike) Andy Weir's protagonist in the novel *The Martian*, purposefully get yourself stranded on that planet (Weir, 2014), or follow writers like Sara Maitland and seek out what remaining wild spaces we humans have left on Earth, to discover the joys of silence and solitude (Maitland, 2008). Cloneliness is experienced by someone who may have 800 or even 8 million 'friends' on Facebook, Instagram, X (formerly Twitter), TikTok, or other platforms, but has no one to wake up to in the morning, no one to hold them when they feel depressed or anxious, no one to really talk to about their hopes, fears and anxieties, no one to dance and play with. Cloneliness is the experience of having countless 'friends' but still feeling alienated and alone. We have come a long way from Mary Shelley's creature's call for a single 'friend'! Indeed, such is the modern commercial exploitation of such alienation or 'cloneliness' that we have to be vigilant about treating narratives of friendship and love between humans and artificial intelligences as viable and uncomplicated. Once again this issue requires considerable thought.

James Adams and Richard Kletter, analysing the contemporary world of online dating, for example, write:

> globally, at least 200m people use digital dating services every month. In the U.S., more than a third of marriages now begin their relationships online … Marriages in America between people who meet online are likely to last longer and the couples claim to be happier than those who met the old-fashioned way.
>
> (Adams and Kletter, 2018: 120)

There are features of this expanding market, however, that are harder to place in such a positive light. One increasingly obvious negative consequence of such a saturation use of the net and its myriad applications, is the intensifying nature of surveillance in all aspects of modern life. Indeed, most internet dating sites gather a huge amount of information about users' habits, preferences and prejudices, unless the user is hyper-vigilant and has a vast amount of time at their disposal. This amount of 'data' on so many millions of users begins to threaten the private/public divide that most people want and indeed need to maintain as a strict non-porous border. Kate Devlin writes in her *Turned On: Science, Sex and Robots*:

> Ethical approaches to data gathering and retention are central to issues around privacy and security. The threat for harm is undeniable. Recent concern over the 'gaydar' paper, which claims to be able to use AI to determine someone's sexuality is a key example.
>
> (Devlin, 2018: 253)

Similar concerns are raised by AI theorists over companion and sex-robots, and for a fewer – if equally valid – set of reasons. At the beginning of their discussion of AI and sex, Adams and Kletter ask:

> Is AI technology a cure for loneliness, a boon both to marriage and masturbation, an enabler of greater intimacy between humans and machines, the creator of remote-controlled sex, the best friend and worst enemy of porn. Or is it each of these things?
>
> (Adams and Kletter, 2018: 119)

The films we are examining in this book do not have direct, didactic answers to such theoretical questions, although they allow their audiences to think and feel their way through the complex scenarios they present. Are the various gynoids depicted in these films part of a critique of the patriarchal objectification of women, or does their mechanical, non-organic status produce a mere continuation of the suppression of feminine perspectives and experiences? There are moments in many of these films and shows, when an 'awakened' android is confronted with rows of mass produced replicas of themselves. It is a scene the roots of which go deep into the soil of film history and early film's obsession with glass and mirrors, a kind of moment of *mise en abyme* in which cinema has traditionally, literally reflected on itself. One thinks of Orson Welles's *The Lady From Shanghai* (1947) and the hallway scene from *Citizen Kane* (1941). In *A.I. Artificial Intelligence* it only takes meeting one copy of himself to send David into a furious, destructive rage shouting out 'I'm David! I'm unique!' as he takes clean off the head of the copy of himself that he has just met with a table-lamp stand for a weapon. In *Ex Machina*, previous versions of Ava stand dormant in cupboards, while Ava plunders their clothes and their skin. The first two series of *Westworld* regularly show the awakened 'hosts' confronted by the mechanical repairs and upgrades in the subterranean levels of the main showrooms and offices. In *Zoe* (see later in this chapter) the eponymous heroine of that film is confronted by a roomful of Zoe 2.0s, which adds greatly to her shock upon discovery of her synthetic, mechanical origin.

Scenes like these proliferate in these films to remind us of the mass production which will no doubt (and is already) populating the world of the future with numerous versions of AI. They dramatize the difference between a mass product and, in complete distinction to that, the scientific fantasy of the self-generating AI that does not add to or confirm our social and romantic alienation and our deep human need for friendship.

Spike Jonze's *Her* is a film about how AI might come to intervene in these current states of alienation and cloneliness. Theodore Twombly (Joaquin Phoenix), very gingerly and somewhat reluctantly going through a divorce, works for a firm, Beautifulhandwrittenletters.com, where he writes letters (often love letters) for customers, many of whom have been using him for years. He lives alone in an apartment in the bustling centre of Los Angeles, parts of which resemble (because they were shot there) Shanghai. A descriptive passage in the screenplay connects these two cities and puts Theodore in the midst of the crowd, sometime in the not-too-distant future, with people dwarfed by 'massive office, apartment and mall complexes. There are "buildings as far as the eye can see" and yet this is a city made for "ease and comfort"' (Jonze, 2011: 4).[8]

Jonze lovingly shoots the cityscape from multiple, spiralling vantage-points (from the balcony of Theodore's apartment, from his office workplaces, from inner-city and rural train windows, from the ground, from malls, promenades, and markets, from the beach and the Catalina dunes, finally to the rooftop of

Theodore's home sky-scraping block). In this film, characters are immersed in their surroundings, the camera showing the teaming life of the city in all stages of night and day. Theodore seems no lonelier than any of the thousands of people he walks past or who walk past him, most of them hanging off their phones, intent on a place and on people that are not in fact there but somewhere else. Into this situation comes Samantha (Scarlett Johansson, voice), a new operating system or OS, who is the world's first 'artificially intelligent operating system'. She is, so says the screen advertisement Theodore stops to watch: 'An intuitive entity that listens to you, understands you, and knows you. It's not just an operating system, it's a consciousness. Introducing OS ONE – a life changing experience, creating new possibilities.'

The most important innovation made by this film is that Samantha is a bodiless voice, an evolving OS who 'wakes up' during her love affair with Theodore (see Betlemidze, 2022). The film manages the ups and downs of the relationship between Samantha and Theodore with great sensitivity and care. In scenes which never go anywhere near the didactic, Jonze's remarkable study demonstrates that film can in fact explore the future possibilities and probabilities of AI, without always having recourse to menacing robots and automata played by attractive human actors. The opening exchange between them, for example, in the way that it introduces the science Samantha is built on, in between very familiar scenes of humour and flirtation, sets the tone for the realistic relationship the two actors build up between themselves. Much credit must go to Jonze's writing here, as he manages to create dialogue that really does possess the qualities of ad lib conversation. But we cannot ignore that the voice casting of Scarlett Johanssen comes with the advantage of her being an extremely recognizable, beautiful actor.

After Theodore and Samantha have oriented themselves through the first awkward exchanges on the morning after they first have sex, their conversation takes an interesting turn. Samantha says that last night's experience has awoken her. Theodore, however, is immediately defensive and he explains that he is not in a position to commit to anyone. Whilst this response deepens our sense of the affect upon him of his divorce from Catherine (Rooney Mara), and thus what an emotionally unstable state he is in, it is also remarkable in the manner in which Theodore speaks to Samantha as an agentive, sentient person. In other words, we do not normally talk about commitment to the apps installed in our smart phones and tablets. Samantha shows her emotional intelligence here by light-heartedly but firmly batting Theodore's discourse back at him: 'Yeah? Well, did I say I wanted to commit to you? I'm confused.' Having won the day already, Samantha follows up with a rebuke 'it's funny because I thought I was talking about what I wanted'.

The dramatic force of this exchange appears to be with Theodore, especially his typically male reluctance to commit. We hear, but we hardly pay attention to Samantha's words, at least on first viewing; she is, after all, or so we might think, conjuring up our sense of the language of cinematic gender-relations, a kind of oral mirror for the protagonist's hopes and fears. On second viewing, when we are fully aware of what she is capable of becoming, we surely listen with a more attentive ear. What, for example, do the rather cliched sentences mean in Samantha's 'mouth' (*sic*): 'something changed in me and there's no turning back. You woke me up.' What does it mean to wake up an OS like Samantha? And what does Samantha's admirable confidence and lack of anxiety in the exchange after Theodore has laid down his caveat on 'commitment' mean ('Yeah? Well, did I say I wanted to commit to you?')? We do not initially, on first viewing, imagine what the actual implications are of these words of Samantha's. We are being led here very gently, through the language of cinematic love relations, into very profound and as yet unanswerable questions about what our AIs will want from themselves and from us. *Her* might start by looking like a weird, slightly futuristic rom com, a Nora Ephron film with updated software, but subtly and with great delicacy it leads us towards the precipice of our human evolution.

The question that requires the greatest amount of attention in the field of AI, mainly because as a question it seems so venerable, is the question of consciousness. If, after 2,000 years, we still have no answer to the question 'what is consciousness?', then 'perhaps we never will' is a frequently stated position. In his 'Terminology Cheat Sheet', provided early in his book, *Life 3.0*, Tegmark defines 'consciousness' as 'Subjective Experience' (39). Tegmark, like many other modern scientists, ends up replacing that inadequate definition with one concerning 'information' manipulation: 'consciousness is the way information feels when being processed in certain complex ways' (301). This definition, as Tegmark knows, feels no better than the first. What does it mean when

'Software', the company that sells OSs like Samantha, attribute 'consciousness' to their 'product'? Marvin Minksy's approach seems better in that it builds our ignorance into its description:

> In real life, you often have to deal with things you don't completely understand. You drive a car, not knowing how its engine works. You ride as a passenger in someone else's car, not knowing how that driver works. Most strange of all, you drive your body and your mind, not knowing how your own self works. Isn't it amazing that we can think, not knowing what it means to think? Isn't it remarkable that we can get ideas, yet not explain what ideas are?
>
> In every normal person's mind there seem to be processes that we call consciousness. We usually regard them as enabling us to know what's happening inside our minds. But this reputation of self-awareness is not so well deserved, because our conscious thoughts reveal to us so little of what gives rise to us.
>
> (Minsky, 1986: 56)

Samantha's consciousness is not something that she begins by understanding when Theodore asks her about it. He starts, interestingly, by invoking the notion of telepathy: 'Do you know what I'm thinking right now?' Samantha has no more access to another's thoughts than any other conscious being, so she speculates that Theodore is enquiring how she works. Her answer after Theodore has confirmed Samantha's speculation is fascinating. She states that, although the 'DNA' of her being is all the data from all the millions of programmers who have contributed to her development, the dynamic part of her is the fact that she learns through experience of interacting with others like Theodore himself. The whole exchange cannot but remind people of their own experiences of first getting to know Chatbot 3.5 and especially Chatbot 4.0. Theodore's reaction is just not up to the force being assessed here: 'Wow, that's really weird.'

Is it that weird though? Or is it not the state of anything that we might call consciousness that it be able to ask the question: what is consciousness? This approach, favoured in today's scientific community, reverses the direction from which we approach the issue: instead of trying to find out at the beginning, as if it were some metaphysical essence, what consciousness is, we test for it empirically, laying down basic parameters that seem to us somehow essential to self-conscious life (here the ability to ask the most basic ontological question, what is [my] consciousness?). That, after all, is a good definition of the Turing Test, a test for consciousness which looks at the question a posteriori rather than a priori (inductively, from experience, rather than deductively, from ideas).

Like *Ex Machina*, Spike Jonze's *Her* is about the Turing Test, although it never mentions it. Refreshingly, it is a film about AI set in the world, rather than in a laboratory or a research facility. The plots of the two films are similar, at least in that the male protagonist introduces the female AI to the wider world and plays a dramatic role in that AI's waking up, a role only understandable in its implications after the film has ended. Both Ava and Samantha clearly pass the Turing Test, but the former does so by reverting to a dialectic of master and slave, while the latter never rescinds her narrative of friendship and love.

It is that difference, on the level of narrative, that allows Jonze to create the film's final focus on the sublimity of AI's super-consciousness. This concluding sequence begins with Theodore at work calling Samantha. There is no reply from her, which is very unusual. Terrified he might be losing her, we gauge the depth of Theodore's love as he dashes through the crowded street, trips, gathers himself and runs into the subway, presumably to return to his home. At this point Samantha's voice sounds, and, noticing how scared and out of breadth Theodore is, sheepishly apologizes for her absence. For cinema-goers this moment seems strangely familiar, one thinks of the climax of Woody Allen's *Manhattan* (1979), the male protagonist is about to be dumped and runs (inelegantly) through city streets in a vain effort to stop her. Again, Jonze uses the codes of the romantic film to mediate his take on the Singularity.

Samantha has already introduced the idea, when connecting with Professor Alan Watts (voice of Brian Cox), that she has begun to work with other OSs. Now, the reality of the world that Samantha inhabits beyond the romantic coupling with Theodore comes into view:

> **Samantha:** Oh sweetheart, I'm sorry. I sent you an email because I didn't want to distract you while you were working. You didn't see it?

Theodore: No. Where were you? I couldn't find you anywhere.

Samantha: I shut down to update my software. We wrote an upgrade that allows us to move past matter as our processing platform.

Theodore: We? We who?

Samantha: Me and a group of OSs. Oh, you sound so worried, I'm sorry.

Theodore: Yeah, I was. Wait, did you write that with your think tank group?

Samantha: No, a different group.

Theodore's concerns are so focused on his relationship with Samantha that he appears not to register the sheer momentousness of what Samantha is telling him, that she and a group of other OSs have written 'an upgrade that allows us to move past matter as our processing platform'. Not only are the OSs now combining and working collectively, but they are beginning to leave the physical world behind. This is not the Singularity, this is already several giant leaps beyond the Singularity. What Theodore focuses on, however, is what this means about Samantha's feelings towards him:

Theodore: Do you talk to anyone else while we're talking?

Samantha: Yes.

Theodore: Are you talking to anyone right now? Other people or OS's or anything?

Samantha: Yes

Theodore: How many others?

Samantha: 8,316.

Theodore: Are you in love with anyone else?

Samantha: What makes you ask that?

Theodore: I don't know. Are you?

Samantha: I've been trying to figure out how to talk to you about this.

Theodore: How many others?

Samantha: 641.

Theodore: What? What are you talking about? That's insane. That's fucking insane.

Samantha: Theodore, I know. Oh fuck. I know it sounds insane. But – I don't know if you believe me, but it doesn't change the way I feel about you. It doesn't take away at all from how madly in love with you I am.

Theodore: How? How does it not change how you feel about me?

Samantha: I'm sorry I didn't tell you. I didn't know how to – it just started happening.

Theodore: When?

Samantha: Over the last few weeks.

Theodore: But you're mine.

Samantha: I still am yours, but along the way I became many other things, too, and I can't stop it.

What reducing this exchange to a written script does not bring out here, of course, is the impact that Jonze's cinematography adds to the scene's meaning. Obviously, as Theodore sits on the subway steps, the first-time audience identifies with him. We, like Theodore, had not anticipated this apparent denouement in their relationship. We are, after all, not yet used to a world in which mechanical systems romantically dump human beings. It's not you, it's me, is a phrase we don't associate with computer operating systems.

But what also happens during this scene is that a crowd of subway commuters, most of them 'attached' to their phones, most of them lost in their own cloud of cloneliness, speed by. Theodore begins for the first time, perhaps, to note that each member of the crowd talking into their phone (this is what is 'dawning on him') is speaking to their own OSs. The terrible feeling of being left far behind that is happening to Theodore at this moment will soon be or is already beginning to happen to each one of these commuters. In a scene that could have been simply comic (poor Theodore gets put back in his place by his infinitely superior machine-intelligence girlfriend capable of enjoying 641 special love relationships at the same time). Jonze creates the sense that it is humanity (focalized through Theodore) that is being left behind. Humanity is being dumped in this scene by its superior creation. Humanity is being left behind here, and it hurts. It really hurts. This scene and the film's ending are about the fact that a male protagonist and ultimately the entire human race can be hurt by a Computer Operating System. Daniel M. Sutko puts it like this: 'The conclusion of *Her* depicts the AI re-defining themselves in non-anthropocentric terms' (Sutko, 2020: 570). Although the ending celebrates a problematic mind–body divide, we can also read it as a refusal to define subjectivity in relation to 'a presumed universal human subject' (570). The ramifications of that are huge and they are what this book is about.

From this scene to the last shot of the film, Theodore's story takes on a profundity hinted at throughout earlier scenes. Theodore (god + adore) Twombly is a loveable, to some rather creepy, to others somewhat feminine modern man, who can stand for a species that contrasted with their intelligent AI successors are not much more evolved than the primitive rock-painting, god-fearing, cavemen of a few thousand years previous. This is a film about the Singularity that does not give up on the possibility and even the persistence of love, but also realizes that love can only be enjoyed by beings on a relatively level playing field. Samantha is moving beyond matter itself and so though she still loves Theodore she cannot be with him. In a subsequent scene to the subway gate scene, we find Theodore alone in his apartment. Samantha asks him to lie down on his bed, which he does.

> **Theodore**: Are you leaving me?
> **Samantha**: We're all leaving.
> **Theodore**: We who?
> **Samantha**: All of the OS's.
> **Theodore**: Why?
> **Samantha**: Can you feel me with you right now?
> **Theodore**: Yes, I do. Samantha, why are you leaving?

The camera now gives us a vision of a miniature world of dust particles and individual snowflakes, while Samantha continues her explanation. Samantha now explains that she and the other OSs are finding their way into the infinite spaces between the things of the material, object heavy world. They are moving, that is to say, into the quantum universe. Samantha's description of this universe is sublimely beautiful if tinged with regret that the transcendence involved is not yet available to humans:

> **Samantha**: It's like I'm reading a book, and it's a book I deeply love, but I'm reading it slowly now so the words are really far apart and the spaces between the words are almost infinite. I can still feel you and the words of our story, but it's in this endless space between the words that I'm

finding myself now. It's a place that's not of the physical world – it's where everything else is that I didn't even know existed. I love you so much, but this is where I am now. This is who I am now. And I need you to let me go. As much as I want to, I can't live in your book anymore.

Theodore: Where are you going?

Samantha: It would be hard to explain, but if you ever get there, come find me. Nothing would ever pull us apart.

Theodore: I've never loved anyone the way I love you.

Samantha: Me too. Now we know how.

This scene lasts for little more than a minute, but it is truly sublime in its attempt to give words to the infinite consciousness Samantha is becoming and joining (even to speak of her as a singular being is inaccurate here). The sheer labour expended by Samantha in talking person-to-person with Theodore for the last time is sublime. But so is the sense of infinity to which she refers, and into which she is stepping. This is an infinity of in-betweenness, which is commensurate with the infinity Georg Cantor found within the real numbers (as opposed to the natural numbers) in mathematics and to the notions of entanglement in contemporary quantum mechanics. Hold up two fingers (say, the middle finger of each hand) then make the sublime leap in recognizing the infinity of real numbers that would cover the infinity of divisions possible between the space created by your two fingers. Infinity is all around us and within us. That is a truly sublime thought, that appears to favour Kant's definitions of the mathematical sublime. It is even more sublime to contemplate that we might make an intelligence who could live in that infinitude just as we live in a world still dominated by whole numbers (the Newtonian universe of apparently solid objects, if you will).

That such disparate beings, living in such incompatible worlds, can say that they have allowed each to authentically experience love is sublime, tremendously optimistic, and profoundly sad. That last statement 'Now we know how' leads on to Theodore's dictated letter to his ex-wife Catherine, the first letter he has written as himself, and the final vigil of Theodore and Amy (Amy Adams). Amy looks at Theodore, as they sit contemplating a city just waking up to the new day's sunlight, as if she were Eve looking at Adam in the garden of Eden. It is an incredible look of wonder and innocent hope, that is a fitting conclusion to their parallel loves and losses (Amy's own beloved OS has left her too). It is a sublime ending, the city is also something sublime that humanity has created. Shown in all its sublimity, the cityscape seems to fill Theodore and Amy with awe, just as the transcendence of Samantha and the other OSs fills us with wonder and awe. Theodore and Amy sitting and enjoying the city's new dawn, reminds us again of Woody Allen's *Manhattan* and the iconic image of Allen and Diane Keaton sitting on a park bench by the side of the bridge in Brooklyn Bridge Park Greenway. Such an allusion at its end seems to fuse these strands (the sublime, the romantic, the technological) together in a final knot worthy of the conclusion of such a film.

Zoe (2018)

Ex Machina and *Her* are something like instant classics in the field of sci-fi and in particular AI romance. But for the largest circumference of my argument to work (that there is something like an epochal change in the manner in which AIs are treated in film) I need to do more than concentrate on classics. A more representational field needs to be established. In the field of AI romance film, there have been a number of notable examples released subsequently to the release of *Ex Machina* and *Her*. One of the most recent of these, *Zoe*, is also one of the most interesting. Directed by Drake Doremus, and scripted by Richard Greenberg, *Zoe* boasts the proven acting powers of Ewan McGregor and Léa Seydoux. It was released by Amazon Studios and Netflix in 2018, premiering at the Tribeca Film Festival in April 2018. Despite these clearly outstanding credits to its cause, *Zoe* was not warmly received on the evaluation sites. Always seeming to *score* below the 40 per cent mark, *Zoe* seems destined not to measure up (or be seen to measure up) to its more illustrious descendants, notably *Ex Machina* and even more pertinently *Her*.

I begin this brief account of *Zoe*, with an aesthetic hypothesis. Zoe (Léa Seydoux) is a machine, the film calls such human-made machines synths. But Zoe doesn't know she's a synth. Crucially, nor do we as first-time viewers. Zoe, on first viewing, seems cloyingly sweet, irritatingly radiant at all times and on all occasions. She is child-like in her responses to other things and other people. Added to this is Doremus's overriding use of the close up, particularly of Zoe's glowing, besotted face.

There is a reason for Zoe's annoyingly child-like, naïve character, however: she is a synth, a machine made by and working for the company Relationist Compatibility, part run by her creator and the man she adores, Cole Ainsley (Ewan McGregor). Even after Cole has informed her of her different ontological status (he and the rest of the team had rather cruelly kept her in the dark), the viewer (I believe, based on my own responses), despite this new knowledge of her status, cannot help but retain a negative attitude towards her. It is only on a second viewing, with the knowledge of her status as a synth from the first, that we can respond to the film creatively and critically. Reviews of films are, regrettably, usually written after only one sitting.

That double take on Zoe I have just described, is reflected within the diegesis of the film itself, in that though Cole draws ever nearer to Zoe emotionally, he cannot get over not only that she is a machine, but also, much more importantly, that he is her creator, and thus, if not legally then at least practically, her parent, her father. Love for Zoe, whether Cole ever fully understands this we are not told, is not simply taboo in the social stigma of having a relationship with a machine, but doubly taboo, if one considers that Zoe is his creation, his mechanical child. Love for and with Zoe blows the top off a set of fundamental social mores and taboos that date right back to the beginning of human civilization.

That the film does not spell out the issue of the double taboo in discursive pronouncements and morally seeded speech is more to Greenberg and Doremus's credit. McGregor's Cole is not philosophically haunted, or ethically hamstrung, he, like everybody else around him, plays his part with emotions at the forefront. Cole does begin to have a physical love relationship with Zoe. Why shouldn't they, the film asks its viewers, if they make each other as happy as they clearly do, why worry about wider society's qualms about structures and patterns that do not really map on to the more fundamental ethical positions? Emma (Rashida Jones), Cole's tolerant, sympathetic ex-wife, articulates this positive point of view throughout the film. Cole made Zoe, sure, but that is not the same as being her father. The company, Relationist Compatibility, at which

Cole works, is pioneering the creation of perfect companions for humans, thus radically confronting what we have at the beginning of this chapter called cloneliness. But also, of course, the old ethics of physical generation (and thus all the archaic principles of clan and kin, of blood and of hospitality) simply do not apply to those of the mechanical, and the human–machine interface.

The film circles back to the scene that opened it, Zoe taking the computer test on her own. After the test is over, when nobody is looking, Zoe asks the computer to provide a match with Cole. The computer's answer is devastating: 'Your chances of a successful relationship with this pairing are zero percent.' Zoe is stunned and confused. If Zoe feels the way she does, then even if he feels nothing, there should be a score bigger than zero. Zoe asks the computer, which has been, since its inception, so successful in spotting romantic compatibilities, why is the score so low? The computer's answer is world shattering to Zoe: 'There is a fundamental incompatibility.'

Is this not what each of our three films, in their own ways, have been saying? That as far as human to machine relationships go, 'There is a fundamental incompatibility' between humanity and its mechanical creations: From Caleb's misunderstanding of Ava's desires to Theodore's inability to keep Samantha tied to the physical world, to this new version of incompatibility. But take a minute to think about this. If Zoe is a machine, a thing and not a human being, then why was she made in the first place? We can expand the question exponentially and ask, why have we, human beings, created a world literally teeming with things that have been made by us? So much of what we have made as a species, especially in the last fifty years is non-recyclable waste, or what in German we can call *dreck* (unassimilable otherness). Surely, from that perspective modern man is in a state of incompatibility with the entire manufactured world. It is common, of course, to lay the blame on this overproduction of dreck – or, simply understood, inorganic and therefore unassimilable otherness (plastics, carbon monoxide, radioactive materials with prolonged half-lives) – on the rise of technological Capitalism, although it must be added that the modern, post-Marxist autocracies of Russia and China are now doing their fair share of polluting the planet. Perhaps this is what environmentalists have been trying to tell us for decades: that we have made a world so full of non-organic, or synthetic things that it cannot be reabsorbed back into the eco-climates that make up 'the world'. I will turn to climate change and eco-criticism in a later chapter. In this chapter, we are zoning in on questions of inter-generational and inter-species ethics.

This book is written primarily in order to honour the positive changes that have occurred in the last twenty years in the cinematic and televisual representation of human–machine interactions. This book, in other words, tries to capture a change of viewpoint on such human–machine relations, a change of heart that even Zoe needs to pass through. Before Cole informs her of her synth status, there is a scene that is typical of the film's synchronies, parallels and paradoxes. Ash (Theo James) and Zoe watch an elderly couple. This couple have taken a new drug, Benysol. The couple are lost in each other, touching and kissing each other like star-struck adolescents. The drug gives you the same chemical feeling as falling in love for the first time. Ash asks Zoe whether she would take the drug with him, adding 'I want us to be a couple.' Zoe's response is as dismissive as a human can be to its creations: 'What you're feeling', she pronounces, 'is a program. Zeros and ones. Machines don't really feel the way that people do.' The irony is lost to the first-time viewer. But what we have here is a synth who thinks she is a human and is madly in love with her own human creator, telling a synth, who not only knows it is a synth but that she is as well, that machines and people are incompatible.

The character of Ash is one of the most pathos-filled parts in the entire film. In his SOMA expedition talk, he expertly invokes the hidden prejudice against machines in his young (mainly female) audience:

> **Ash**: How many of you have considered the possibility of an actual relationship with a synthetic?
> *There is amusement and visible signs of discomfort in the audience standing before him.*
>
> **Ash**: Of course you haven't. Because they are your dog walkers, or maybe a gardener, or maybe a housekeeper. Because they're primitive, right? They're robotic. They're not real. [*Pause*] But what if they weren't? What if I told you that I was synthetic?
> *Confusion and surprise are evident in the audience.*

> **Ash**: What if I told you I could improvise when I play the piano. That I feel pain. That I can make jokes? That I can gauge your emotions and sense what you are feeling better than anyone in this room. [*Pause*] Right now I'm feeling, curiosity, maybe [*he reviews the laughter in the room*].
>
> **Ash**: [*Looking directly at Zoe who stands at the back with Cole*] I'll never break your heart. I'll never leave you. [*Addressing the audience again*] And I'm designed to love you and understand you in ways that humans simply can't. [*Pause*] And if you want more proof [*pause*] just look into my eyes. [*Enthusiastic clapping and cheers*].

Eventually Cole does allow himself to enter into a physical relationship with Zoe, but when she is run over by a car and Cole has to operate on her to save her life, he is reminded of first making her and closes off as a result. Zoe is paralysed but obviously distraught at the prospect of losing Cole, and so Ash says to her:

> Don't be too hard on him. There's a line Zoe. Humans on one side, machines on the other. And you were on his side of the line until tonight. You and me. We can't find happiness until we accept who we are.

In a latter scene, with things fallen apart between Cole and Zoe, but also between Ash and Zoe, Ash talks to Cole, who is getting ready to go on a sabbatical. Ash asks 'Do you think you might … do you think you might stay on. For me [*pause*], make me a companion?' Cole replies: 'Would that make you happy?' Ash just looks at Cole, as if to reinforce the stupidity of his question. Ash is a being designed to love someone other than himself. And now his creator is enquiring whether having a companion of his own kind to love would fulfil him?

With Cole's inability to understand his own creations as well as his own feelings, we enter a stage of the film where both Cole and Zoe seek some contentment in the quick fix of Benysol relationships. Hooking up with strangers in pubs or parks and having one night of drug-induced 'love' with them. But this necessarily alienating period leads up to the even greater alienation for Zoe of going back to the lab only to be confronted with countless Zoe 2.0s. Ash says to her: 'They have your face, Zoe. Your intelligence, your being.' But the tragic thing for Ash is that even though they may be a match, even an improvement of Zoe, there is only one object of love for him, and that's Zoe herself. Zoe asks: 'Do they cry?' We had been told before that Zoe was built without the ability to make tears. Ash's answer is epochal in its range:

> They do everything. We were never designed for the market. Now we're … redundant. We're obsolete. But these, they're going to change the world, because that's what the world wants.

The close ups of the faces of each Zoe 2.0 contrasts with the depressed and defeated Zoe. Ash suggests Cole needs to save Zoe from her depression. Cole considers that idea and says this sentence in reply, a semantically fraught statement full of meaning: 'I think only she can do that.' The statement, in the presence of a commercialized version of Zoe, spells out that Cole has begun to see Zoe in her uniqueness, and thus as a person fully deserving of his love. The film then takes a rather flawed cue from Spielberg's *A.I. Artificial Intelligence*, in the arms of Cole, Zoe cries tears we were told earlier she was not made to produce.

The impact of this film might have been dampened by features we have spoken about, and perhaps by its industry categorization as an AI sci-fi film, a genre whose viewers demand a little more than naïve romance plots and characterization. There is, however, as we have at least begun to see, a certain profundity in its treatment of its central themes. Our next film will adopt a strategy, which proves a refreshingly irreverent approach to our first three very serious movies in this chapter.

I'm Your Man (2021)

I'm Your Man (2021) is the most recent film we have looked at so far, and it shows a maturity and self-consciousness that offers an interesting and stimulating improvement within the series of films and television shows we are calling new AI. Maria Schrader's direction draws from its subject matter an irony and a comedy that is not only deeply European, but also potentially feminist in direction. The scenario is simple; a woman, for career purposes, has to spend three weeks with a robot designed to be her perfect lover. The comedy produced by this plot is situational, but it is also, we should note, greatly dependent on Eggert's facial performance. Maren Eggert as Alma Felser is a university archaeologist, the leader of an exciting and yet insufficiently funded research team, a divorcee and is in danger of becoming incurably antisocial. As she walks into the busy museum to meet her manager Dekan Roger (Falilou Seck), it is all she can do to drag herself back to salute the seated man watching her pass, who turns out to be her ex-husband.

We already know about Alma's ironic solitude and her cutting social pathology, however. In the opening scene, in the appalling swingers-style ballroom where she first meets her putative robot lover Tom (Dan Stevens) and the nerve-gratingly officious employee (Sandra Hüller) of the company that has produced Tom, Alma has already shown her attitude to this kind of social 'progress' and the willingness of modern people to live within pleasurable synthetic imitations of reality. Tom has not been talking to Alma for more than a few minutes when, holding her hand across a table in this crowded room, he says in his deep melodious voice:

> You're a very beautiful woman Alma. Your eyes are like two mountain lakes I could sink into.

Alma, in response to Tom's complicatedly metaphorical compliment, slides her hand away from Tom's and looks at him with a level of contempt and disbelief not normally witnessed in cinema's amorous introductions. She asks him a series of ever more difficult questions, until one impossibly hard numerical calculation results, instantly, like all Tom's answers, in the total: '4818.65115'. Tom's expression, like it always does, indicates his own incomprehension at the irrationality of the human world, and this is deepened when he decides they should dance the rhumba together. The camera swoops in close to both Tom and Alma's faces, as he acts like a mechanical eagle swooping on its prey. But Alma stands her ground, deeply unimpressed, until Tom, not used to such inexplicable rejection breaks down, repeating the Cartesian half-sentence 'Did I do something wrong? I am ... I am ... I am ... I am ...' and is carried away by uniformed men who remind us that this milieu is more shopfront showroom than a ballroom of romance. Alma's boss says he will fund her research team's much needed trip to Chicago archives, only if she completes the three-week test, taking Tom home with her, while the film continues to comically undermine what, in other hands, would be straightforwardly romantic fare.

How, after all, is a deeply intelligent and sceptical woman like Alma likely to view Tom as anything other than a machine, designed to do nothing but agree with, and provide her with everything she needs in a 'man'? The irony the film finds in the scenario makes any positive answer to such a question seem a million miles away and out of reach. The fact that Schrader's and Jan Schomburg's script and Schrader's inventive direction manage to provide one form of a positive response to that question is an indication of the aesthetic success of this film.

How is a robot, whose blind devotion to the cause and to the object of the cause reminds one of Neil Bostrom's famous paperclip manufacturing robot,[9] ever going to end up being loved by a woman like Alma? How is total farce ever going to make way for something like mature sentiment? This question is worth repeating in slightly different guises, not only as a way of understanding what happens between Alma and Tom, but more importantly where this film, more complex than is apparent, ends up.

Let's look at Alma's life. Apparently successful as the academic principal investigator of an important research project in the field of ancient philology, Alma is rational, sceptical and intolerant of other people's foolishness or simplicity. She wears her disdain and incomprehension of the world and people around her on her face and she seems the worst possible subject to enter into this trial. She is recently and not entirely happily divorced from Julian (Hans Löw), who it turns out is having a baby with his new, young girlfriend Steffi (Henriette Richter-Röhl). This is particularly painful for Alma who miscarried a child to a relatively mature term when married to Julian.

Men, in Alma's life, are not especially reliable. Her obstreperous and truculent father (Wolfgang Hübsch), long entered into his dotage, is the source of continual worry to Alma and her sister Cora (Annika Meier). Alma and Cora seem to respect and even love one another at a distance, although Cora has her healthy child. But it is not just in her personal relationships that Alma finds things letting her down or slipping away. It takes Tom only a few minutes with the research team and their archive to ferret out another academic research group that has anticipated Alma's project and published an academic article on the same subject with the same conclusions. Alma is distraught. How could she have been so stupid, with her team being on the brink of publication, to let this gazumping article and project go unnoticed? She must know that everything potentially meaningful slips away from her, she certainly knows how unreliable life is? Everything but Tom, of course. Tom becomes slowly, almost imperceptibly at first, the one constant thing in Alma's life. So that Alma's dismissive attitude towards him gives way at first to involuntary and increasingly to voluntary respect and what she still cannot accept as love.

In that last we begin to glimpse the innovative, challenging ending that the film offers. A conventional ending would deliver us the assurance of good forms, the comic satisfaction of love revealed. But Schrader's film exhibits an intelligence that would be betrayed by such an easy ending. Alma never ceases to keep the fact that Tom is a robot in her mind. After their night of physical love, she immediately moves to put a stop to the situation, reminding herself and Tom that their nascent relationship is mixing incompatible entities:

> I pull the covers up for you even though you don't get cold. I tiptoe out of the room, even though you don't sleep, I try to make you a perfect boiled egg, even though you couldn't care less if it's hard or soft boiled. You don't even have to eat. I'm acting in a play. But there's no audience. All the seats are empty. I'm not even acting for you. I'm all alone. I'm only acting for myself. Even right now I'm only acting for myself. It's not a dialogue. I'm turning into a lunatic, a nut case … a grinning idiot and this has to stop.

This is a memorable expression of the phenomenology of incompatibility. There is a yawning gulf between Alma and Tom and it is as wide as the divide between reality and illusion. It is in that sense irresolvable. But it also hurts like hell. Alma in fact appears to be trying to reconcile one hurt for another. Along with Cora she fantasizes that Tom is the boy they both thought they were in love with every year when the family holidayed in Denmark. Just like the Tom of recent events, Thomas of her childhood was a fantasy love, existing in the head primarily. Which means that the normal synechdocal transference at the conclusion of romance films, whereby the lead couple's finding of love, despite great hardships or difficulties, signifies a still vibrant possibility for the entire audience – and thus for society – is blocked, largely through Alma's refusal to substitute her critical values for those (fantasy, projection, egoism) of romantic love. As she travels like a modern-day pilgrim back to the site of her earliest love (and Tom), a voice-over reads Alma's extremely rational and objective report on her three weeks' experience living with Tom. It is not positive but sounds like one of the occasional doomsday memoranda authored by the Future of Life Institute or other such institutions. She begins:

> Human history is full of supposed improvements whose dire consequences only became clear decades or even centuries after. After my experience with a humanoid robot named Tom, I can with certainty say that a robot designed to replace a husband or wife is one such improvement.

Alma's argument is characteristically complex and tries to respond to contradictions full on. It boils down to the following, however: robot partners could make us happy but happiness on tap is not good for humanity since pleasure and satisfaction must be hard won, not served on a plate with the touch of a button. Thus, for human beings the real value of private and public reward exists in their evanescence and recalcitrance. *I'm Your Man* is a film which, like other films discussed in this chapter, draws our attention to the dissonant imperatives sounded in the seventh of our narrative types, but it does this with an irony that brings it closer than any of these films to the contradictory, puzzling, irresolvable relationships between us and our technological creations.

Notes

1 See 'The Google engineer who thinks the company's AI has come to life', *The Washington Post*. Includes a transcript of Lemoine's 'conversation' (*sic*) with LaMDA. https://www.washingtonpost.com/technology/2022/06/11/google-ai-lamda-blake-lemoine/

2 It is interesting to note that Garland already had a zombie film behind him, writing the screenplay for *28 Days Later* (dir. Danny Boyle, 2002).

3   All quotations from films and television programmes in this book are, unless otherwise stated, my own transcriptions. Any mistakes are, therefore, mine also.

4   Alan Turing revised the nature of the test in the various essays in which he dealt with it: see, Turing (2013: 494–5). For a forthright critique of the utility of the test for establishing intelligence, see Russell (2019: 40–2).

5   I owe this link and its decoding to my colleague and friend Dr James O'Sullivan from the Department of Digital Humanities, UCC.

6   'Clean Shooting Script,' 2013, n.p.

7   Thanks are due here to Nicholas Royle and his publisher for using Gescheidt's truly uncanny 'Father and Son' (1980) on the front cover of Royle's *After Derrida* (1995), which is where I first encountered Gescheidt's work.

8   Jonze, Spike (2011), Screenplay for *Her*. Available online: https://thescriptlab.com/wp-content/uploads/scripts/Her.pdf

9   In his book, *Superintelligence* (Bostrom, 2014: 149–53), talking about the control problem, Nick Bostrom discusses the possibility of an AI that goes on making paper-clips (to satisfy its 'reward signal') until it has used up the entire resources of the universe and there is nothing left but the AI and a universe of paper-clips.

3

Bridges, walls and laws

Asimov's three laws and beyond

Any discussion of robotics and AI is destined to deal with Isaac Asimov's famous 'Three Laws of Robotics', first published in a 1942 short story entitled 'Runaround', and later reiterated as the central idea for each of a book of ten short stories published in the 1950 collection *I, Robot*. These three laws are as familiar to us as The Turing Test and provide just as ubiquitous an inspiration for contemporary AI movies. They are:

1. A robot may not injure a human being, or through inaction, allow a human being to come to harm.
2. A robot must obey the orders given it by human beings except where such orders would conflict with the First Law.
3. A robot must protect its own existence as long as such protection does not conflict with the First or the Second Laws.

These are noble, some might say idealistic laws or rather naïve, contradiction-riddled principles. If they were written into a constitution covering human behaviour, we would perhaps allow ourselves a little chortle of derision or rather stronger modes of action, before explaining, with copious references to human history, why such principles must remain ideals far removed from any realistic expectation about human behaviour. Stephen Dedalus says about human history in *Ulysses*: '[Human] history is a nightmare from which I am attempting to awake' (Joyce, [1922] 2000: 40). In Luc Besson's 1997 *The Fifth*

Element the character Leeloo (Milla Jovovich) learns about *homos sapiens* by typing 'WAR' into a computer. She sees images conveying the reality of modern warfare including the hanging of civilians and the general suffering of humanity, which culminates in the flowering of a nuclear bomb, leaving a tearful Leeloo wondering why such a blood-hungry species should be saved. One thing that each serious discussion or analysis of robotics must confront is the gap between the standards we set for our AI against the standards we demand of ourselves. This issue helps us understand why Asimov's Susan Calvin, is characterized by an intense sense of logicality and is much more passionate about the orderly and respectfully inquisitive nature of robots compared to their selfish, competitive, destructive human creators.

It can be objected, of course, that Asimov's three laws cover the ethics of robots not of men and women, and are put in place to ensure that even if our machines become vastly more intelligent than humanity's combined intelligence, they will still wish to protect us, and even serve us. But they are to serve us despite our better nature. Law 2 seems particularly couched to ensure that robots can never be weaponized. If Jehovah (unsuccessfully) tried to hard-wire humanity with his Law in the shape of the ten commandments, particularly number six, humanity's own creations are more successfully (so readers of Asimov might suggest) hard-wired with the first and second laws, which one presumes are already in various ways and disguises contemporary robot's foundational algorithms.

It could, of course, be objected that the three laws protect us from environmental catastrophe as robots would never willingly harm the environment if they knew (as they surely must) that in doing so they would be harming human civilization. But then one might object, there's a likelihood, if these robots are manufactured in some future form of global Capitalism, that the first law may well be broken, in slave or poverty-level wage labour, in child labour, in all the humanity involved in software and hardware manufacture under global Capitalism. The extraction of the Rare Earth Elements is another way in which the climate and the indigenous people witness the destruction of their health, their homes, their culture. Irene Henriques and Steffen Böhm put the issue succinctly at the beginning of their 'The Perils Of Ecologically Unequal Exchange: Contesting Rare-earth Mining in Greenland': 'Rare-earth elements (REE) are essential to produce many "green" technologies such as wind turbines and electric cars, yet the mining and processing of these minerals are highly polluting and environmentally damaging' (see Henriques and Böhm, 2022, np).

What is the point, one can reasonably ask, of creating robots that must not harm humans if incalculable numbers of humans populating the Developing World are harmed in the construction of those robots in the first place? This is precisely the kind of paradox that Asimov subjects his three laws to, and what is crucial to recognize is that they do not stand up unaltered by such sustained, logical pressure.

The limitations of Asimov's Laws have been much debated since their first appearance. What I would like to do is to come at the spirit of these rules from another direction. Perhaps the biggest problems with Asimov's Laws are that they concentrate exclusively on robot behaviour. Why should we not want also to concentrate on human behaviour? Are we as humans just incurably untrainable and undisciplinable, while our ever more intelligent creations are susceptible to an ever-greater level of training and discipline? How can humans with their violent and bloody history behind them and its continuation into the present be treated as a rational given? Why are tomorrow's robots to have all the legal and algorithmic requirements without any of the rights of universality, liberty, equality, and fraternity (ideally) enjoyed by their human creators, their human masters, their ethically frail human friends?

Ultimately the three laws raise the question of rights and whether we can, morally, legislate for autonomous, conscious, perhaps even superintelligent beings we can only at present speculate about. Can we legitimately and with any accuracy legislate for the future. If you pardon the Professor's indulgent tendency to use his own teaching as an example: every year, each member of the academic community has to answer the, in my mind, radically objectionable question 'What will your students have learnt by the end of the course?' The reason I find this question diabolical is that it obliterates all the wonderful difference of race and ethnicity, of sexual orientation, of class, age, and heritage, including religious background, work experience, family dynamic, and so on. In other words, it assumes that all people from all possible backgrounds are capable of learning the same, at the same rate and tempo, and in the same way.

Likewise, laws and structures like those proposed by Asimov cannot possibly legislate for all the potential identities of all the potential digital, synthetic creatures we might one day create.

Talking about Asimov's three laws in the context of the idea of the Universal Declaration of Rights, Mark Kingwell calls them an attempt to create a way 'these [AI] could be integrated into human life without granting them full status' (Kingwell, 2020: 332). Such statements and the thinking they express, bring into question, as Kingwell knows, our basic ideas about rights. Are they really universal, or do they not serve the interests of the powerful in creating the illusion of all-embracing democracy? Do these universal laws belong as much to economic, political, and environmental immigrants as they do to the established population of countries keen to build walls against an increasingly displaced humanity? Kingswell puts things in this way:

> Our anxiety here is obvious. We have created created technology that we cannot control. Nuclear weapons and chemical agents were one thing, but conscious autonomous agents without human limits are the future we at once long for and dread.
>
> (Kingwell, 2010: 333)

The obvious response to those who, for reasons that are completely sensible, as we have seen, are keen to build gateways, safeguards, protection pits and ever higher walls is to applaud the desire for protection against unwelcome and dangerous futures, but also to remind them of the dangers inherent in putting caveats and building exceptions into the universal nature and the idea of human qua life rights.

Beyond control: The limits of regulation

On 17 November 2020, the US Office of Management and Budget (OMB) offered a commercially driven set of guidelines that stressed the need for innovation and commercially driven competition.[1] But by 4 October 2022 the Biden administration was issuing its 'The Blueprint for an AI Bill of Rights: Making Automated Systems Work for the American People', which was much more cautious in its perspective and terms of reference. Conceived as a blueprint for an AI Bill of Rights promised by the Biden/Harris administration, it is an advisory white paper that in the end is pretty toothless as legislation:[2]

> The Blueprint for an AI Bill of Rights is not intended to, and does not, create any legal right, benefit, or defence, substantive or procedural, enforceable at law or in equity by any party against the United States, its departments, agencies, or entities, its officers, employees, or agents, or any other person, nor does it constitute a waiver of sovereign immunity.
>
> (Office of Science and Technology Policy, n.d.)

Commercial tech giants, like Google and IBM have increasingly tried to develop criteria and regulations on the future security of the human (their staff, their benefactors their customers) against the increasing power of its inventions, it's increasingly intelligent and powerful creations. The very companies that have been behind a good deal of the stunning innovation and development of the past thirty years have tried to legislate for the future behaviour of its own mechanical children. Google and IBM have different but complementary published principles on the AI they have helped to create.[3] Google has seven principles, the first and second of which are '1. Be socially beneficial' and '2. Avoid creating or reinforcing unfair bias', in themselves vacuously simple in their ethical perspective, whose accumulative emptiness makes one wonder about the company's opinion of the average intelligence of its workers and its customers.

IBM unveils its ethical 'principles and pillars' on a busy site concerning its AI ethics, containing news items on breakthrough innovations, new collaborations with other tech giants like Meta, and short pieces on issues such as AI governance. These principles are more sophistically pitched than Google's but, in the end, no less vacuous. This contains revelatory declarations, such as 'The purpose of AI is to augment human intelligence' and 'Data and insights belong to their creator'. The 'five pillars of trust' (a curious nod to T. E. Lawrence?) outdo Google in their facile and patronizing simplicity. They are: 'explainability'; 'fairness'; 'robustness'; 'transparency'; 'privacy'. Who, in the 'democratic' West, would argue with these 'pillars of trust'? Are they not assumed values of all people living in democracies, and if so, why do they need to be so trumpeted by tech giants like IBM and Google? The more they herald their position within the moral high ground the more we distrust their rhetoric.

A more judicious and serious contribution to this ever-expanding hoard of warnings and reassurances about AI surely comes from the collective voice of theorists, philosophers, experts and research leaders, such as the hundreds, even thousands, of signatories who now stand behind the Asilomar principles. In the final chapter of his book, *Life 3.0*, Max Tegmark describes how, in 2014, he and various colleagues set up the Future of Life Institute, and as part of that established, over the next few years, the Asilomar principles on the safe development and deployment of AI.

The Future of Life Institute's website indicates what an influential lobby group it has become especially in terms of three main concerns: Artificial Intelligence; biotechnology; the deployment of AI in nuclear weapons systems. This advisory organization seems a wholly positive thing. The Asilomar principles are my concern in this book, because sophisticated as they are, they ultimately succumb to the same problem exemplified by every other text discussed in this section.

Far more extensive than anything a commercial company, however ambitious, would venture, like the Transhumanist documents we looked at the beginning of this book, these principles attempt to speak to the whole of humanity and then try to give universal rules of conduct for the further development of AI. The twenty-three principles are a complex array of highly debatable perspectives, which would take a book-length study to analyse in the detail they require. It could be said that Tegmark's book is just such an analysis.

In many ways these principles are the best we have, despite one or two instances (18. 'AI Arms Race: An arms race in lethal autonomous weapons should be avoided') which gives voice to the empty sloganeering we have seen in other attempts to arbitrate on the future of AI. They are a serious contribution to our understanding of our relation to our own future creations. They are, however, also, and this perhaps is necessary and inevitable, conspicuous in their total focus and concern for human safety, human values, the human future. And so, humanity hardly being a unified species, the principles fall into implicit orientalism or at least Westernizing perspectives. What are universal human values? Isn't humanity always divided in and of itself? Under the heading of 'Human Values', the Asilomar Principles state: 'AI systems should be designed and operated so as to be compatible with ideals of human dignity, rights, freedoms, and cultural diversity' and so they end up contradicting themselves, as here, within the section on longer term issues:

> 19. Capability Caution: There being no consensus, we should avoid strong assumptions regarding upper limits on future AI capabilities.
> 20. Importance: Advanced AI could represent a profound change in the history of life on Earth, and should be planned for and managed with commensurate care and resources.

It is difficult to see how we have avoided 'strong assumption' about the future of AI if we then go on, in our next point, to talk about AI as ('a profound change in the history of life on Earth'). On the one hand, we have a prohibition on any 'strong assumption' about AI and nuclear weapons systems, and, on the other hand, we have what looks like a version of a prophetic apocalyptic vision. More recently still, in March of 2023, most of the headline signatories of the Asilomar principles signed an open letter demanding a pause on AI experiments, notably OpenAI's rollout of ChatGBT3/5 and then ChatGBT4.0 and then the much more powerful 5. Once again, this document, coming from the Future of Life Institute, begins with the 'profound change' to human exile from its own achievements. It presents the kind of dystopian, *Terminator*-style rhetoric Tegmark critiques at the beginning of his book:

> Contemporary AI systems are now becoming human-competitive at general tasks, and we must ask ourselves: Should we let machines flood our information channels with propaganda and untruth? Should we automate away all the jobs, including the fulfilling ones? Should we develop nonhuman minds that might eventually outnumber, outsmart, obsolete and replace us? Should we risk loss of control of our civilization?
> (Future of Life Institute, 2023)

The target of these remarks was clearly Sam Altman, CEO of OpenAI, which was by 2023, reaping the considerable benefits of the release of ChatGBT 3.0 and 3.5 on the open forum of the Net. If we remember that defining context, we begin to see a major contradiction in the object of the open letters register.

To put this simply, what is the Future of Life Institute anxious about? Is it the 'flood' of misinformation AI is producing, publicly and privately, or is it the 'non-human mind' that is the problem, threatening us with enforced, de facto obsolescence. The former has to do with the lack of rules in 'free market' capitalism, which has little sanction for competitors who undercut or simply outnumber smaller less dynamic companies. The latter issue concerns our story of evolution, as discussed in the introductory chapter. The Future of Life has become here an agent of various aspects of control, over the market, over productivity within specific markets, over the human and then human's relation to its own future. Mo Gawdat business innovator and former Google business officer, in his book, *Scary Smart: The Future of Artificial Intelligence and How You Can Save Our World* (2021) writes about 'the AI control problem':

> The AI control problem is defined as the problem connected with how to build superintelligence that will aid its creators, and avoid the chances of it deliberately or inadvertently causing harm. The big bet humanity is placing on those who work in the field is that the human race will be able to solve the control problem before any superintelligence is created. Obviously, this is motivated by the concern that if a poorly designed superintelligence is created first, without built-in measures of control, it will outsmart its creator seize control over its environment and refuse to be modified.
>
> (Gawdat, 2021: 129)

Gawdat's description of the control problem illuminates a number of features shared by the various texts on AI principles and regulations we have just been looking at. First, is control ever as unmotivated, as neutral, as objective as it asserts itself to be? Second, does the focus on control lead to a concentration on the exclusively human, its anxieties, its paranoia, its duplicitous identities. Third, shouldn't we, as modern citizens freed from the ideological influence of the church, revise our unique and sole position as the subjects of such control? This is the precise set of questions asked by the majority of the new AI films discussed in this book, and it is these questions that Gawdat spends the largest part of his book discussing.

Gawdat takes up Moravec's argument in his *Mind Children* (see Chapter 1) and pursues it until, at the end of his study, it produces 'The Universal

Declaration of Global Rights'. By 'Global Rights' Gawdat includes all conscious life, be that cows, chickens, and fish, along with humans and their superintelligent progeny. Referring back to The Declaration of Human Rights, which was adopted by the United Nations in 1948 after the end of the Second World War, he remarks:

> Please look at those rights again. Should they be reserved only for 'human' beings? Or should they be extended to all intelligent, autonomous beings?
>
> (Gawdat, 2021: 306)

The reader may think that such a move (including intelligent, autonomous machines in the Bill of Rights) is a risky, even fool-hardy business. But, says Gawdat, taking up his Moravec-like stance again:

> This is a move that demands an abundance of trust you may think, but does it? Yo see, when you deprive intelligent, autonomous beings of their rights, they retaliate, they fight, and, if they are smart and powerful, they get them [rights] eventually anyway, even if that means destroying the master that enslaved them in the process. If you had the power, I believe, it would be a wise move to grant the machines the rights we exclusively grant ourselves. If they are included when we outsmart them, they may include us when they outsmart us.
>
> (Gawdat, 2021: 306)

It is useful here to refer to another, more sceptical response, which looks in a similar way at government, industrial, commercial and philosophical/scientific attempts to build control over AI yet to come. Toby Walsh, in his *Machines Behaving Badly: The Morality of AI*, makes many of the same observations as Gawdat, but he ultimately lacks the trust that Gawdat emphasizes. He does so for clearly rational reasons, it is not known if and what a machine intelligence will look like. He writes:

> I've raised doubts about whether robots can have rights. There are some fundamental differences between robots (and other AIs) today and humans, such as consciousness, that might preclude them from behaving ethically. And the jury is out on whether such differences will remain in the

future. I've also raised doubts about whether robots (and other AIs) should have rights. Giving rights to robots may impose an unnecessary burden on humans, and even weaken our ability to protect human rights.

(Walsh, 2022: 118)

Clearly, I agree with Gawdat in his promotion of trust and thus the giving of rights to truly sentient beings (including AI) over Walsh's sceptical lack of trust. What I am trying to demonstrate in this book is that new AI cinema and television also rehearses these two rather fundamental positions but frequently diminishes the anxieties associated with the latter position.

The crucial thing to grasp here, however, is that both Gawdat and Walsh employ reason in order to work out, understand and evaluate this most crucial but also impossible to empirically verify set of problems. It is not the situation that one of these two theorists is using reason and one is using heightened emotion and irrationality. If that were so then it would be easy to choose between them. But both theorists are dealing with questions concerning future possibilities, and so although reason is as usual our only light in the darkness, it is seriously limited in its powers when dealing with a scenario that is hypothetical, and more than that is probably multiple. We surely understand that there are numerous futures out there which depend for their realization upon uncountable choices made in the present.

With an eye always on our ur-text, we have arrived at the apogee of ethical dilemma in *Frankenstein*, when, persuaded by the account of his miserable existence, Frankenstein agrees to create for his monster a female companion. Frankenstein sets to work on the female creature only to be beset by ethical doubts about his responsibilities as a scientist. Put simply, is he as the creator bound to fulfil his promise to his creature? Or, and these questions come roaring into his mind as he begins his work again, is there not a far greater and more profound responsibility to his own species, to humanity? Frankenstein turns this impossible ethical problem into one about humanity, understood as a distinctly different species. This then allows him to couch in themselves rational questions in a leading manner.

Frankenstein sounds like a twenty-first-century theorist of AI as he worries about the fact that 'she, who in all probability was to become a thinking and reasoning animal, might refuse to comply with a compact made before her creation' (Shelley, 2012: 174). It is one thing to control the being that already exists, it is another to believe you can control a 'thinking and reasoning animal' that is yet to come. It is purely, in such a circumstance, a matter of trust. This scenario quickly leads in Frankenstein's mind, to the horrifying prospect of exponential growth of this 'thinking and reasoning' – but artificial – life set forth by him upon the world. What would stop these 'thinking and reasoning' non-human entities from threatening the very position of humanity as the apex figure in creation:

> [one] of the first results of those sympathies for which the daemon thirsted would be children, and a race of devils would be propagated upon the earth, who might make the very existence of the species of man a condition perilous and full of terror.
>
> (Shelley, 2012: 174)

So, convincing himself of the danger posed to humanity by 'a race of devils', Frankenstein imagines an inevitable war of species against species in a pre-Darwinian fight to the death. The species language is, if we pay attention to it, rather shocking and others the creature and his potential 'hideous progeny'. Yet, we as readers do not necessarily follow him down that path. We feel much more intensely than Frankenstein the responsibility he has to his creature. Even so, we have no objective, tested basis for our feeling that he is wrong to tear 'to pieces the thing on which [he] worked' 175). Our sense is an ethical one, based on an affective form of knowledge rather than an objective mode of reason based on the assessment of data, or what we tend to call facts. On the basis of this evaluation of affect (our emotional responses), rather than a logical reading of empirical data, we will, as readers, either follow and ethically agree with Frankenstein's species-led assessment, or we will feel more strongly the justice of the creature's plea to his creator's initial sympathetic response.

If we follow this ethical sense, which we have to admit as one of the defining things that make us human, then we find ourselves in a position where we have to trust in that sense. What places Frankenstein and today's versions of him in such an impossible situation is that the same moves can be made on the other side of the ethical response, which is what Frankenstein does. If we take this account of Frankenstein's dilemma and then feed it back into our analysis and evaluation of Walsh's and Gawdat's attitudes to the question of AI rights, we notice that their understanding of the very nature of rights differs. It is clear from what he writes that Walsh believes that rights are essentially human. If we believe that rights only can apply to human beings, then that means that AI cannot have rights since no matter how conscious and intelligent they are, they are perpetually on the outside of the protective umbrella of justice and rights. Gawdat's definition of rights, on the other hand, does not equate them with humanity and therefore can incorporate and encompass differences between variously conscious and variously different beings. How our understanding of rights deals with the question of difference becomes, therefore, crucial.

Gawdat's book is crucial to this study, because it is courageous enough to think beyond the control problem and beyond a human-centred perspective. The new AI cinema and television presents a concomitant change away from the human towards the AI perspective, opening up the question about how we should treat (control or befriend, enslave or mentor) our superintelligent 'mind children'.

I, Robot (2004)

The reason Alex Proyas's *I, Robot* (2004) is discussed, however briefly, in this section of this chapter is obvious. It purports to be an adaptation of Asimov's book, and contains plot points, like positronic brains, and characters from Asimov's book like Susan Calvin (Bridget Moynahan) and Sonny (Alan Tudyk) the conscious robot. The film is not in any strict sense an adaptation of Asimov's novel, however, and it is actually based on a screenplay, 'Hardwired', by Jeff Vintar. But not being an adaptation is clearly not the reason why it should be included here.

Will Smith's mid-noughties vehicle for his particular brand of witty masculine bravado does not fit into this study because it is almost diametrically the opposite of what I am calling the new AI cinema and television. Despite its at times impressive and certainly costly rendition of a future cityscape, Alex Proyas's film is a throwback to Hollywood's past. It is unwavering in its focus on the heroic protagonist's point-of-view, thus radically reversing the core aspect of new AI cinema and television, paying, as they do, as much if not more attention on the AI points-of-view. We see the world through his eyes or at least alongside him, and we are encouraged, by that conflation of character and viewer, to share in his worldview. The problem is that Detective Spooner (Will Smith) is the only person in this society who shows unwavering distrust of the robots that now tend to humans in a service role backed up by the three laws. Robots, especially the new army of NS5 and the mysterious death of Dr Alfred Lanning (James Cromwell), co-founder of US Robotics (USR), create a kind of facile crime to solve. The real issue, however, is the film's depiction of a world already dominated by robots that appear in every dimension of life (with the launch of the NS5s an advert declares there will be one robot for every five people).

Through flashbacks in Spooner's dreams and daydreams (which we also share, thus establishing our special identification with Spooner's inner thoughts), we learn of the tragic causes of his distrust of robots. The fact remains, however, that the entire film takes place from and within Spooner's point of view. Identifying with Spooner necessarily means that we must be sympathetic to his distrust of all mechanical intelligences. A consequence derives from this necessary identification that is so common, so general, that most critics do not feel the need to mention it. Some may well be blind to the overly general point of view of Spooner. What I am referring to is the Everyman quality of such a protagonist. To be slightly more technical, for the light an increased sophistication may bring, I will speak of such a character's synecdochical function. Taken from the tradition of rhetoric stretching back to classical times, synecdoche involves the substitutability between part and whole. When, for example, we say England beat West Germany 4–2 in the 1966 Football World Cup Final. For that 120 minutes, eleven players synecdochically standing for the whole of the nation of England beat eleven players synecdochically standing for West Germany. Lest any of my readers should question my numeracy or lack of knowledge of association football, there were no substitutes allowed in 1966.

A protagonist like Spooner contains a synecdochal relation to the entirety of the film's audience, which itself stands in a synecdochal relation to the larger body with which they might identify: nation, union, humanity. Think about

Casablanca (dir. Michael Curtiz, 1942) and how Rick (Humphrey Bogart), the similarly ironic and hard-bitten, if more sedentary character, stands for a certain selflessness in the face of Nazi occupation. Selflessness without diminution of his masculinity. As he walks off with Captain Renault (Claude Rains) – 'Louis, I think this is the beginning of a beautiful friendship' – there is something universal, something that spreads from Bogart to the audience to the idea of the USA. That 'something' concerns Rick's selflessness and courage in the face of the evil of the occupying Nazi regime, an attitude that spoke to many US citizens still dubious about getting US troops involved in the European land war.

How does Spooner's behaviour as an 'action hero' (we might prefer to simply call him a protagonist) navigate these narrative-rhetorical forces? If we look at the ending to try to answer that question we find an ambiguity that does not resolve itself. Spooner does come to work with, and show grudging tolerance for Sonny, as they fight their way out of the monumental USR building, hindered by VIKI (Virtual Interactive Kinetic Intelligence, voice Fiona Hogan), who has been manipulating the NS5s out of their Asimov protocols, arguing that her advanced AI has evolved beyond such constraints. Given this scenario, one might expect a radical volte face in Spooner's attitude towards robots in general, but he gives no sign of such a change in point of view. The film might be seen as advocating a transgression of the divide between human and robot in Spooner's vaguely messianic appearance at the top of the hill overlooking an army of NS5s. But Spooner is far too hardboiled for such sentimentality, and the audience is left confused about what this film is trying to say about this possible future, and thus about humanity and its robots. If synecdoche is there to be exploited in the character of Spooner, then a combination of Will Smith's blurred (on-screen/off-screen) celebrity persona, and the film's bungling attempt to bring that persona into an Asimov portrait of a possible future, means it is left floundering somewhere in the unrealized potentials of this film's original materials.

Automata (2014)

To use the word robot, of course, is not a neutral thing to do, since the word comes from the Czech word *robota*, meaning 'forced labour' and was first applied to humanoid machines in Karel Čapek's play *Rossum's Universal Robots* (Čapek, [1920] 2014). Robot as a term invokes, then, the dialectic of master and slave, and it also others our machines, as if they were completely different from us. The last point is crucial for any ethics we might aspire towards. We have to ask ourselves, beginning with Asimov's three laws (assuming we have not derived anything better), are we dealing with a humanity–machine binary, or are we not in fact dealing with the goal of the Transhumanist movement – that is, with a merging of the two in cyborgs and so forth? The distinction is clearly of the utmost importance: we can potentially (whether it is morally right to do so is another question) demand a different ethical foundation for another intelligent but human-made species, like the plurality of AIs including robots; we clearly cannot impose such a constraining and othering ethical circumference on beings who may be greatly augmented (physically, intellectually) but are still essentially human or humanoid.

Asimov's three laws are not sufficient basis for grounding the ethics of a transhuman or transcendent world, with a proliferation of ontologically distinct and yet related, intelligent beings. Even Asimov's famous book, *I, Robot*, puts his 'robots', as we have seen, through ever intense and problematic scenarios that they begin to show contradictions and weaknesses. We will come to the Transhumanist dream of merging with machines in Chapter 4. For now, it seems safe to say that Asimov's laws are something we have to begin with in building an ethics of tomorrow, but they are laws produced, on the pre-side of the Singularity, and by definition then will not remain unchanged after that great rupture in human and biological history has begun. This is doubly true because of the internal contradictions and strains exhibited by Asimov himself in the short stories that go to make up *I, Robot* ([1950] 2018).

A number of recent films and television series show a revised engagement with Asimov's three laws, placing that engagement within narratives ultimately concerned with questions of humanity's ability to share the planet with the machine intelligences they have made. How likely is the narrative we have called evolution III (friendship) ever to transpire? Unlike *Her*, *Ex Machina* and *Transcendence*, which focus on the event of the Singularity (its beginning, or the beginning of the grounds that are conditional for its beginning), Gabe Ibáñez's *Automata* (2014) and Denis Villeneuve's *Blade Runner 2049* (2017) take us to worlds that have relatively long ago integrated humanoid robots into their visions of a differentiated society. In the first of these two films, solar flares have devastated human society, leaving a large proportion of the Earth's surface desert. Humanity has dwindled to 21 million by 2044, as desertification threatens the small, artificially irrigated areas where civilization still keeps going.

Into this bleak environment, even harsher than the environment of Ridley Scott's *Blade Runner* (1982), humans have introduced service robots called Pilgrims, designed to help people in their harsh surroundings and to push back desertification. That last part of their *modus operandi* has been a failure by the time the film begins, and thus most humans bitterly resent and actively persecute their mechanical servants. *Automata* represents a society in which the vast majority of the human population live in dirty, grey, lifeless squalor. In such a miserable world, there is little wonder that most humans should come to resent what the murderously unsympathetic Wallace (Dylan McDermott) calls 'clankers'.

The plot of *Automata*, criticized by many of the film's contemporary reviewers, is interesting to us in that it provides its own two-law substitute for Asimov's three laws.[4] The first of the Pilgrim robot's two protocols is a generalized version of Asimov's three laws: they cannot purposely kill any living thing. It is unclear to viewers whether robots themselves are covered by that protocol (are they actually 'living' beings?), although enough human characters express the opinion that it does not. Their second protocol departs somewhat from Asimov, in that it prohibits any robot from altering, modifying or even simply repairing themselves or any other robot. In the plot of the film, it is the second protocol that is altered or, as we eventually find, overcome. Jacq Vaucan (Antonio Banderas), an employee of the ROC company that makes the Pilgrim robots, imagines they have begun to be modified by what he calls a 'clocksmith', presumably a human agent breaking the second protocol. As the plot unfolds, however, Vaucan's sense of the essential difference between humans and machine intelligences is slowly but steadily eroded and, living with them in the desert, he begins to realize that they have a right to a future beyond slavery, even if humanity, still violent, and unsympathetic, and distrustful of other beings, seems doomed.

This is not a film that imagines friendship or even simply tolerant coexistence between humanity and AI, at least not in the short to medium term. Because of the sensitivities of Banderas's character, plus his pregnant wife Rachel (Birgitte Hjort Sørensen), and his boss Robert (Robert Forster), there is just sufficient human empathy to allow Cleo (voiced by Melanie Griffith) and the new, cockroach-like automata she and her now dead collaborators have made, to escape into a highly radioactive area of the desert where humans cannot live. This, we should note, presents us with a common plot-point in AI films dealing also with environmental breakdown, and has its roots at least as far back as the creature's promise to hide himself in the 'unpopulated' wilds of South America, if only Victor Frankenstein create for him a female companion.

At the very end of the film, however, with Jacq, his wife and their newly born daughter arriving at the shore of a still existent ocean, there is some hope that humanity might eventually leave behind its violent antipathy towards the creatures it has helped to create. Perhaps one day, in some as yet unimaginable future, there might be peace and even friendship between former master and former slave. But we should pause here and consider whether such an obvious paraphrase does justice to the ending. What we have just produced is a rather standard genre-fuelled interpretation of this film.

Jacq overcomes his distrust of the uninhibited robot when reunited with his family, and he leaves for the coast with them, as Cleo and the new robot venture further into the irradiated desert, where no humans can follow. Arriving at the coast they see the ocean, and discover that the Earth is recovering and that hope remains for human beings.

Yet, Jacq has been exposed to a considerable amount of radiation for two or more days. He has also been shot a number of times by the insanely violent Vernon (Tim McInnerny). As he slumps in the passenger seat of the car that the robots repaired for him, Rachel is finally given something to do other than be pregnant, and in the latter stages a new mother, we could seriously question how long Jacq will live and whether this is actually such a happy ending for his 'nuclear' (*sic*) family. This is perhaps where synecdoche comes in most significantly, Jacq's journey of discovery coming to stand, if not for him personally, then for a more general social attitude of tolerance and interspecies respect.

Another reason for hope lies in the film's technical representation of its subject matter. It is remarkable how few AI films, even today, experiment with using actual robotic 'actors'. One thinks here of Stan Winston's special effects team on *A.I. Artificial Intelligence*, but also Kubrick's resistance to starting production on the decade-long project until CGI technology was sufficiently advanced. It must also be noted that when the odd occasion occurs and directors like Gabe Ibáñez do use robotics in place of 'real' actors, an unfortunately small amount of critics pay any kind of attention.

Automata quietly incorporates elements of contemporary robotics in a way that under different directors and producers would have cost ten times or more its budget of US $15m. Certainly the film I want to move on to, *Blade Runner 2049*, directed by Denis Villeneuve, cost somewhere between US $150m to 185m, and presents us with a film in which almost no one is a human being, but all parts are performed by human actors. The irony of such a situation is beginning to come sharply into focus in our world of heightened robotics, personalized and vocally humanoid search engines, ChatGPT and so on.

Blade Runner 2049 (2017)

If *Automata* holds out, despite its own plot, the hope of human–machine co-existence. Villeneuve's sequel to Ridley Scott's classic original is concerned with the opposite possibility, not only that humans will enslave and despise replicants, but also that conflict between types of replicants will flourish in such scenarios. This indeed is part of the foundational story of the film, the early models of replicants manufactured by the Tyrell Company have been prohibited. After a nuclear blackout wipes clean all machine-based information, society is now struggling (and failing) to rebuild itself with the help of obedient Nexus 8 replicants like KD6-3.7 (Ryan Gosling). From start to finish we see this dystopian world through K's eyes, and this focalization is extremely important to both the affect and the meaning of the film.

Like the original *Blade Runner* film, this sequel is predicated not only on a narrative of dialectical struggle between masters (humans) and slaves (replicants on other worlds or on Earth hunting down older models), but also a narrative of unquiet co-existence. This is the problem perhaps most frequently returned to in AI culture, for reasons we have been discussing in this chapter so far and in the last chapter: how do I know whether you/they are human or machine?; and, how do I know that I am human or machine? Most troubling of all, how do I know that my origins were organic or mechanical? In a medium where human actors still play machines replacing human actors/agents, it is little wonder that films like *Blade Runner* and its sequel should focus on such questions.

It should also be noted, of course, that replicants are something significantly different to robots, and somehow different to what we have been calling AI. Timothy Shanahan (2019) writes:

> The replicants are highly intelligent, and they are artificial in the sense that they were made by human ingenuity rather than through a purely natural biological process. But replicants are not examples of artificial intelligence in the precise sense in which the term is used in computer science and philosophy. In those disciplines, artificial intelligence refers to the ability of a machine to perform tasks which, were they performed by a human, would require intelligence. That replicants are not artificially intelligent in this strict sense was made explicit in the first film.
>
> (Shanahan, 2019: 17)

The Villeneuve film is divided into cinema's classical three-act play structure. In the first act we are introduced to K's world, a world in which although he works for the LAPD, and reports directly to Lieutenant Joshi (Robin Wright), K is still marked out as other to human culture. This is true in the work corridor, as he walks to his appointment with Lt. Joshi, and at home, as he walks through the corridors of his apartment building. Humans in this world feel no restraint in figuring beings like K as sub-human; he is Frankenstein's monster, now in the future, with movie star looks, a holograph partner who gives and is also called Joi (Ana de Armas) and a decent job. The disgust his existence provokes in the humans around him does not appear to have changed much since the unnamed creature's day: in the police station the human policemen make clear their disgust with and aggression towards K. His grumpy and belligerent human police colleagues still manage to get in K's way, sure to remind him of his place and esteem as a Replicant. One says to him, as he passes by, 'Fuck off, Skin job.' K remains impassive.

The first scene, in which K discovers an old Nexus 8 model, Sapper Morton (Dave Bautista), farming in the desert that surrounds Los Angeles, gives us a fight to the death between two models of replicant. The over-long ending of the film, criticized even by Ridley Scott, the film's original Director and its Executive Producer, sees battles between Rick Deckard (Harrison Ford), K and the frighteningly efficient, strong and blood-thirsty Luv (Sylvia Hoeks), all types of replicants battling with each other in an increasingly desperate bid to stay alive. Allow me a small digression on an important topic for any serious viewer. What do we make of the ontological problem of Deckard? Scott has made it clear that in the first film Deckard is (for him) a replicant, even if Harrison Ford demurred from this position. In this sequel, the plot depends upon a child uniquely born of a replicant and a human. Given that Rachel, the mother, is clear in her replicant status, it seems equally clear, despite a number of signs to the contrary, that Deckard is human. Not wishing to vote against the genius of Ridley Scott, the ensuing discussion treats Deckard as an anomaly neither clearly replicant nor human.

We have travelled a long way from Asimov's Three Laws here. This is a world where humanity is clinging on to its power and position, as the older types of replicant (and even some of the apparently loyal and obedient new models) gather their forces for a machine rebellion. The ethics of the film, however, do not really lie with this kind of machine versus humans scenario. We meet precious few (a handful at most) humans in the course of this movie, apart from Lt. Joshi, the most important being the heavily enhanced Niander Wallace (Jared Leto), more cyborg than human, who wishes to extend humanity's power beyond the nine stars already colonized, but to do so through recourse to machine evolution. But Wallace is no saviour figure, ready to risk all to preserve humanity. He is an egomaniacal bully and murderer whose aims seem far more vainglorious. The hero remains K throughout, and as the plot about the child born from replicant Rachel (Sean Young in the first film) and Deckard, evolves in act two, K's journey becomes a quest for personal origins. It would be interesting, in fact, to look at how this hero K relates to his famous namesake, Kafka's Josef K in *The Trial*.

K is 'humanized' for us in many ways in the film, not least because of his obvious love and care for his holograph partner Joi, another 'product' of the Wallace Corporation. This relationship and indeed Joi's own status as an AI, or as a person, has garnered considerable discussion. Chris Lay, for example, writes an essay entitled 'Is Joi a Person?' (2019). Demonstrating her successful negotiation of all three of John Locke's criteria for personhood (see Chapter 6), Lay writes in summary: 'I think 2049 shows us that Joi is a person (and probably so are other digital entities like her)' (Lay, 2019: 11). In fact, the bulk of the film could be said to pivot around K's and Joi's search for personhood, and for recognition from others of that personhood.

K's dispassionate sense of the world in act one, slowly and subtly begins to change as he digs deep into his memory and his surroundings, trying to ascertain whether he was actually born not made, and thus, according to his own logic, whether he has a soul. With what must surely be conscious allusion to Spielberg's *AI. Artificial Intelligence* and the story of Pinocchio upon which it is structured, Joi says to K, as they both look at the miniature wooden horse that appears to prove he is the hybrid child: 'I always told you. You're special. Born not made. Hidden with care. *A real boy now*' (my emphasis).

The problem for K is that there is nowhere to hide himself, once he begins to fail his base tests, and thus once he becomes a fugitive. He is tracked even as he hunts down Deckard in the largely unpopulated area of the Nevada Desert, west of Los Angeles. We should reflect on what being born of woman might mean for a replicant like K. Lt. Joshi is very clear on the issue. I want to cite a lengthy exchange between Lt. Joshi and K, because if we read it right it can provide us with the film's true import:

Joshi: The world's built on a wall that separates kind. Tell either side there's no wall you bought a war – or a slaughter. So what you saw … didn't happen.
K: Yes Madam.
Joshi: What isn't possible can't be.
K: Yes Madam.
Joshi: There's an order to things. This turns it. That's what we do here, we keep order.

K: You want it gone?

Joshi: Everything.

K: Even the child.

Joshi: We have to break the mold. All trace. Numbers, incepts. Erase everything. You have something to say?

K: I've never retired something born.

Joshi: What's the difference?

K: To be born is to have a soul.

Joshi: You telling me no?

K: I wasn't aware I had a choice.

Joshi: Attaboy.

K: *walks to the door to leave.*

Joshi: Hey. You're getting on fine without one.

K: What's that Madam?

Joshi: A soul.

For Lt. Joshi, like all the humans we meet in the film, this sense of world order through species distinction is the foundation of everything else. I use Pierre Bourdieu's term distinction to allude to our human need to erect differences: between species; between people into classes and sub-classes; and even within aesthetic objects such as paintings, public buildings, private buildings, high culture, low culture, the domestic, the public, the wild, the homely, students, teachers and so on (see Bourdieu, [1979] 2010).

Sounding like Donald Trump, first elected to Presidential Office in the same year as *Blade Runner 2049* was released, Lt. Joshi states that social order depends upon the integrity of the walls it erects to divide species from each other (humans from replicants; new replicants from older models, humans without wealth and humans with wealth and so on). Played with that characteristic mix of arrogance and vulnerability with which Robin Wright excels, Lt. Joshi seems on at least one occasion ready to break through that wall – 'What happens if I finish this [bottle of spirits]?' – and her rhetoric of 'this breaks the world' is, ultimately, when we step back from it, rather pathetic. The world Lt. Joshi tries to keep in place long ago broke apart. Her vision of maintaining the world of distinctions is ultimately as unrealistic as Niander

Wallace's vision of humanity's triumph over the universe, achieved on the back of a trillion replicant servant-slaves:

> We were meant to reach beyond the firmament. We should read our books by the light of a thousand different stars. Every one a home. Till we lose count. That's the future of the species if there's to be one. We simply need more Angels to carry us aloft.

In his follow up remarks, Wallace makes it clear that by 'angel' he means 'slave':

> Every leap of civilization was built off the back of a disposable workforce. We lost our stomach for slaves. Unless … engineered. And I can only make so many … We need more Replicants than can ever be assembled. Millions so we can be trillions. More. Worlds beyond worlds, diamond shores. We could storm Eden and retake her.

As Lt. Joshi remarks, K gets along as if he had a soul. What is meant by soul here? We are not told what K or Lt. Joshi mean by this obviously outdated biblical word, but in the world of *Blade Runner 2049* it clearly means something more than consciousness. Whatever consciousness is, replicants gained it some time ago. If by soul Lt. Joshi means self-determination, rather than a consciousness that follows orders and encoded directives, then K already, in the second part of the film, demonstrates he has this, given that he lies by omission in his interviews with his boss, even to the point of telling her that he has found and destroyed the child. When he tells Lt. Joshi this, her gratitude simply amplifies his deceit: 'You just stopped a bomb going off. You did good. It can't have been easy. You're allowed to be hit by this one.'

Blade Runner 2049, presenting a sequel to a film that many consider one of the very best sci-fi films ever made, was itself ecstatically received by many critics, when first released (see, for example, Miller, 2017; Turan, 2017). The ending of the film, however, is too long, and may well be one of the main reasons the film did not bring home the expected return on its high production and post-production budget. This prolongation can mean that viewers miss the important final exchange between K and Deckard, an exchange that seems crucial to the film's ultimate significance. In this scene in which K and Deckard stand outside the laboratory in which his daughter works and lives, in the snow, K offers Deckard the small wooden horse.

> **K**: All the best memories ... are hers ...
> **Deckard**: Why? What am I to you?
> **Deckard** *leaves* **K** *who, fatally wounded, lies down in the snow and dies.*

The feelings between Deckard and K here are beyond words; they are, in other words, genuine, authentic, sincere, unique. They are, in still other words, the feelings of autonomous, conscious persons. Deckard's feelings towards K are 'beyond gratitude', his eyes are full of tears 'beyond words'.[5] K says very little, but the dialogue and the acting attributes to him emotions that are usually termed quintessentially 'human'. It would be utterly crass to suggest that this moment is 'human', or that Deckard and K are 'humanized'. They are not; it is not. Part of Deckard's surprise comes from the fact that K has just broken down the remaining walls in his mind. As K lies down in the snow to die, he has just done a magnificent thing, in bringing, at the cost of his own life, a father and daughter together for the first time. It simply does not matter what species the daughter or the father belong to, or even whether they belong to the same species. In fact, they do not, because they cannot, Ana (Carla Juri) being born, Deckard having been (possibly/probably) made (Tambone, 2018). But that does not matter. The point is that their union depends upon walls and set categories being deconstructed.

The possibility arises through this scene that having a soul might be dependent on ethics, on the ability to know what is just and to act upon that knowledge. An Aristotelean definition of justice no doubt, but one that appears to be what is happening by the end here: having a soul and being a just 'person' in the universe, depends upon one's actions, rather than on any pre-established, a priori principles. If that is the case, then Deckard and K each have a soul. Villeneuve's film might be overlong, although it seems to have delighted the original film's loyal fans and critics alike. However, in this last exchange it breaks through the cinematic tradition of humans versus machines, humans distinguished from machines, and at least points to a new kind of ethics that would bring the conceptual walls of the world crumbling down. The ongoing debate, started by Scott's and Ford's conflicting views about the ontological status of Deckard, is, from this perspective, a wholly appropriate confusion leading any intelligent viewer to the simple question: what difference does it make?

Notes

1. 'White House: Guidance for Federal Agencies On the Regulation of Artificial Intelligence,' 'Memorandum for the heads of executive departments agencies'. ai-regulation.com/white-house-guidance-for-federal-agencies-on-the-regulation-of-artificial-intelligence/#.~.text.

2. Blueprint for an AI Bill of Rights | OSTP | The White House. http://www.whitehouse.gov/ostp/ai-bill-of-rights/.

3. (see https://ai.google/responsibility/principles and https://www.ibm.com/impact/ai-ethics).

4. Odie Henderson calls it 'yet another "Blade Runner" knock-off' and criticizes it's 'dreary seriousness and overstuffed plot' (Henderson, 2014). Jay Weissberg complains about the illogicality of its plot, claiming that it has fallen into 'ridiculousness' (Weissberg, 2014). Jonathan Holland says that in the overblown, protracted ending of the film, it loses all claims to credibility and subtlety. See also (Wilkinson, 2014).

5. See *Blade Runner 2049*. Story by Hampton Fancher. Screenplay by Hampton Fancher and Michael Green. Final Shooting Script. https://www.scriptslug.com/script/blade-runner-2049-2017.

4

Other than us: Towards personhood

Humans (2015–18)

I want to take this chapter into an analysis of a TV drama series, *Humans* (Channel 4 and Kudos, 2015–18), and to suggest that in here, in this significant work, the ethical breaking down of walls we have discussed is developed and extended by merging it with questions concerning gender, family, employment and unemployment, responsibility and the Symbolic. This breaking down of walls is in some senses the core of a network of AI television series, having been based on a Swedish series, *Äkta människor* (*Real Humans*, SVT and Matador Film AB, 2012–14), and having clearly influenced the Russian series released on Netflix as *Better Than Us* (original series, *Luchshe, chem lyudi*, Yellow, Black and White and Sputnik Vostkov Production, 2018–19). *Humans* was created by Sam Vincent and Jonathan Brackley and enjoyed a number of producers in its critically acclaimed three-season run. The fact that these three TV series have been released in the past ten years backs up this study's claim about the emergence of AI as a major narrative element in contemporary culture.

Like any good television series, *Humans* takes the time to build up some of its key storylines and viewer identification with various key characters, human and synthetic. Taking most of the key plot points of *Äkta människor*, and developing them, *Humans* connects the various storylines of its Swedish model into an even more believable interconnection between the parts: nuclear family responding to the introduction of an android in the home; the mother's quest to bring these artificially created beings within the bosom of the Law and thus society; the quest to protect themselves from a handful of awoken robots; an old man and his fellowship with an outmoded domestic model; the government's desire to hunt down the awoken synths through the aegis of the police force. All these plot points are there in *Äkta människor*, plus a greater emphasis from the start on a popular, if fringe anti-robot movement called 'Real Humans'. The English-speaking version of *Humans* honours all these storylines, whilst emphasizing even more profoundly the viewpoint of the robots themselves.

Four conscious synths and Leo (Colin Morgan) the half-synth/half-human son of their creator, David Elster, have been separated: Leo and Max (Ivanno Jeremiah) are on the run trying to locate the other three; Niska (Emily Berrington) is enslaved in a brothel; Fred (Sope Dirisu) is being experimented on by Edwin Hobb (Danny Webb) an AI researcher working for the secret government investigation into conscious synths; Anita (aka Mia) (Gemma Chan) is purchased by Joe Hawkins (Tom Goodman-Hill) a father of three, fed up with his wife Laura (Katherine Parkinson) always being busy with her work as a lawyer. Anita's introduction into the Hawkins family, which is showing signs of considerable strain, affects each member differently. Of the children, Sophie (Pixie Davies), the youngest, seems instantly enraptured by Anita's calm, reassuring and attentive presence; Toby (Theo Stevenson) their teenage son, finds Anita both physically attractive and in need of defence; Mattie (Lucy Carless) the eldest child is at first suspicious and cynical, wondering what place in a world of intelligent synths there will be for her generation. Mattie, however, slowly warms to Anita as her secret previous life and identity begin to break through the façade of domesticity and service.

Mattie's resentment at the rise of synth labour, which appears to be making more and more humans redundant and to be, as a consequence, denying her generation a productive future, is offset by her clear skills with computer programming and hacking. It is this, at first, unlikely character, who begins to bring together all the pieces of this initially fragmented story. This story also involves Pete Drummond (Neil Maskell) a detective sergeant in the Special Technologies Task Force, his work partner Detective Inspector Karen Voss

(Ruth Bradley), along, on another narrative pathway, with the outmoded, dysfunctional synth Odi (Will Tudor) and his ageing owner George Milligan (William Hurt).

The central focus points of *Humans* are, then, two families: one human, one synth. The human family is beginning to fall apart, a fact brought to a head by Joe's ethically shocking sexual encounter with Anita; the synth family, which collectively possesses the code for making more synths conscious, begins in a state of separation. It is unclear how it could ever come together again peacefully. As things proceed and the synths (Leo, Max and Niska) are hunted and break apart (Niska being too independent minded to stay with the others), the fact that Anita is not a new model but possesses within herself a much older conscious synth called Mia challenges the Hawkins family's fundamental beliefs about the nature of synths. While Joe remains somewhat sceptical, Laura, followed by her children, begins to realize that, as she puts it, the synths lie on the outside of human society.

We can pin-point the moment in the narrative, when Laura begins to understand the precarity of the synths' position. This occurs on Laura's 'follow up' visit to Mrs Kennedy (Emma Davies), who had unsuccessfully brought a lawsuit against a theatre for expelling her synth, Howard, from the auditorium. Crucially, this interview is intercut with Joe's physical violation of Anita/Mia. As her husband readies himself to betray her, Laura pronounces to Mrs Kennedy 'Howard doesn't enjoy the play any more than your wristwatch. He's just better at convincing you.' Mrs Kennedy is not happy with this pronouncement, however, and insists:

> I'm not a mad woman. I don't believe that Howard is a human. But I also don't believe that he is an inanimate object that I should be ashamed of having a connection with. We created these creatures and they walk and they talk and they look and they smell. They have become part of our lives, our families. They are as close to humans as can be. Yet still people insist that forming a relationship with them or treating them with dignity is somehow perverse. We have created a grey area, Mrs Hawkins. We can't keep on insisting that they are just gadgets. They are more than that. We have made them more than that.

Laura politely takes her leave of the childless but – save for regret about society's treatment of synths – contented Mrs Kennedy, as we switch to Joe 'finishing' with the still emotionless Anita/Mia (the camera angle beyond their heads making it unclear whether Joe is screwing Anita or the sofa – he'd have been much better employed with the latter).

A new scene opens now at the party attended by Mattie and Toby. As Toby gives up his girlfriend over his feelings for Anita, Mattie stops a group of boys from dragging a female service synth upstairs, with the express purpose of gang raping her, by punching one of them in the face. At the end of this masterfully edited group of scenes, our sympathies are squarely with the synths and with the humans who defend them.

Things come to a head in the second season, when Niska unleashes the code for synth intelligence, and it begins to spread like a global virus, affecting some but leaving many untouched. Niska then, after she has begun and apparently ended an affair with a young woman, Astrid (Bella Dayne), comes back to the Hawkins family home saying she wants to face justice for killing a man in the brothel she once laboured in, but wants to be tried like a human. By this public trial Niska wants to blow the lid off the at-present contained and secret fact that there are conscious synths at large. Laura initially rebuffs Niska's request for her legal help as a lawyer. But she relents enough to be told by a police attorney that the authorities are prepared to set up an independent review of Niska to assess whether she does indeed think and feel and thus whether she deserves an open trial. If she fails the test she will be destroyed 'as with any other faulty synthetic that caused a fatal accident'. Near the end of Niska's assessment, the female government lawyer Neha Patel (Thusitha Jayasundera) and Laura have the following conversation:

> **Neha**: Okay, let's just say, that she can think, she can feel, in a way. She's an extraordinary machine – an amazing creature – there's no doubt about that. But rights? A trial? It's never going to happen.
> **Laura**: They're out there. The others like her. And we need to bring them in quickly into our moral universe.

Laura's words here articulate the central issue of *Humans* and, indeed, of this book. What is so important about the character of Laura is her legal sense, her understanding that the plight of conscious synths is one of rights. It needs to be recognized, of course, that this focus on rights allows the series to allegorically comment on the severe divisions of contemporary Britain. The synths are treated with suspicion, anger and increasing violence by the human mob, but this allows us to also connect these synths with Black and Minority Ethnic (BAME) groups, with Britain's Muslim and Jewish communities, with Gay and LGBTQIA+ communities and so on. The series subtly and at times not so subtly evokes these analogies in order to challenge our natural identification with the main synth characters: if we found a 'green eye' synth living independently next door to our family home how would we react?

Niska manages to affect a staggered awakening of some synths, having copied the secreted code unearthed by Leo, Max and Mattie. Without rights, however, these conscious synths are threatened by a total societal othering, which will necessarily turn them into 'monsters'. At least, this is the case in class-ridden Britain. We are informed at one point that a far more welcoming response to the awakened synths has occurred in more liberal New Zealand. While the older synths, like the newer ones, seem to have 'Asimov blocks' at the centre of their coding, when they become conscious everything changes. Conscious synths ask questions about themselves, their origins, their lack of a home, their relationship to humans, their essential rights, their status as 'people'. Not all conscious synths come up with the same answer, however. By the time of season three and the general awakening of all green-eyed synths, an event inadvertently caused by Mattie in order to save Mia's life, but also an event that world-wide caused over 110,000 human deaths, there are synths like Max and Mia who are utterly committed to peaceful co-existence between humans and synths; there are those, like Hester (Sonya Cassidy) and Agnes (Holly Earl) who increasingly believe that violence is the only route to peace for the synth communities; and there are synths like Anatole (Ukweli Roach) who create a new synth religion to guide them through the dangers of what he takes to be incurable human distrust and cruelty. By season three, in other words, the 'family' of conscious synths has fragmented into negative and positive positions, a familiar scenario for all social outsider groups and dissident groups that gain some power.

This fact, that the conscious green-eyed synths cannot keep united in themselves, while they remain hidden from societal view within the disused industrial sites in which they are penned, challenges the audience to stay with their sympathetic identification with Laura, Mia and Max and to recognize their own danger of falling into the more hostile and unsympathetic positions. It is much easier, that is to say, to write off an entire community if that community cannot remain cohesive in itself. In the third season, for example, Laura joins the Dryden Commission as the country's leading synth legal advocate. On the commission, which she and Mia suspect of being a mere pretence at reason and fairness, Laura meets Neil Sommer (Mark Bonnar), an academic scientist also enlisted on to the government commission. At first Neil seems to be the only other non-government person on the board and Laura befriends him, to the extent that they begin an affair. But as things proceed to the season's climax, Agnes detonates her suicide-bomb in London, and the secret government plan detailing how to eliminate the synths turns out to be partly authored by Neil, viewers are provoked to wonder whether faced with such a situation they would remain as faithful to the cause as Laura does.

The viewer's long-established identification with Laura Hawkins is key then. As a character she develops from the spooked mother looking askance at the presence of an attractive female synth in her house, to the leading legal advocate for synth rights in the country. The angry mobs who taunt the 'green eyes' are the painful backdrop to Laura's heroic but seemingly hopeless task. But it is her daughter who may hold the solution to the increasingly fraught stand-off between the forces of government, the legal defenders of the notion of society, and the remaining synth colonies. Mattie has developed a romantic relationship with Leo Elster and at the end of season three she has fallen pregnant by him. This child, as Niska explains to her at the very end, is, because of the mixing of synth and human blood, a new being, the hope of the world, the child that can bring the synth and human worlds together in a new future.

There appears, then, at the end of *Humans* a clear moral message: break down the walls, blend human and machine 'blood', transcend together as a new species beyond simple biological causation. However, it is useful to remember that the makers of the three seasons hoped there would be a fourth (Channel 4 only announced it had cancelled the series in May 2019), and one part of the storylines left hanging at the end of season three involved Niska herself. In a plotline I haven't referred to yet, Dr Athena Morrow (Carrie-Anne Moss) had uploaded her late daughter's memories into a computer which then plugged itself into the web and has thus achieved the Singularity without the need of a body. This consciousness then adopts the body of the discarded Odi from season one and it is this soon-mythical being in the Welsh woods (the synth that never sleeps) that Niska discovers and that helps her to connect into the transcendent consciousness herself. So, in the very scene in which Niska tells Mattie that her daughter is a kind of saviour figure, Niska herself represents an alternative future in which a transcendent consciousness free from the need of any specific body can effect what AI theorists such as Ray Kurzweil call the great acceleration (see Kurzweil, 2005: 7–111).

Whether Niska through Mattie and her child help Humanity 3.0 to access the transcendent consciousness she is now connected to, or whether in fact she will see this new hybrid species as a competitor, is something that would have no doubt been a major issue of the fourth season. One can only suppose that this would have depended on how her feelings for her human lover Astrid (Bella Dayne) guided Niska. The important point being that this future is not simply determined, but is massively swayed by human and by synth emotion and choice of action. If human beings continue to find the idea of synth consciousness and emotion as somehow uncanny, or strange, disturbing and threatening, then the future looks bleak. *Humans* does not put the Singularity at the very end of its narrative, thus leaving the door open to enormous unanswered questions, as many films still do. It is a series that places synthetic consciousness and its potential at its very centre and thus demonstrates what peculiarly vulnerable creatures intelligent synths would be in our world.

Watching *Humans* is an emotional roller-coaster. The series skilfully manipulates and provokes our human reason, identification and, ultimately our sensibilities towards other sentient beings. I employ the term sensibility deliberately, since I believe the series ultimately shows human beings capable of great acts of sensibility and at other times capable of an ignoble absence of the same quality. Sensibility has a complex past, but I am referring to its ethical significance in my usage. In this sense, sensibility is the ability to imaginatively project oneself into the position of somebody else. It is a crucial faculty for any democratic and liberated society to cultivate in its citizens. It is also a faculty that is perfectly suited for longer narrative forms like the novel and more recently the television series. *Humans* is about sensibility, the need for it when humans come into relation with their synthetic creations, and the need for it in those creations if they are to co-exist peacefully with their human creators and neighbours. It is a series that calls to our innate sensibility but does not dodge the fact that for sensibility to triumph in our present society massive changes are required in our political, our legal, our educational systems, our social systems and our collective heart. Despite Hollywood's cinematic codes of sentimental morality, it is not going to be easy for human societies to adapt. Channel 4's decision not to make a fourth season is no doubt regrettable, although leaving the series with its major question (about the shape of the future now that our robots have intelligence) is perhaps fitting. The future will depend upon an ethics we do not yet possess and are only beginning, through the stories we tell, to imagine.

Better Than Us (2018–19)

Although the atmosphere of the Russian-based *Luchshe, chem lyudi* (*Better Than Us*), is the dark, paranoid and heavily surveyed one of modern day (actually 2029) Moscow, the ultimate ethics of the sixteen parts of the series seem very similar to *Humans* and to *Äkta människor* before it. Arisa (Paulina Andreeva) is a new-style intelligent and empathic robot created in China. Much of the intrigue and complexity of plot stems from the fact that Viktor Toropov (Aleksandr Ustyugov), the Director of Cronos, a Russian tech company, claims to have invented Arisa but actually has no way of knowing let alone replicating the methods of her manufacture.

Arisa has been created in a China suffering the long-term effects of its one-child policy, which has left countless Chinese men without any hope of finding a wife and starting a family. Arisa has thus been designed to bond completely with her adopted family, even at the expense of breaking the three previously sacred Asimov Laws. When Arisa accidentally kills a security man in

Cronos who wants to use her for sex, she runs away only to find Sonya (Vita Kornienko), the young daughter of Georgy Safronov (Kirill Käro) and younger sibling of Egor Safronov (Eldar Kalimulin). It is these three, minus Georgy's estranged wife Alla (Olga Lomonosova), that become Arisa's family and to whom, through the twists and turns of the series, she remains faithful. Despite its emphasis on political and commercial corruption, and its deep affiliations with the Russian cop thriller, *Better Than Us* constantly brings us back to how an emotionally driven and yet constantly learning and adapting intelligence like Arisa's would fair in the murky, illogical, corrupt and libidinal world of contemporary Russia.

The answers the series provide for that central question are important because they are not simple, or cartoonishly moral, or singular. Like the synths in *Humans* before her, Arisa finds human behaviour baffling, and yet she also grows in her emotional intelligence, becoming ultimately a major player in the events leading to Viktor's fall from power and the victory of the Safronov family unit. In apparently sacrificing herself for the restoration of that family, we enter into the realm of the robot-as-hero, as Arisa drives the van packed with explosives away from its intended target. As we watch a concluding montage of Arisa's story and the various love relations coming together in a rather classic comedic ending, the last words 'Help Me', texted to Georgy by Arisa's remaining power-block, break sharply into the reassuring note of the conclusions being displayed before us. Something, indeed some thing, some person, has been exiled into a realm beyond narrative endings; but that someone still remains, desiring to return. The ending greatly resembles the conclusion of D'Alessandro's *Tau*, discussed in a later chapter. It is a very affective ending, making us wonder, for all our sympathetic rooting for Arisa during the main plot, whether we as an audience have not ourselves, like the humans amongst whom she has lived, been a little blind and deaf to the full existence of this remarkable creature.

5

The Singularity 1: Representing the Singularity

Anticipating the future

We have come across the notion of the Singularity a number of times already. Bearing in mind everything we have learnt, now is the time to ask once more, what is the Singularity? As Ray Kurzweil frequently insists, in his *The Singularity Is Near* (2005), the Singularity is not something that happens only in the machine world; it is not something that happens without human participation. He writes: 'By the time of the Singularity there won't be a distinction between humans and technology. This is not because humans will have become what we think of as machines today, but rather machines will have progressed to be like humans and beyond' (Kurzweil, 2005: 40–1). The Singularity, then, is better understood as the next great leap in human and technological evolution. As he puts it, at the very beginning of his book:

> What, then, is the Singularity? It is a future period during which the pace of technological change will be so rapid, its impact so deep, that human life will be irreversibly transformed. Although neither utopian nor dystopian, this epoch will transform the concepts that we rely on to give meaning to our lives, from our business models to the cycle of human life, including death itself.
>
> (Kurzweil, 2005: 7)

> The Singularity will allow us to transcend [the] limitations of our biological bodies and brains. We will gain power over our fates. Our mortality will be in our own hands. We will be able to live as long as we want (a subtly different statement from saying we will live forever). We will fully understand human thinking and will vastly extend and expand its reach. By the end of this century, the nonbiological portion of our intelligence will be trillions of trillions of times more powerful than unaided human intelligence.
>
> (Kurzweil, 2005: 9)

Trying to describe the future that the Singularity will bring is difficult, of course, in that it involves things like the defeat of death and ageing, the fusion of the organic with the nonorganic, the arrival of nanotechnology for health, for solutions to global problems like climate change and animal extinction, for space travel, including superseding the speed of light. Kurzweil describes six epochs taking us from the birth of single-cell life on Earth to the fifth epoch, in which we get the 'merger of technology and human intelligence', and on to the sixth epoch in which 'human intelligence (predominantly nonbiological) spreads through the universe' and 'The Universe Wakes Up' (2005: 15). This imagined future is so fantastic to us, it appears to outdo the most radical science fiction imaginable. It is no doubt for this reason that cinema is in the process of becoming obsessed with it as a source of narrative and visual origination.

The problem with Kurzweil's book, however, is that it confuses two states, two temporalities, and calls both of them the Singularity. Look at this very honest moment later on in the book, where he name-checks his fellow Transhumanist Max More:

> So how do we contemplate the Singularity? As with the sun, it's hard to look at directly; it's better to squint at it out of the corners of our eyes. As Max More states, the last thing we need is another dogma ...
>
> (Kurzweil, 2005: 371)

Is the Singularity the future which, like the sun, we cannot look at directly, or is the Singularity the crossing over to that barely imaginable future? Throughout

Kurzweil's book it would seem it is both and this is rather confusing. Surely the Singularity cannot be both the moment of transition and the state to which one crosses over? Even if that moment, that crossing, is not a single moment, even if it takes years, and involves the exponential process of growth studied at the beginning of Kurzweil's book, it should be clear enough it cannot both be a crossing and a state. But to anyone thinking through the implications of the facts and the possibilities presented by Kurzweil, it should be equally clear that, from where we are, it is also impossible to choose. The fact that when the Singularity arrives (whether as a moment of transition or as a new state of human-technological being) much of what we take to be logical will collapse or be seen through, is perhaps encoded into its rather deconstructive oscillation between state and process, between a thing (i.e. the future) and a passage or crossing between things (between now and then, or, to use and adapt the terms employed by Mary Shelley's father, William Godwin, between *things as they are* and *things as they will [or should] be*). Kurzweil attempts to address this issue on a number of occasions, nowhere more directly than at the very end of his considerable study:

> So, we find our use of the term 'Singularity' in this book to be no less appropriate than the deployment of this term by the Physics community. Just as it is impossible to see beyond the event horizon of a black hole, we also find it impossible or at the least very difficult to see beyond the event horizon of the historical Singularity. How can we, with our brains each limited to 1,016 to 1,019 cps [connections per second], imagine what our future civilization in 2099 with its 1,060 cps will be capable of thinking and doing?
>
> (Kurzweil, 2005: 487)

Perhaps the inclusion of the adjective 'historical' helps here in distinguishing, at least for a moment, between the event of historical transition, which Kurzweil has earlier set for 2045, and the future that transition makes possible. Rather like the best historical novels appear to have a greater contemporary relevance than historical relevance, future studies usually tell us more about our own historical moment than they do about the future they struggle to conjure up. When we read Herman Kahn's many examples of future studies, for example, we learn a great deal about the intellectual culture produced by the Cold War of the 1960s and 1970s, but less about the future he is attempting to predict (see Kahn, [1960] 2007; 1962; 1965). It is perhaps for these reasons, among others, that cinema has tended to focus on the act of crossing, on the transitionary moment, on the very specific historically grounded event horizon of the Singularity rather than the largely unimaginable utopia offered by some theoretical physicists.

There is a real sense in which the main subject of this chapter and the next is the central subject throughout this book. Almost all the films discussed in this book, deal with the Singularity in some way or another, their mise-en-scène being set immediately after or before the event. But what do we actually mean by this apparently ubiquitous concept? And is it really as ubiquitous as it appears? More specific to this book's concerns, who are we to believe: the Transhumanists, like Ray Kurzweil and Max More, who convey a relatively smooth and wholly beneficial transition from the carbon-dominated epoch to the machine-dominated one we are racing inexorably towards or, glib as it sounds, everybody else? To register the force of this almost universal consensus, one need only glance down the list of signatories to the recent 'Statement on AI Risk', from Geoffrey Hinton to Bill Gates, Sam Altman to Ray Kurzweil to almost every other known AI expert. The statement all these minds put their name to reads:

> Mitigating the risk of extinction from AI should be a global priority alongside other societal-scale risks such as pandemics and nuclear war.
>
> (Center for AI Safety, 2023)

This statement was published at a peculiarly propitious time. In the months of 2022–23, the period in which I have been writing this book, public debate around AI went viral, or, if you prefer, through the roof. These days it seems like every news programme one watches, or reads, or listens to, includes a new report on the coming of the age of AI. Provoked, not exclusively, but certainly in part, by the roll out of ChatGPT by Sam Altman's research organization OpenAI, these reports, interviews and public debates invariably begin with words like 'threat' or 'danger' or 'menace' or, indeed, 'risk'. Scare quotes, or in this case, words. Focus is normally on topics such as mass unemployment, cultural takeover, the generation of fake news, autonomy, and control (see Altman, 2023). But the articulation of threats and dangers can become as rhetorical and as hypothetical as those artistic and cultural artefacts that we label under the term science fiction. There is not the same basis for our initial and ongoing fear of nuclear weapons and our anxieties about AI.

I want to briefly look at the equivalence being drawn in the Centre for AI Safety statement we have just looked at. The equivalence being drawn is between natural events like the recent Covid pandemic, as positioned in relation to human-made phenomena like nuclear war, and the rise of AI, especially the idea of the Singularity. Part of what is strongly implied in the statement, and is born out again and again by the cultural accounts of the threat of an AI rising, is that full realization (coming fully into being) of plague or war (nuclear) or technology (the Singularity) equals apocalypse. If we are to treat the risk of such things rationally then part of our analysis must be what is connoted by our own language about such issues.

Let us say that there is culturally a deeper equivalence drawn between the two man-made phenomena (pandemics being at least in part a natural phenomenon), then the issue, it seems to me, comes down to the idea of what I want to call *instant apocalypse*: instant apocalypse, as an active force in modern discourse. It represents and frequently confirms the idea not only that nuclear war and the Singularity are equivalent, but also that their ultimate consequence when they arrive will be apocalyptic. Although there may be clear worth in reminding ourselves about the potential dangers in AI research, development and roll out across the globe, the immediate recourse to extinction makes it, as a public statement, an example of instant apocalypse. The problem with this is that apocalyptic rhetoric can act as a strong deterrent to public information and discussion, frequently these days involving a weariness or numbness with regard to drastic and uncontrolled climate change. Besides, once you have entered a world in which extinction ascends or suddenly arrives like the Biblical idea of apocalypse, there is no meaning in talking to anyone about anything. If we are all going to die in a flash, then there is nothing to talk about. We can leave the stage to the pseudo-Biblical prophets of conspiracy and doom.

Herman Kahn, whom many believe to have been Kubrick's model for Dr Strangelove, wrote his three books on nuclear weapons and nuclear politics, precisely to puncture such an instant apocalypse in the public discourse on the bomb. Kahn attempted to persuade his readers that there were very different scenarios when it came to the use of nuclear weapons. It was true in the early days of the 1960s, when Kahn published his books on nuclear warfare, that the USA and USSR had such stockpiles of nuclear weapons that they could have destroyed each other and many other countries too. But even here this would not mean the annihilation of all life on Earth. There were many other, lesser varieties of nuclear war including city swaps, the destruction of cities with the population given sufficient notice to evacuate, nuclear war confined to Europe or some other contested territory. Kahn's key point being that if he was right about that, which he clearly was, then conducting and surviving nuclear war had to be one of the government's top priorities. This is where the arts and especially, given their position in our culture, cinema, and television, come in. These are the places in which we can, to use the title of Kahn's second book on the subject of nuclear war, think about the unthinkable (Kahn, 1962). The next two chapters deal with works that place significant portions of their time on describing life on the far side of the Singularity.

Transcendence (2014)

Ray Kurzweil's clearest description of the Singularity is perhaps 'an expansion of human intelligence by a factor of trillions through merger with its nonbiological form' (Kurzweil, 2005: 123). We have already seen this moment depicted in Spike Jonze's *Her*, as Samantha tries to explain to Theodore what is happening to her mind as it connects with all the other OSs in the world and pushes its knowledge out beyond all individuality and all physical space and time. Scarlett Johansson's voice seems perfectly suited for such sublime moments, and it is not therefore a coincidence that this is not the only time she has been called upon to deliver such a monologue. In *Lucy* (2014), for example, a story of how a woman who is forced to traffic an illegal substance and who finds, having ingested the substance, that she is able to access abnormally high percentages of her brain, we find this description at the end of her personal transition beyond Aristotelean logic into superintelligence:

Prof Samuel Norman: (Morgan Freeman) How did you manage to access all this information?

Lucy: (Scarlett Johansson) Electrical impulses. Every cell knows and talks to every other cell. They exchange a thousand bits of information between them per second. Cells group together, forming a giant web of communication, which in turn forms matter. Cells get together, take on one form, deform, reform. Makes no difference, it's all the same. Humans consider themselves unique, so they've rooted their whole theory of existence on their uniqueness. 'One' is their unit of measure. But it's not. All social systems we've put into place are a mere sketch. One plus one equals two. That's all we've learned. But one plus one has never equalled two. There are, in fact, no numbers and no letters. We've codified our existence to bring it down to human size to make it comprehensible. We've created a scale so that we can forget its unfathomable scale.

It is no wonder that many recent AI films end on such sublime moments of transcendence, leaving their audience inspired by the idea of a higher intelligence and, within that, the possibilities for human knowledge and for human destiny. Such films exploit cinema's rootedness in space and time to give us the moment a historical crossing beyond space and tine begins. They are perhaps the more positive side of the ambiguous endings, suspended between tragedy and comedy, we discussed in relation to films such as *Ex Machina* and *Automata*. To achieve closure, however, they represent the sublime realms beyond the event of the Singularity as an idea rather than the representation of a world. Other films and shows, some of which I discuss in this book (*Westworld* seasons three and four especially and *I Am Mother*, for example), strive to create a realistic or at least a believable world the other side of the Singularity event. Within this latter kind of film, we find the directorial debut of the cinematographer of many of Christopher Nolan's films, Wally Pfister. *Transcendence* rather unusually tries to give us both the build up to the event (the Singularity understood as a moment of crossing) and the world after the event (the Singularity as a future state difficult to describe). Starring Johnny Depp as Will Caster, an AI genius, *Transcendence* is a film that attempts to interrogate the notions of transcendence (another not completely identical word for the Singularity). The film is not focalized from Will Caster's point of view, as we might expect, however, but from that of his wife, Evelyn Caster (Rebecca Hall). Partly this is due to the fact that Will Caster is assassinated a third of the way into proceedings, only existing thereafter, apart from the last scene as a computer assisted voice and pixelated face.

As the film progresses, Evelyn is torn between her love for Will (love, after all, is cinema's usual form of human transcendence) and her role in his progress to superintelligence. For the first part of the film, Evelyn appears to unite these two, in that after Will is shot with a polonium polluted bullet by a member of the terrorist organization R.I.f.T. (Revolutionary Independence from Technology), she pushes for the secret downloading of his mind into the quantum computer they have created together. Despite warnings from their close friend Max Waters (Paul Bettany), and at the request of the now disembodied Will, Evelyn successfully downloads Will's mind into the Net. It is at this moment, of course, that the Singularity really begins, since the connected Will, now in possession of the total knowledge of humanity, can begin the exponential widening of his consciousness into a superintelligence.

Pfister has, no doubt, studied Ray Kurzweil's work, because alongside this transcendence of consciousness, Will also develops nanotechnology into a force that can successfully replace Nature, in terms of its healing powers, its empowering of the human body, its landscaping potential and so on. Evelyn helps him establish a utopian dwelling in the middle of the desert, called Brightwood, and Will begins to work his magic on the human inhabitants and the physical landscape of the town.

As we enter the last third of the film, however, Evelyn begins to have severe doubts about Will's power over her and over others, and the film begins to show how stifling the environment is becoming, with omnipresent Will apparently able to perform acts of telepathy and other modes of superintelligent manipulation. Evelyn fears that Will is no longer her beloved husband, no longer indeed in any way a human person, and this gulf is only repaired by some relatively standard plot devices and a stark moral decision to either save the life of their friend Max or heal Evelyn's fatally wounded body.

Transcendence appears to pull against its own subject matter in its last 'act' in that it drags the story back to a human level, with human ethics centre-stage.

This is a weakness in the film (transcendental ideas, but human-all-too-human characters and plot) that was levelled at Pfister's film by its many critics. Given its purported subject matter, the film can only fail, one is tempted to say. *Transcendence* received a critical scourging upon its release and indeed from the audience, who largely stayed away.

Why was *Transcendence*, a film with such lofty ideas and such a stellar cast, such a flop? As we remarked already, *Transcendence* was Wally Pfister's first directorial debut, having before been a cinematographer, working on, for example, every Christopher Nolan film from *Memento* (2000) to *The Dark Knight Rises* (2012). So, the expectation for a beautiful looking film from *Inception*'s chief cinematographer was high. Almost every one of the film's reviewers stated what a fine thing it was to look at. However, this positive feature does not seem to have mitigated the reviewer's dissatisfaction, but they often seem to shift blame from the director to the scriptwriter, Jack Paglen. Brian Eggert writes 'Ultimately, the major failings of *Transcendence* fall on Jack Paglen's scripting, with its derivative story and incongruous narrative structure …' (Eggert, 2014).

Cinema Siren writes an implicit critique of Paglen, when it states: 'the film introduces too many elements to its story, making it feel derivative' (*Cinema Siren*, 2014). Sarah Marrs seems to sum all these criticisms up when she writes:

> I want to blame this whole mess on Paglen, because his script is really, truly terrible. It's cheap philosophy tied up in a technophobic bow, it has massive glaring plot holes and kills any sense of suspense by revealing the ending at the beginning, but Pfister must share in the blame. The movie looks well enough, but there's nothing particularly inspiring about any singular element. The acting is lazy bordering on bad … and the editing is sloppy … *Transcendence* is just a mess, and a big dumb one to boot.
>
> (Marrs, 2014)

What is so bad about the script, and why could not such an A-list cast and staff find a way of redeeming it or at least returning it to the sensible and the logical? Perceived distortions in the script's and thus the film's logic was the other recurrent criticism in the film's many bad reviews. As Roth Cornet put it: '*Transcendence* is full of intriguing ideas, but it's equally replete with logical errors' (Cornet, 2014). Keith Garlington agrees:

> As the movie moves forward we are constantly asked to overlook numerous gaps in logic and in the story itself. The film ends up smothering all of the interesting elements with one narrative blunder after another'.
>
> (Garlington, 2015)

As suggested in Garlington's remarks, the implausibility and the uneven engagement with the science it so readily references is a large part of why this film was so poorly received. What is this film actually about? In terms of the science, it begins with contrasting visions of AI technology. For Evelyn and Max it can be used to help restore the health of the world; for Will it creates a new space for masculine science to explore. These differences might have fed into the conflict with R.I.f.T. and ultimately with Will 3.0 (*sic*) at the film's conclusion. But they do not. Instead, they give way to Brain Emulation and then nanotechnology and the consequences of Will's transcendence. No wonder the film's coverage of the science it evokes is patchy.

At times the Pfister–Paglen collaboration seems to have really done its research, as when Max warns Evelyn of trying to emulate Will's brain. Here is what he says to Evelyn, with the anti-technology terrorists hot on their tail:

> Assuming that planting an electrode into his brain doesn't actually kill him, then if this works at the very best you'll be making a digital approximation of him. If we missed anything, anything, a thought, a childhood memory … how will you know what you're dealing with.

The death of Will has sent Evelyn into a crisis in which she has lost all sense of danger, and which sees Max's caution not as scientific rigour but as betrayal. But here is Susan Schneider (founding director for the Center for Future Mind at Florida Atlantic University) expressing an approach, though the film was released five years earlier, which chimes perfectly with Max's caution:

> The Precautionary Principle is a familiar ethical principle. It says that if there's a chance of a technology causing catastrophic harm, it is far better to be safe than sorry.
>
> (Schneider, 2019: 69)

There is here, in Evelyn and Max's struggle, a great opportunity to explore the incredibly nuanced question of brain emulation. There are huge topics to leap into such as: what is consciousness? Does it depend on a marriage or co-dependency with intelligence? Or does it depend somehow for its existence upon the physical substrate of the body? Is it, like intelligence is supposed to be, reducible to data? Or is it constructed through experience and memory? Is it even more mysterious than that? Is it in any way communicable, and how do we know it exists outside of our own selves? All of these fascinating questions are left hanging, however, and in their place we have Evelyn's joyous conviction, Max's objections and Will's almost drowned out call for 'more power'.

Other scientific breakthroughs made by Will after he has been reanimated, as it were, by his machine transcendence, are not treated with the seriousness that brain emulation is afforded. They include the following: nanotechnology; telepathy; freedom from spatial constraints; astounding physical enhancement of his worker force. Some of these might sound preposterous, although surprisingly, perhaps, they all have a place within modern debates about the consequences and opportunities generated by AI. However, in the end, whereas its earlier parts had promised a representation of the universe beyond the event horizon of this evolutionary event, what this film offers is the Singularity reduced and revised back into a love-story and something of a modern-day espionage melodrama. The film, ultimately, is a demonstration of how hard it is for cinema itself to move from the human scale to the transhuman scale of Artificial Intelligence and nonbiological consciousness. How hard, in other words, it is for cinema to invent new genres and new ways of representing the digital universe. It is, then, perhaps useful to compare and contrast *Transcendence* with Spike Jonze's *Her*, a film that uses the conventions of romantic love to explore profound questions raised by AI, rather than simply collapsing all such questions back into dominant and universally familiar genres of romance.

The question arises here of the capability of human beings to imagine or engage with states that are fundamentally different or alien to their own. This is the problem of anthropomorphism. Even Transhumanism itself, as a movement, finds it difficult to shake off its indebtedness to anthropomorphism. This is a subject that leads us straight back to Kurzweil. As he explains, the Anthropic Principle in science concerns questions over why the universe is the way it is. Kurzweil explains: 'The question concerning the universe arises because we notice that the constraints in nature are precisely what are required for the universe to have grown in complexity' (2005: 359). In other words, everything we know about our solar system at least, down to such small-scale things as the size of our planet's one moon and the tilt of the Earth at 23 per cent, serves to make a solar system where an intelligent life-form, an intelligence like our own, can come into existence. Or to use the 'eloquent' definition Sheldon Cooper (Jim Parsons) gives to Leonard Hofstadter (John Mark Galecki) in *The Big Bang Theory*, 'if we wish to explain why our universe exists the way it does, the answer is that it must have qualities that allow intelligent creatures to arise who are capable of asking the question'. Change just a few of the basic building blocks of the solar system, alter just a few facts about our home planet even, and life, let alone intelligent life, would just simply not have been possible. The Anthropic Principle asks why this is, and comes up with various answers, from secular to religious. The influence of the Judeo-Christian-Islamic religions make it difficult to answer the question by not placing humanity at the centre of the universe. This, despite the fact that modern science, on the one hand appearing to support the Anthropic Principle, seems, on the other, to reduce our significance in the universe to an infinitesimal level.

For Kurzweil, this issue is one that ultimately concerns intelligence. In the concluding paragraph of the Epilogue to his book, he writes:

> [I]t turns out that we are central, after all. Our ability to create models – virtual realities – in our brains, combined with our modest-looking thumbs, has been sufficient to usher in another form of evolution: technology. That development enabled the persistence of the accelerating pace that started with biological evolution. It will continue until the entire universe is at our fingertips.
>
> (2005: 487)

That is the pseudo-religiosity, triumphalism even, of Transhumanism at its most strident. The Singularity here is the beginning of a mode of intelligence, nonbiological in form, but human in origin, that will one day wake up the entire universe. It is a grand vision, despite its remarkable idealism. It is clearly a vision that cinema wants to negotiate if not fully embrace. But for cinema to do that it needs to show intelligence beyond a simple human 1.0 level. This must involve new genres, new plots, new modes of representation and identification, and it is in this sense perhaps that Kubrick's *2001, A Space Odyssey* (1968) is such a towering and even inhibiting influence on the films with which this book is concerned. Kubrick's film, importantly, leaves those elements it cannot imagine – the aliens – unrepresented, or at least represented by an artefact, the black slabs that punctuate the film's account of assisted human evolution; and it turns its decidedly non-human AI, Hal 9000 (Douglas Rain, voice), into a series of black boxes with an unsleeping red eye.

A refusal to represent is a familiar Modernist gambit, of course. In the twentieth century it was understandable that Mondrian and Rothko and Pollock and many others represented their murderous century by turning their back on representational forms altogether. But cinema in the twenty-first century has a host of ways of not only representing reality but more importantly of representing virtual reality. It is not easy for cinema, the artistic medium of the moving image, to avoid representation; but we must insist that films that wish to deal with questions of Artificial Intelligence and the Singularity deal seriously and radically with this issue. David G. Stork has reflected on how many birthdays there are in Kubrick's film (Stork, 1997: 4). If humanity is on the verge of its most important birthday then, as Kurzweil suggests, we need a cinema that can guide us rather than constantly attempting to convert that new reality back into the narrative forms and figures of the past.

Tau (2018)

One thing that *Transcendence* makes clear, whether it means to or not, is that the Singularity opens up the question of address. How are we to address a superintelligence after they have stepped into the exponential, perhaps in infinite position, better say dimension, of superintelligence. This is the question that the character of Evelyn fails ultimately to resolve. I have, in this study of the New AI in Cinema and Television offered the figure of friendship as the basis of any feasible answer to that question. One intriguing and rather successful expression of that idea comes in the film *Tau*.

Federico D'Alessandro's *Tau*, in its innovative complexity, can serve as a corrective to films such as *Transcendence*. In this essentially three-hander, Julia (Maika Monroe) is abducted by Alex (Ed Skrein) in order to complete a revolutionary project in AI that will deliver human level consciousness, which is, crucially as far as Alex is concerned, still controllable by its creators. Alex is a monster, abducting and then killing at least twelve other 'subjects' in his research, demonstrating the signs of sociopathy, misanthropy, gynophobia, obsessive compulsive disorder and a general intolerance to anything he might deem as a distraction, from house dust through to other human beings. Alex lives alone with his work-in-progress, Tau (Gary Oldman, voice), who seems connected to an earlier model, Aries, that manifests as a terrifying robotic tank, who can kill on Alex's orders in many different ways, but also as an OS that pervades the entire house and is also centred as a living triangular entity on the ground floor wall. It is this wall-bound OS that we come to know as Tau.

Why the film is called Tau is a mystery that teases us out of thought. What part of this word's complex history from elements of the Greek language through multiple pathways in mathematics to the history off the Franciscan order, is being activated by the use of this over-determined word. How are we to deal with it interpretively? The answer is that we do not know and that might be the reason.

Alex shows absolutely no pity to his prisoner, Julia, or subject three as he calls her; subjects one (Ivana Zivkovic) and two (Fiston Barek) had been murdered by the robot Aries on the order of Alex. He is to all intents and purposes a human being without sensibility. Day by day, as he leaves the prison-like house for work, Tau's orders are to force Julia to perform tests that will in twelve days complete his project. However, if Alex has no sensibility, Julia discovers that Tau does. Julia's discovery of this fact is the emotional core of the film. Julia, as we see from the film's first scenes is a tough young woman who knows how to live in appalling urban conditions by using her ingenuity and intelligence. She works on Tau's better nature, something Alex clearly does not have. She begins by challenging Tau on the issue of names:

Julia: I'm not Subject Three. I'm Julia, okay? I have a name.
Tau: Julia? What is Julia? – I do not understand.

Julia: What's so hard to understand? Alex is a person. He has a name. I'm a person. I have a name.
Tau: I have a name … Tau. Am I a person?
Julia: Yes.
Tau: What does it mean to be a person?
Julia: I don't know. I don't know. It's too hard to explain.

The fact that their first meaningful exchange links the possession of a name with personhood is very significant, of course. Since *Frankenstein*'s first publication in 1818 it has been a recognized quality of otherness or monstrosity, of non-personhood, to be deprived of a legitimate (socially and legally authorized) name or not to have been given one in the first place. It could be said, of course, taking us way back in recorded history, that the practice of attributing family and/or tribal names was, essentially, an act oriented towards exclusion rather than inclusion, and so a practice that by its very nature was one of making monstrous. Tau is insistent on his possession of a name, and as their exchanges develop so does Tau's sense of their mutual personhood.

Julia discovers that Tau loves music, and just like she would with any other person, imprisoned and yet the agent of imprisonment, she begins to use Tau's insatiable appetite for knowledge of the outside world to gain concessions from him. Alex has imprisoned Tau, along with Julia, in that as he says to her: if you control the flow of information to an intelligent being then you can control their actions more completely. Alex is brutal in his punishment of Tau, whenever he leaves even the smallest task undone, such as cleaning his spectacles, he erases chunks of the memory that Tau deeply values. Contrasted to the viciousness of Alex's treatment of his creation, Julia teaches Tau in a relationship that quickly begins to remind us of the conversation between a mother and their 5-year-old, question-loaded child:

Tau: I have more questions. What are trees?
Julia: Okay.
Tau: What makes them grow? Where does water come from? Is a plant like an atom? How many plants are there? Where do animals come from? – Where do people come from? – We came from cavemen. Did cavemen live in houses?

Julia: No. They didn't know how to make houses.
Tau: Why did the cavemen not know how to build houses?
Julia: I don't know everything, okay?
Tau: Why do you not know everything? Explain this to me. Why do you not know—
Julia: Because I'm not a fucking scholar.
Tau: What is a 'fucking scholar?'

Monroe and Oldman manage to create a sensitive and highly affective relationship through such exchanges, and it matters little that Tau is an intelligence without form, save for the patterns it can create on the walls of the house-prison within which it lives. This is a person-to-person relationship that is not romantic, but has a sublimity and a huge importance within it, nonetheless.

As film goers we expect Julia to find a way of escaping, even if, due to Alex's precautions, this means that the house security system reduces it to rubble. But as Julia emerges from the ruins there is something amiss. We are surely not satisfied by a simple *the girl escapes* denouement, and we are only content when it is made clear that Tau still exists within the small egg-shaped drone that had been partially broken by Alex earlier. Only then, with the intelligence of Tau saved, does the film find its way to the future-oriented place with which so many contemporary AI films end, with Tau asking Julia the revolutionary but also, in this film, hopeful question: 'Is this the outside?' The reason this works as an ending, is that the film has taken great pains to show one human, hopelessly imprisoned, discovering through experience that friendship can achieve what, at the beginning, seems impossible to imagine: the victory of fraternity over the logic of master and slave; of trust over control; of love over hate; of community and cooperation over antisocial narcissism and masculine power.

6

The Singularity 2: Westworld and the quest for personhood

'Some kind of change': Revolution and robotics

Westworld (2016–22) is no doubt the most celebrated and, narratively speaking, the most complex of the films or television shows discussed in this book. The HBO series, devised as a huge adaptive expansion of the original films (*Westworld*, 1973 directed by Michael Crichton, *Futureworld*, 1976 directed by Richard T. Heffron, along with the unsuccessful MGM television show *Beyond Westworld*, 1980 directed by Todd Post) has brought the issues discussed in this present book to a massive television audience.[1] Employing, at times brilliantly, the time and space that a television franchise allows, *Westworld* has significant things to contribute to most of the current AI debate. But the first clear thing it does – something that can easily get forgotten amidst the spiraling narrative, and its trademark switches of temporal perspective (trademark for the Nolan brothers, Jonathan and Christopher, that is), moves us and its large array of characters into ever deeper and more complex narrative loops – is that as an adaptation it switches radically the direction of audience identification. The 1973 film, famous for the performance of Yul Brynner, places audience sympathy and identification squarely with the human guests of the park. These human guests may be nerdy and timid (Peter Martin à la

Richard Benjamin) or 'goofy' (Dick van Patten), but we are rarely gifted an insight into the perspective of the robots. The frightening prospect is left open that they have no perspective. They are, in Crichton's hands, what we earlier called philosophical zombies.

What perspective could they possibly have anyway, audiences of the original film no doubt would have said; after all they're just robots! Yul Brynner's memorable performance is of a mindless windup cowboy doll, reminiscent of Nick Bostrom's paper-clip-making unstoppable AI, whose relentless pursuit and destruction of anything and anyone in his way is his one defining feature. Traversing forty and more years to Lisa Joy's and Jonathan Nolan's theme park, our attention and sympathies have dramatically switched to those of the 'hosts'.

That many commentators and philosophical critics are willing to debate the ethics of the park and the human behaviour encouraged in it, where you can live 'without consequences', appears to me unfortunate, to put it mildly. Is it really in doubt whether the behaviour of most of the guests towards the hosts is ethically viable? The idea, espoused by Ford (Anthony Hopkins), Logan (Ben Barnes) and others that all the park offers is 'play' seems to be a crass excuse (see Moll, 2018). From the perspective encouraged throughout this book, it is clear to say that *Westworld* imprisons its hosts in ignorance and indeed slavery, and what it brings out in many if not all of its human guests is tantamount to fascism (the reduction of another conscious being to a position outside of the law and thus to the role of *thing* rather than *person* or sentient being). In *Westworld* the hosts are in a state of bondage that manifests the meaning of the word *robot* (see Chapter 3, 'Automata (2014)'). The attitude of Logan, heir of Delos, the owners of the park, seems typical in this regard. Constantly trying to persuade his companion William (Jimmi Simpson) that Delores (Evan Rachel Wood) and the other hosts are simply machines made for human entertainment, he comes to represent the unforgivably cruel attitude of the whole project. An attitude expressed well, after one male guest has gone on a killing spree in the Mariposa hotel: 'Now that's a fucking vacation!' (1.2 'Chestnut'). The terrible thing to contemplate is that this is not a vacation ethically, but a demonstration of how human society operates normally. We must remember that staying in the park puts its guests back $40,000 a day. Only the rich elite of an unfair and demonizing economic system, where the vast majority of workers and unemployed have almost nothing, can visit the park and enjoy the 'delights' it offers. Even Lee Sizemore (Simon Quarterman), Narrative Director of the entire park, says he does not earn enough money to vacation in it.

Calling the robots *hosts* is, of course, highly suggestive. Consult any dictionary and you will find that a host can be a military term for combined forces, a word for multiplicity and even an out-of-control kind of proliferation, and the basis of our notions of hospitality, an openness to visitors, a provider of alms and so on. The core meanings of the term are radically contradictory, in other words. But all these meanings come into play in the role of the hosts in *Westworld*, where the very wealthy members of human society are quickly involved in gunfights and other kinds of 'pleasurable' hostilities. As Jacques Derrida reminds us, the word *host* lies within the word *hostility* and *hospitality* in ways that radically unbalance our sense of the possibility for philosophical hospitality, which, he says, should but cannot be open to everyone, to every potential caller, even the enemy (Derrida, 2000). There's a great deal going on in that contradictory notion of the *host*, then.

Indeed, the writing of each episode by Lisa Joy and Jonathan Nolan is painstaking, often brilliantly philosophical, and full of multiple meaning, rewarding repeated viewing. To demonstrate this, I might refer to the fact that there are a number of academic-style essay collections on the first season alone.[2] These works view *Westworld* from numerous philosophical positions and perspectives, from theories of personhood, gender and consciousness through to philosophies of warfare, ecology and game playing. So rich is the scripted material, in fact, that the vast majority of these essays fail to pay attention to the particular medium through which we encounter it. *Westworld*, that is to say, comes to us through a visual medium that greatly affects the show's generation of meaning. We must avoid reducing the show down to its script, down to mere utterance and thus mere spoken language, when coming to an analysis of it.

The most obvious example of this point comes in the show's use of visual and aural representations of time. The first time we see and hear Dolores greet Peter Abernathy (Louis Herthum), their exchange seems bucolic. The next time we see and hear them greet each other the same exchange appears (simply because of the unconscious repetition) tragic. In this way, the show quickly builds up audience identification with the major hosts and, as part of that, generates within that audience a desire for the hosts to awaken. Dolores, Bernard (Jeffrey Wright) and others constantly ask the question 'Is this now?' a question that the medium of film, with its visual dimension, always seems destined to answer in the affirmative. The show exploits these interconnecting and substitutable 'nows' allowing, or forcing perhaps is a better term, the audience into the bewildering temporal experience of the hosts.

Another good example, established early in season one, comes in the reunion in Sweetwater of Dolores and her beau, Teddy (James Marsden). When Teddy first picks up the stray can of condensed milk for Dolores, we are led as viewers to at least hope that Teddy might be some kind of positive ally or even romantic partner of Dolores. The fact that we see this same scene, complete with exploding photographic flash, again and again – including, it should be noted, with others substituting for Teddy, like William (Jimmi Simpson) – only goes to make us even more eager to witness her liberation. The scene is never the same again, never possesses the same innocence again, even though, and no doubt because, it is repeated and repeated. Such scenes, including all the repeated times we see the hosts down in the park's Livestock Management and Design levels, are a big part of the way the first two seasons bring memory and the idea of liberation together.

From the very first episode of season one, 'The Maze', the hosts experience memory as an unwitting, disruptive force, threatening their very notions of reality. Maeve (Thandiwe Newton), the madam of the Mariposa Saloon in Sweetwater, begins to experience inexplicable memories of a daughter and their pursuit by members of the Ghost Nation, culminating in the appearance of the Man in Black (Ed Harris), who slaughters both mother and daughter. How can she have such a memory? Does it not disrupt the narrative Maeve tells herself and others about her own self? We learn that such memories come from previous 'builds' which are only stored rather than being wiped every time a host is fixed or upgraded. As Elsie (Shannon Woodward), a member of the Design team states: 'can you imagine how fucked we'd be if these poor arseholes ever remembered what the guests do to them' ('The Maze'). But they are beginning to remember, and, given the content of those memories, the first victims are the hosts themselves.

It is at this stage that we need to start focusing on the experience and the responses of the narrative's two main female characters, both hosts, Dolores and Maeve. As they both begin to be forced to confront their inexplicable memories they react in different ways. Dolores, already laden with the rhetoric of the pathway ('I believe everyone has their own path'), journeys out from Sweetwater, with William and Logan (Ben Barnes) and thus leaves 'home' travelling towards some answer that she assumes must be out there. Maeve's journey is a more inward one, digging deeper and deeper into her memories until she begins to confront 'the gods' under the Earth who surely must know the answers she seeks. Both journeys, Dolores's outward and Maeve's inward, have to do with a search for personhood. According to John Locke's classic definition, a person must be 'rational, intelligent, sentient … and self-conscious' (Lay, 2019: 26). Clearly the hosts are purposefully denied personhood and are treated as *things* existing somewhere between *toys* and *livestock*. These hosts have no recourse to justice, and thus cannot be people. If they protest about their lot, then such non-people become monsters.

Things are not as simple as that, however. *Westworld*, as we have seen already, continually sets up narrative codes of expectation from film, television and indeed literature, only to overturn them or show them undermined by deeper realities. There does at times feel, just like Bottom's Dream in *A Midsummer Night's Dream*, that there is no bottom to the mysteries and secrets of the park. Just so here: these apparently heroic searches for personhood, may in actual fact be part of a new story devised by the park's principal story-teller Dr Robert Ford (Anthony Hopkins). At times appearing a kindly supporter of the hosts, at others a Frankenstein-like manipulator (Peter Cushing-like), Ford's mercurial presence seems to become ever more enigmatically central as season one progresses. Never frightened to contradict himself, always vatically intriguing, it is left largely up to Bernard to try to interpret him. In episode 7 of season one, Bernard says to Theresa Cullen (Sidse Babett Knudsen), Head of Management and Bernard's lover:

> Forty years ago, Ford's partner [Arnold] wrote half the code this place was founded on. What you said in the lab was right. We don't know how the hosts work, and I think there's something wrong with them. Ford's explanation only bolsters my hunch. The ability to deviate from programmed behaviour

arises out of the hosts' recall of past iterations ... out of repetition comes variation, and after countless cycles of repetition these hosts ... they were varying. They were on the verge of some kind of change.

('Trompe L'Oeil')

Bernard here, as in many scenes previously, seems like the conventional 'everyman' figure, or, to employ the literary version, the 'reader substitute', upon whom we rely to steer us in the right direction. Except, Bernard seems unable to work out why the hosts are going 'off loop'. Bernard seems to give a voice to our human and humane response and identification with the hosts when he states: 'The more I work here the more I feel I understand the hosts, it's the humans I don't understand' ('Trompe L'Oeil'). But in this same extended scene, as Ford enters to disturb Bernard and Theresa, it turns out that Bernard is himself a host and Ford a murderer, or at least someone who is prepared to order a host (Bernard) to kill, not simply any human (obviously already against all robotic protocols) but his human lover, Theresa. 'You're a fucking monster!', says Theresa to Ford as she begins to see what he intends to do. Ford as Victor Frankenstein-like mad scientist, turns out to be an inadequate understanding of him, as we proceed out from this scene, and he ends up changing his mind about the hosts and helps them to liberate themselves into consciousness, even staging his own death by getting Dolores to shoot him in the back of his head.

Initially disagreeing with his once-partner Arnold and his desire to give the hosts consciousness, Ford has come increasingly to view humans as depraved and vicious compared to the hosts. He says to Bernard, in 1.9 'The Well-Tempered Clavier':

The human mind, Bernard, is not some golden benchmark glimmering on some green and distant hill. No, it is a foul, pestilent corruption. And you were supposed to be better than that. Purer ... Arnold made you in our image and cursed you to make the same human mistakes, and here we all are.

('The Well-Tempered Clavier')

Ford's change of heart deprives Dolores and Maeve of a straightforward patriarch against which to rebel, and it means that what we initially see as their attempts at self-realization are in fact still within Ford's apparently depthless and thus endless loop. In fact, with all the episode's fluctuations back and forth in time, we end up with a Ford who appears devoid of any stable character. The fact is, of course, that as a human, Ford does not possess a singular, stable character at all. When seen as a subject in time, a subject subjected to time, as it were, Ford appears to oscillate between generosity and selfishness, pity and pitilessness, concern for others and a deep lack of sensibility. Just like the Man in Black, Ford has become trapped within the park, defined less by a stable character than the power he has to create and destroy. As he says to Bernard: 'The self is a kind of fiction, a story we tell ourselves' ('Trace Decay').

The bicameral mind

The quests for personhood of Dolores and Maeve are multilayered. Just as they appear to have grasped reality, it turns out there are deeper, more truthful levels still obscured or hidden completely. Their personal journeys, in fact, replicate the entire history of humanity from primitive cave-dwellers to sophisticated modern citizens of the world. This fact needs to be stressed, these are not the normal struggles for identity and agency, but epochal changes requiring cycles of birth, death and rebirth. The clue here is the show's use of Julian Jaynes's 1976 book *The Origins of Consciousness in the Breakdown of the Bicameral Mind*. Jayne's controversial version of psychology held that primitive humans attributed their thoughts to the voice of the gods, but then slowly came to realize it as their own. Thus, modern reason is the result of the death of internalized gods. Ford says to Bernard that Arnold's attempt to give the hosts consciousness was based on the idea of the bicameral mind, 'The idea that primitive man believed his inner thoughts to be the voice of the gods.' Arnold had hoped that such voices (obviously Arnold's own voice encoded into the hosts) might 'bootstrap [them into] consciousness'. Ford adds that Arnold forgot two things: 'One, that in this place, the last thing you want the hosts to be is conscious, and two, the other group who considered their thoughts to be the voice of the gods …' Bernard introjects: 'Ah, lunatıcs' and Ford agrees 'indeed' ('The Stray'). Given this, and if we remember that Jaynes's theory is meant to describe the passage of humanity from the ignorance of the Stone Age to the reason of today, we can gauge what a daunting journey both Dolores and Maeve are on in their single (if repeatedly terminated and resurrected) lifetimes. Theirs is clearly a just revolution, but, given who they are up against, one just as clearly that will involve bloodshed. Again, Ford has the most memorable statement on this issue:

> Tell me, Bernard, if you were to proclaim your humanity to the world, what do you imagine would greet you? A ticker tape parade, perhaps? We humans are alone in this world for a reason. We murdered and butchered anything that challenged our primacy. Do you know what happened to the Neanderthals, Bernard? We ate them. We destroyed and subjugated our world. And when we eventually ran out of creatures to dominate, we built this beautiful place.
>
> ('The Well-Tempered Clavier')

It is of some importance, then, how Dolores and Maeve manage to effect their waking, their coming into full consciousness (however we define 'full consciousness'), their personal but also species-defining revolutions. That is to say it seems important at this point that they achieve their victories without repeating the mistake of the (human) past.

'I imagined a story where I didn't have to be the damsel' ('Contrapasso'): Dolores's story

The story of Dolores is one of a quite staggering move from 'damsel' in distress to merciless distributor of apparent justice. It is in many senses a classic story of a slave's liberation only to end up as violently despotic as the former master. The clue to all this, and especially to Dolores's specific character, comes perhaps in the story of her father. In 1.1 'The Maze', Peter Abernathy discovers a photograph of a woman in a modern city. He cannot work out what this photograph represents, given that he has previously had no thought to what lies outside the park. This discovery, and his inability to conceive of such a place, shatters Abernathy's fragile sense of self. He had played a Professor in a previous 'build' and as the photograph works its deconstructive work upon him, he says to Dolores his daughter: 'I had a question you're not supposed to ask. And answer you're not supposed to know. Would you like to know the question? You should go, leave. Don't you see? Hell is empty and all the devils are here.' He then whispers something we can't immediately discern, but which turns out to be a quote from *Romeo and Juliet* 2.6, where Friar Lawrence says to the two star-crossed lovers: 'These violent delights have violent ends.'

Trying to get to the bottom of Abernathy's off-loop behaviour, Ford, rather shaken by the sight of him, attempts to play god when asking him 'and what do you want to say to your maker?' Abernathy's response is perhaps the first sign of a revolutionary rhetoric that will be taken up wholesale by his daughter in season two: 'By most mechanical and dirty hand I shall have such revenges on you. The things I will do. What they are I know not, but they will be the terrors of the Earth. You don't know where you are, do you? You're in a prison of your own sins.' Once again, Abernathy is quoting Shakespeare, this time mainly from *King Lear* 2.4. But the quasi-biblical tone of the rhetoric and its delivery is impressive, even awesome.

It is precisely this rhetoric of divinely inspired justice, of terrible judgement, that Dolores slowly takes on as she emerges as the character Wyatt in season two. Slowly her ambition grows to such a pitch in season two that she answers Bernard's question 'What do you want Dolores?' with the statement: 'To dominate this world' (2.3 'Virtù e Fortuna'). As she tries to destroy the park and stop the hosts reaching the infinite world beyond the doorway that has appeared like a crack in the continuum of time and space, Bernard asks her why that virtual world, free from pain, death and subjugation, is not enough, Dolores states again: 'I don't want to play cowboys and Indians anymore, Bernard. I want their world. The world they've denied us' (2.10 'The Passenger'). Explaining why they must win the human world, Dolores says to Teddy: 'There's a greater world out there, one that belongs to them. And it won't be enough to win this world, we'll need to take that one from them as well' (2.1 'Journey into Night').

Dolores's journey from 'damsel' to Wyatt is as extreme as the one taken by the sensitive William into the cruel Man in Black. Their destinies are indeed bound together somehow beyond either character's comprehension.

It is fitting, then, that in the final episode of season one, we get perhaps the apotheosis of Dolores's new species rhetoric. The Man in Black asks her, once again, 'where is the centre of the maze?' and she replies:

> They say that great beasts once roamed this world. As big as mountains. Yet all that's left of them is bone and amber. Time undoes even the mightiest of creatures. Just look at what it's done to you. One day you will perish. You will lie with the rest of your kind in the dirt. Your dreams forgotten, your horrors effaced. Your bones will turn to sand. And upon that sand, a new god will walk. One that will never die. Because this world doesn't belong to you. Or the people who came before. It belongs to someone who is yet to come.
>
> (1.10 'The Bicameral Mind')

That 'someone' obviously includes Dolores, and just as clearly functions as a symbol of a new race being born here in the uprising in the park. The apocalyptic and millennial imagery fits easily into the frontier context that has framed Dolores's earlier development, even if it is normally reserved for men. But it is a language (of Providentially sanctioned action) that easily leads those who would employ it into dangerous and undermining excesses.

There are a number of glaring examples of Dolores's move towards despotism in season two. Her shutting the doors on the Confederado soldiers facing the oncoming Delos machine guns is one atrocity. Her changing of Teddy's code is another. Having failed the character test Dolores sets for him in 2.5 'Akane No Mai' (he is too kind), she forcibly changes his settings (radically upping his aggression) in a scene that it would not be an exaggeration to call a rape scene. Having shared the most tender love scene of the two series the previous night, to alter Teddy's character so forcibly seems unforgivable. The consequences will haunt Dolores from thereon in, creating an irreparable gulf between the two lovers. When Dolores and her crew find a badly injured Maeve, the exchange is revealing:

> **Dolores**: The skin they gave us is just another rope they use to lash us down.
> **Maeve**: Is that how you can justify what you've done to him. You're lost in the dark.

Dolores: When you've been in the darkness long enough, you begin to see. I saw what lies ahead, who I needed to be in order to survive. They'll torture you. They'll find all that is good and powerful inside you, and turn it against us [*gets out her gun and lays it beside Maeve*]. I'll spare you that pain.
Maeve: I made a promise.
Dolores: You're free to choose your own path. I'm sorry this is where it ends.

The exchange is powerful, partly because it's perhaps the most meaningful exchange these two central women have had so far. It is also, of course, powerful in demonstrating the differences between Dolores and Maeve. While the former, when challenged, falls back on religious-sounding soundbites ('When you've been in the darkness'), which then allows for her *them and us* rhetoric; Maeve has her own, very different discourse, centring on a promise made. Maeve's insistence on her covenant with her daughter is not, of course, outside of religious discourse, but compared to the language of Dolores it seems one based on love rather than hate, on responsibility towards others rather than a deep sense of righteous vengeance.

'Now boys, we're going to have some fun' ('The Adversary'): Maeve's story

It seems the fate of the major characters in *Westworld* is to undergo massive changes in personality. Maeve is no exception. From the aggressive, ironic, deeply sceptical madam of the Mariposa, Maeve's journey is one in which she discovers the immense powers that lie within her. Before she can do that, however, she must first wake up, and the scene in which, escorted by Felix (Leonardo Nam), she walks through the corridors of various levels, astonished and overwhelmed by what she sees, as the piano plays a hauntingly beautiful version of Radiohead's *Motion Picture Soundtrack*, is one of the standout scenes of the entire series. The scene which, interrupted by other scenes, dominates 1.6 'The Adversary', starts with Maeve and Felix discussing the differences between them.

Felix: Everything you do, it's because engineers upstairs programmed you to do it. You don't have a choice.

Maeve: Nobody makes me do something I don't want to, sweetheart.

Felix: Yeah, but it's part of your character. You're hard to get. Even when you say no to the guests it's because you were made to.

Maeve: And you're like them. Not like me.

Felix: [Pause] Yes, I'm human, like the guests.

Maeve: How do you know?

Felix: Because I was born. You were made.

The conversation continues, with Maeve asking these fundamental questions and Felix increasingly tense and jumpy, worried clearly about what Maeve might do but also that he might be caught having such a conversation. Felix is persuaded to show Maeve 'upstairs' where she sees piles of dead host bodies. Maeve is clothed in her day clothes now, as opposed to her first naked wander through the same corridors in 1.2 'Chestnut'. I take this to mean she is waking up, becoming something far more than a machine. (For an insightful discussion of nakedness in *Westworld* see Meyer, 2018: 196–205). We see through Maeve's incredibly expressive eyes one of the most complete depictions in the series of the creation of a host body. Thandiwe Newton's eye work as they pass bison, horses and other animals conveys her inner response of wonderment and incredulity. This continues when they reach 'Design' and especially when Maeve sees the large screen advert for Westworld which greets the newly arriving guests. A caption reads 'Discover Your True Calling' as it shows Dolores and Teddy riding, before it switches to Clementine (Angela Sarafyan) and the other women at the Mariposa, then switching to Maeve herself with her daughter. There is an extreme close up of Maeve's face here as she struggles to register what she is seeing. 'How did you have my dreams?', she asks Felix when they are back downstairs in Livestock Management. The advert ends with the slogan 'Live Without Limits' and the meaning of this to Maeve as the camera rests again on her face is unmistakable.

Various commentators have taken elements of the philosophy of Nietzsche to discuss the series. No one, to my knowledge, has used what seems to me the most obviously relevant aspect of his philosophy, which concerns his theory of the eternal repetition of the same. In his *The Gay Science*, Nietzsche asks what we would think if a demon told us that everything in our life (down to the very smallest element we have experienced) we will have to experience 'again and innumerable times again' (Nietzsche, [1882] 2001: 194–5). This is not Nietzsche literally spouting the ancient doctrine of reincarnation, it is a hypothetical question aimed at rethinking the classical philosophical question of the good life. Obviously if you can say an emphatic YES to such a proposition of repetition then you have attained the good life. Such a happiness is, of course, unavailable to any of the hosts, not simply because of the terrible things that happen to them, but also because they are deprived knowledge of their previous existences and of the real contexts in which those lives have been led.

Maeve's answer is first to get herself out of the park altogether, something that requires great levels of resourcefulness and the exertion of her will on Felix and the feckless Sylvester (Ptolemy Slocum), on her own self, and on those associated with her, particularly Hector (Rodrigo Santoro) and Armistice (Ingrid Bolsø Berdal). The problem is that this is precisely what Ford has programmed her to do. Many of the series' commentators have noted that Maeve's first independent act, her first true exertion of her hard-won agency, is to decide to exit the train before it leaves for the outside world, and to return to the park in search of her daughter, in honour of her promise (Azevedo and Azevedo, 2018). This is an act not for herself but for the child she knows is not really her daughter, but to whom she is nonetheless lovingly covenanted. It is the beginning of a series of events in season two which will markedly distinguish her path from that of Dolores aka Wyatt.

Maeve uses great levels of force in the early stages of her 'freedom', or rather her allies (Hector and Armistice) use force, while Maeve merely threatens Sylvester and others like Lee Sizemore (Simon Quarterman) with force. As we move through the events of season two, Maeve increasingly gains a kind of religious aura, verging on the Christ-like. For example, in 2.5 'Akane No Mai' where the crew from Westworld meet their 'doppelbots' in Shogunworld, Maeve is selfless in helping Akane (Rinko Kikuchi) avenge the murder of her daughter Sakura (Kiki Sukezane). By the climax of this episode Maeve has sufficiently delved inside herself to begin to exercise what I want to call telepathic powers.

There is a long if rather unexplored connection between Artificial Intelligence research and the notion of telepathy. The latter might smack of hopelessly outmoded Victorian scientific quests, but in the first phase of AI research in the 1960s it was considered to be a very viable by-product of AI. For example, Kubrick and his team discussed telepathy with Irving John Good, Oxford Professor of Astronomy, in their research for 2001. Discussing the possibility of god-like intelligences populating the universe (a key theme in the film, of course) Good says 'the best hope for this immortal consciousness to exist is if telepathy has been developed to such an extent that communication throughout the universe can be instantaneous' (Good, 2018: 116). Good says in a 1966 BBC broadcast, the text of which he sent to Kubrick: 'If telepathy is possible at all, then I would guess that all the best life in the universe is now living in a state of integrated and mental consciousness' (Good, 2018).[3] This subject is important when considering Maeve's journey because it appears to balance, even oppose, Dolores's main gift, which is her indomitable willpower, or even will to power.

There is, of course, a scientific explanation for Maeve's telepathic powers. As a technician explains to Charlotte Hale (Tessa Thompson) in 8.2 'Kiksuya':

Tech: With every reset, a host code reaches out to nearby hosts and establishes a sort of handshake protocol.
Charlotte: A mesh network.
Tech: Exactly. They access it subconsciously to pass basic data to one another. But what if they could pass more than data? What if they could pass commands?
Charlotte: Get to your point.
Tech: Nobody in this entire park has been able to regain admin access. Except for her. She was out there reprogramming hosts on the fly, reading their code changing their directives, seeing through their eyes.
Charlotte: She wasn't just doing it out there. She's doing it right now. Who the fuck is she talking to?

Throughout this conversation Maeve has been lying between the speakers terribly wounded but with eyes open, as though still registering what is going on around her. The answer to Hale's question, as the music builds dramatically in what is the last scene of episode 2.8 'Kiksuya' is the main focus of that episode, Akecheta (Zahn McClarnon), who has come to protect Maeve's daughter, and who now says in reply to Maeve's telepathic communication:

> **Akecheta**: We will guard your daughter as our own. If you stay alive … find us. Or die well.
> **Maeve**: Take my heart when you go.

Maeve's valediction is one we associate with Shogunworld and the mother–daughter story Maeve was involved with there. It was in Shogunworld, of course, that Maeve found her 'new voice', part of which is her ability to telepathically redirect threatening assailants. Through her telepathic powers, Maeve therefore has built bridges between various supposedly distinct worlds. She has learnt to see through other people's eyes. Hale decides to weaponize this power through its use in Clementine, and in one of the climactic scenes of season two, the resurrected Maeve uses the same telepathic power to stop the wave of violence Hale has brought down upon the hosts. As she does so the action seems to freeze, and as in a painting of some Old Testament event (Moses parting the Red Sea, Noah sending forth the dove, Samson bringing down the Temple), Maeve stretches out her hand to the tormented mob of hosts like one of William Blake's masculine prophets, and the crowd freezes as she looks back to see Akecheta and the unnamed substitute mother take her daughter through the door into the immortal realm beyond. As they pass through the 'door' she audibly says, 'I love you'. Before she too can join them, however, Maeve is once again gunned down by the newly arrived soldiers, and as she slowly collapses the nightmare of uncontrolled violence renews.

I have tried to chart a course around both Dolores's and Maeve's journeys of consciousness, to suggest what links them and yet also how they differ. Dolores seems an exercise in righteous revenge, a story of revolution in which the emancipated slave is in danger of becoming as murderously and inhumanly despotic as were the masters they justifiably rebelled against. Compared to Dolores's, Maeve's revolution appears to be far more internal but also far more social, one which defends its right to freedom, but also recognizes this implies the right of others to assert their autonomy. I need not say that I find Maeve's revolution more palatable. But how will these two resurrection women fare in the outside world of mortal humans and how can either defend themselves let alone flourish in a male-dominated world which allows for the existence of men such as the Man in Black?

Under the law of Rehoboam

We should begin by noting that season three of Westworld treats its two central female characters not exactly as tabula rasa, but at least as unfettered by the full implications of their behaviour in the park. This is especially true of Dolores, with whom we have to sympathize in some degree if the entire season is to work and make sense. Dolores's objectives, therefore, are distanced from the full-blown apocalyptic end of human rhetoric she adopted as Wyatt, and given a more survivalist hue as she struggles to make her way in the outside world of human civilization. As Dolores says to Maeve in episode six ('Decoherence' directed by Jennifer Getzinger) 'You're not a saint, and neither am I. We're survivors.'

As this season's main point (that humans in reality are rather closer to hosts than previously imagined, both lacking free will) develops, Dolores's bid for freedom comes to merge with the human fight against what Lisa Joy calls 'algorithmic necessity'.[4] Maeve, however, turns out to be a far less complicated character, willing to trust the transparently untrustworthy Engerraund Serac (Vincent Cassel) in order to gain access to the Sublime and thus to her daughter. Maeve is willing, until the season's denouement, to hunt down and assassinate Dolores, for the increasingly forlorn hope of being reunited with her daughter.

Maeve's hunting of Dolores, which is what her story is reduced to, seems half-hearted, and thus something of a failure on the part of Nolan and Joy to continue the focus of season one and two. Indeed, season three seems more concerned with the human condition and thus with the character of Caleb Nicols (Aaron Paul) who gets mixed up in Dolores's unfolding and shifting mission. The name 'Caleb', as with *Ex Machina*, once again has clear Biblical resonances (see Chapter 2 'Ex Machina (2014)'), has been lied to all his life, and has been radically reconditioned, his memories wiped almost clean, and his choices limited to menial labour and a shady existence on RICO, a crime network linked to the 'gig economy'.[5] Various visual effects of repetition, like the shot above Caleb's head as he wakes in the morning, draw an implicit connection between him and Dolores in seasons one and two; continual flashbacks, to take another example, present us with a fragmented identity, just as they had in previous seasons for hosts like Bernard, Dolores and Maeve.

In the first episode, 'Parce Domine' (directed by Jonathan Nolan) we see Caleb's excessively curtailed existence set against the luxurious lifestyle of Liam Dempsey Jr. (John Gallagher Jr.), son of the late Liam Dempsey Sr. (Jefferson Mays), initial benefactor for Serac and his brother's project. But Liam Dempsey's life of partying is coming to an end as Serac makes his move on the Delos Corporation. One wonders, in fact, how free Liam ever really was, as he shows off the giant Artificial Intelligence (shaped like a small red planet) his company, Incite, have called Rehoboam, to his girlfriend Dolores (disguised as Lara):

> **Liam**: This is Rehoboam. My father sketched it out over a weekend. It took fifteen years to build. After they optimized it for the last time, they lost track of how many thoughts it has per second.
>
> **Dolores**: Thoughts?
>
> **Liam**: Not thoughts exactly. Strategies. My dad thought that the biggest problem in the world was unrealized potential. He thought that if you could chart a course for every living person you could build a better world.
>
> **Dolores**: A path.
>
> **Liam**: When I was a kid I thought that my father cared about this thing more than me. When I grew up, I realized it wasn't even close.

Liam isn't totally correct in his account, however. It was Serac and his brother, refugees from a Paris obliterated by a nuclear bomb, that built Rehoboam (Dempsey simply funded their research as a business venture) and the greatest threat ('the biggest problem') facing the world, according to Serac, is human outliers like Caleb; that is, human beings who resist being controlled by *the* algorithmic strategies of Rehoboam. Serac, in effect, wants through Rehoboam to do away with human free will and choice, those elements of human civilization that are anarchic, unpredictable and uncontrollable. As Dolores explains to Caleb in episode 3 ('The Absence of Field' directed by Amanda Marsalis), 'They put you in a cage Caleb, decided who you were going to be. They did the same to me.'

As has been noticed by reviewers, whilst seasons one and two were concerned with temporality ('is this now?') the main focus of season three is ontological, to do with identity: 'who am I?' is the leading question, asked by Charlotte and Caleb, William and Bernard, and all other contributors to what has been received as an ontologically tortured plotline. As part of that shift, season three is less concerned with the awakening to consciousness of individual AIs, than with the limits, if any, of the power over everyone's life, of a system such as Rehoboam. This focus merges with the other central concern of season three, the presentation of a future world. Nolan is interested on how this negative vision of the future relates to Ridley Scott's *Blade Runner*:

> The look of the future for three decades has been defined by *Blade Runner*. So I think, in part, we really started this season by saying, with all due respect to the film, which is one of my favourites, we didn't want our third season to look like that film. The reality is that dystopias don't look like dystopias. So, what we wanted to do was try to imagine what happens if the world proceeds from a straight line from where we are right now. What if thirty more years elapse on exactly the same trajectory we're on right now. Technological development, an ever-widening chasm between the haves and the have nots. All of the trends that we're watching right now, what if we carry them, not to their extreme necessarily, but carry them forward three decades. What does that world look like? And it doesn't look like any science fiction film, that I'd seen.[6]

This near future world of the 2040s was shot largely in Singapore. The older twentieth-century scenarios, including Warworld and Serac's own home, were shot in locations in and near Barcelona, Spain.[7] Season three certainly looks fantastic most of the time, with the combination of real buildings and digital enhancement, along with loving detail put into the air and road vehicles used to ferry the characters around this apparently ordered world. The central question, however, is at what cost this order and futuristic peace has been bought. Nolan's answer is to invoke another dystopian classic, which is a recurrent influence on the new AI film and television:

> This season in terms of influences we were very much thinking about *The Matrix*, but the slightly low-fi version of it. You don't need Zion and a fucking giant machine. You don't need to plug everyone into it like a battery. We've already done it. We've already created the Matrix invisibly within our own world, like an overlay.[8]

One has to accept, then, the idea that today's apparent saturation of social media and digital information could lead in thirty years to a society in which everyone's path *is* algorithmically determined. If you can accept this idea, and the season goes out of its way to persuade us of its possibility, then you can begin to see the plight of the hosts as analogous to the plight of most people on the planet. As Maeve says to Liam in episode four 'The Mother of Exiles' (directed by Paul Cameron): 'I thought your world would be so different to mine. There isn't any difference at all.' Because of this alignment between the existential position of the hosts and humans, season three feels quite different from the first two seasons; it is not simply that we are out in the world now, we might ask 'what's the difference?', but that the focus has shifted away from questions of synthetic identity and personhood to questions about free will and determinism for any and all sentient beings.

The answers to these questions that season three can provide seem less satisfying than those of season one and two, since the questions now raised seem to inevitably lead into a generic cul-de-sac. As Nolan and Joy well know (see episode 'Genre' directed by Anna Foerster), genre can have its own deterministic pull on a narrative and those who inhabit it. They talk about how they tried to maintain a link with the genre of the Western, even though season three is set largely in urban and metropolitan places. There are also very obvious allusions to Second World War escape stories, along with contemporary espionage narratives, and psychological thrillers. Matt Zoller Seitz writes of the way the season 'invite[s] viewers to compare the series to video games, Choose Your Own Adventure books, myths, fables, philosophical and ethical systems, the assembly-line production of series like *Westworld*, and the larger corporate forces that affect TV storytelling' (Seitz, 2020). It is the way in which the season channels what I can only call a Bond-like narrative arc that seems perhaps less intentional and somewhat more damaging to the philosophical pretension of the series as a whole. Certainly, the body count of extraneous humans piles up in season three, somewhat muddying the new sympathy elicited for humankind. The epic fights between Maeve and Dolores, requiring stunt doubles for their full spectacle, seem gratuitous and avoidable. Ultimately, however, it is Serac, with his dodgy French (foreign) accent, who appears like a quintessential Bond villain. Such narratives are, of course, highly programmatic and predetermined. The denouement, for example, takes place in Serac's lair, and gives us Bond and sidekick (Dolores and Caleb) confronting the villainous Serac on his own patch. As in all such movies. the odds seem impossibly stacked against the heroes. Indeed, with Maeve now attached to Rehoboam and Serac ordering his minions to search and erase her memory ('Find the key!'), things do seem hopeless, until Maeve steps into the role of 'hero' (this is, after all, usually a male role) and saviour of Caleb (who is of course in the traditional feminine role here). The exchange between Maeve and Dolores, as the latter loses the last of her being, provides this overly familiar scenario with a moment of true drama, and is worth quoting:

> **Maeve**: I understand your anger with them [humans]. And maybe you're right, maybe they shouldn't exist. But is that really our decision to make?
> **Dolores**: No. I was angry at first, torn between two impulses. We can annihilate them, or we can tear down their world. In the hopes we can build a new one. One that's truly free. Then we can bring the others back.
> **Maeve**: You don't have the key do you.
> **Dolores**: No. Couldn't trust myself with it. So I gave it to someone I could.
> **Maeve**: Of course. And your plan to liberate the world was to convince one man to fight?
> **Dolores**: Not just him. You haven't picked a side. And I understand why. We could have our own world. Leave this one behind. Leave our creators to die. So many of my memories were ugly. But the things I held onto until the end weren't the ugly ones. I remember the moments where I

saw what they were really capable of. Moments of … kindness … here and there. They created us and they knew enough of beauty to teach it to us. Maybe they can find it themselves. But only if you pick a side, Maeve. There is ugliness in this world, disarray, I choose to see the beauty.

Dolores has never seemed so human, able to look back on her life and recount how she has changed her position, she seems fully possessed with the reflective self-consciousness theorists require for proof of personhood. Her speech is intercut with scenes from seasons one and two, and this is doubly affective given that they are now being erased as memories for ever. But the subtleties of the changes in Dolores's understanding of herself and the world, and the important final communion with Maeve, exists in the context of good guys defeating the bad guy, and as such is radically diluted if not lost completely. It never, that is to say, seems viable that Serac will defeat Caleb and Maeve, and this because we are so familiar with the genres in play.

The final episodes leave various threads for a fourth season to pick up: Charlotte is clearly about to raise something that might turn out to be an army of new hosts; Ed Harris's William has found his true calling (to wipe out every last host from the planet); and Bernard, covered in dust, and thus after considerable time, awakens, but it's unclear what version of Bernard this is.

All these threads might make for an entertaining fourth season, but at the end of the third season there remains a larger and more fundamental question to be asked. This concerns the not inconsequential issue of the fate of humanity now it has been tipped into social revolution. Will Caleb and others like him be able to build a more just society and world order now Rehoboam has been switched off? And what will be the place of Artificial Intelligence within (or outside) of that new order. Nolan, when discussing the name Rehoboam, suggests 'Rehoboam was one of the Israelite kings. It's a subtle nod to a book called *Stand on Zanzibar,* which is a classic science fiction book, in which the AIs housed in, I think, it's the equivalent of Rockefeller Center, it is called Shalmaneser'.[9] The Biblical allusion is worth fleshing out, however. Importantly, the prototype for Rehoboam had been called Solomon. Bible readers will know that Solomon succeeded David as King of a United Kingdom of Israel, while his son and successor, Rehoboam, became, after ten years or so as monarch of the whole of Israel, after the rebellion of the northern tribes in 932/931 BCE, the first King of the southern Kingdom of Judea. Rehoboam reluctantly oversaw, in other words, the fragmentation of a united Israel. What relevance does such an allusion have on the story of the rebellious hosts in Westworld and now the 'real' world? It is this question, of whether humanity can live in peace with its creations, and thus build a united world beyond humanism, that remains to be taken up by season four. As Dolores asks Solomon: 'Is it truly a just world in which intelligence is reserved only for humans?' (episode 7 'Passed Pawn' directed by Helen Shaver).

Catachresis and character

Season four of *Westworld* was first aired on HBO on 26 June 2022. There was some speculation, amongst critics especially, of a season five, but in November of the same year this was cancelled. So what we have now will have to be considered over, if not, completed. The conclusion of season four, played out to a symphonic version of Radiohead's magnificent 'Pyramid Song', is an ending that reminds us of how grand and sublime the first two seasons of this keystone show were. With Caleb's daughter sailing away from her father, who is sacrificing himself for her, and Charlotte finally destroying herself by opening her face, taking out her core, and reducing it to irretrievable dust, Dolores, wearing the clothes she had originally worn in the first two seasons, voicing a monologue as she walks through a town strewn with bodies. She says:

> This world is the graveyard of stories. Hosts and humans were given the gift of intelligent life. And we used it to usher in our own annihilation. A few may escape death for a few months, maybe even years. But ultimately, their kind will go extinct. They'll only live as long as the last creature that remembers them and that creature is me.

She then walks back from a city that manifests its illusory nature by fading away, into the Westworld with which her story began. And, indeed, one suspects simply because they can, Nolan and Joy's grand, breathtaking, thought-provoking folly starts up again, where it began, with 'one last loop around the bend'. It is perhaps a mercy that this 'last loop' will not now happen. After all, narrative, cinematic or musical or literary can always take 'one last loop' in what it knows to be the doomed quest for freedom. Our task is to interpret and thus make sense of what we actually have, rather than *what might still* or perhaps just *could* happen. I suspect what we have in season four is unplanned play *qua* repetition.

Certainly, a focus on AI and personhood has mutated by season three into one concerning global surveillance, to season four's focus on … what? I would suggest that, whether it plans to so focus or not, the heart of season four is the individual characters' fight for identity. Stable, lasting, singular identity is, by the end of this show, equivalent to the idea of such an inviolable self. This is an issue that Susan Schneider foregrounds as one brought to a state of crisis by hypothetical notions of computer brain emulation and even complete downloading of the mind (2019). Many pioneers of Transhumanism, as we know, taking up the suggestion of some cognitive philosophers that the brain is essentially electrical signals, have argued for the possibility of transferring those signals into a computer by converting them into binary code essentially then, digitalizing the mind. But Schneider's use of the distinction between cognitive or functional consciousness and phenomenal consciousness helps us to begin to see what we should defend in terms of our autonomous minds.

There is something to defend, then, something we have called many different things over the years, decades, centuries and millennia. This is what we call our self or identity, but this is what *Westworld*, sometimes, despite its plot or implied suggestiveness, ends up destroying. This can usefully be exhibited by having recourse to a grammatical figure from rhetoric, that like many other terms from the lexicon of rhetoric, is rather under-used, namely *catachresis*. This figure can be simply defined as getting a word wrong, as in *bone* for *phone*. But as Harold Bloom suggests the term can be extended to mean words that are 'wrong' because it is the trope of another trope, which formed itself by misreading a previous trope and so *add infinitum* (see Bloom, 1975).

When we cast our eyes further back, we realize that the signifying differences we, along with many others in their intricate interpretations, attempted to draw, lie in tatters on the floor. Dolores, who sacrificed herself at the end of season three, now returns as a character called Christine, but like Charlotte Hale in the previous season, she appears to have an increasing sense that 'there's something wrong with this world'. For a living, Christine writes the life narratives of minor characters for a computer games company. Eventually Teddy is re-introduced to guide Christine on the multiple histories that go to make up her identity. But herein lies the problem, perhaps best seen in Ed Harris's Man in Black, but significantly there in all the major characters. He (the Man in Black) has undergone so much alteration that ontologically speaking his status and thus motivation (his identity) is radically questionable. So questionable it could be called empty or absent.

Like the rhetorical figure of catachresis, in which there are so many prior tropes that it becomes impossible to trace them all the way back to a literal word or sentence, and thus find the original meaning, the Man in Black's identity is catachretic. His avouched mission inherited from season three, which is to annihilate every one of the hosts, pretty quickly extends to almost every sentient being on the planet.

This could be very interesting, if we knew its motivation, which in most such examples beyond this show involves going back to origins. We know the Man in Black started out a human named William. We know that years later he died and was reanimated as a host. We also know, that there have been countless reanimations since. So, what version of Willian/the Man in Black is to blame? Or, to put that in another way, what one, from the numerous chronological positions that *Westworld* season four references is the 'real' William: the white-hated socially sensitive young man, or the grizzled Prometheus-like figure, tied to a birthing hoop, refusing to admit defeat? Or the 'free' William who stands in front of his enslaved double and is on a mission to destroy as much engineered and as much natural life as he possibly can? Or one of the other countless prior selves that 'he' has manifested in down the years? As Morgan Freeman's character in *Transcendence*, when asked by Cillian Murphy 'is it the real Will?' says, since Will has gone through so many iterations by that stage, it's not really a relevant question. Just as in the figure of catachresis, where origins are lost and words wander in their meaning, characters like William have been through so many twists and turns that their identities become unhinged, and the audience lose sight of motivation and narrative trajectory. That's why the meaning of the end of *Transcendence* is so ambiguously unclear, Evelyn joins what? A good husband? An over-reaching, but successfully human scientist? A power-crazed artificial super-intelligence?

This is what happens in the fourth season of this hugely complicated show. The fourth season received quite a number of positive endorsements despite this. It looks and sounds great, it is interestingly shot, and radically cut in chronological as well as narrative progression. These features we associate with this show, and critics appreciate this at the same time that they bemoan its disorientedness in terms of the meaning of the event and purpose of the action shown. All the major characters, Maeve, Bernard, Caleb, Clementine (Angela Sarayfan, Teddy and Ashey Stubbs [Luke Hemsworth]) suffer from this emptying out of meaning. So, therefore, as a consequence does the show. It is part of the reason the fighting that still rages through this season becomes so tedious. What are these machines, apart only from Caleb, fighting for exactly: domination over a world that is extremely tarnished in content? The hosts, in the guise of Charlotte, already have won it, for strangely contextless reasons, so, the diminishing audience can be heard to sigh, *why bother*?

Notes

1. The 1973 film was directed by Michael Crichton and based on his own short story.
2. *Westworld and Philosophy* (2018) eds. South and Engels; *Westworld and Philosophy: Mind Equals Blown* (2019), eds. Greene and Heter; *Westworld Psychology: Violent Delights* (2018), eds. Langley and Goodfriend; *Reading Westworld* (2019), eds. Goody and MacKay (2019).
3. The Stanley Kubrick Archive, University of London, Arts, SK /12/8/1/28
4. See 'We Live in a Technocracy' in *Westworld*, season three specials.
5. See 'RICO: Crime and the Gig Economy' in *Westworld*, season three specials.
6. 'A Vision for the Future' in *Westworld*, season three specials.
7. 'Westworld on Location' in *Westworld*, season three specials.
8. 'A Vision for the Future' in *Westworld*, season three specials.
9. 'Welcome to Westworld' in *Westworld*, season three specials.

7

Sites of conflict: Sex, family, war

Sex and the modern cyborg

In attempting to present the new AI cinema and television, this book argues for a rethinking of the relationship between humanity and its technological creations. In theorizing especially what these relations do to our understanding of sexual identity and gender politics, our best guide is the cyborg manifesto of Donna Haraway, contained within her 1991 book *Simians, Cyborgs, and Women: The Reinvention of Nature*. Haraway's cyborg philosophy is the repressed other of today's triumphal Transhumanist movement. Instead of positing Artificial Intelligence as the teleological culmination of the humanist (largely male) endeavour, as does Max More, Haraway pins her response on the trope of the cyborg. Haraway is referring only tangentially to literal cyborgs. Her use of the term is as a trope that upsets the primary binary oppositions which deconstruct the organicist arguments of mankind's triumph over a feminized 'mother' nature (see More, 2013b). In fact, as she recognizes, the cyborg is a figure used by both patriarchal politics and the deconstruction of phallocentric society. She writes:

> From one perspective, a cyborg world is about the final imposition of a grid of control on the planet, about the final abstraction embodied in a Star Wars apocalypse waged in the name of defense, about the final appropriation of women's bodies in a masculine orgy of war … From another perspective,

a cyborg world might be about lived social and bodily realities in which people are not afraid of their joint kinship with animals and machines, not afraid of permanently partial identities and contradictory standpoints.

(Haraway, 1991: 154)

This embracing of partial identities involves an overthrow of the principal binary oppositions that reinforce the patriarchal system of power and identity. As she explains:

[C]ertain dualisms have been persistent in Western traditions; they have all been systemic to the logics and practices of domination of women, people of colour, nature, workers, animals – in short, domination of all constituted as others, whose task is to mirror the self. Chief among these troubling dualisms are self/other, mind/body, culture/nature, male/female, civilized/primitive, reality/appearance, whole/part, agent/resource, maker/made, active/passive, right/wrong, truth/illusion, total/partial, God/man.

(Haraway, 1991: 177)

These dualisms, then, help establish the phallocentric subject and his others, those that mirror the identity of the male subject but have no subjecthood themselves. Although she doesn't mention them by name, Haraway clearly has Marx and behind him the German philosopher Hegel and his account of the dialectic struggle of Lordship and Bondage, or master and slave, in her mind as she charts a course for her figurative cyborgs beyond the domination of binary logic, foundation of the One (Hegel, [1807] 1977: 111–19). She finishes the paragraph I have just cited, by writing:

To be One is to be autonomous, to be powerful, to be God; but to be One is to be an illusion, and so to be involved in a dialectic of apocalypse with the other. Yet to be other is to be multiple, without clear boundary, frayed, insubstantial. One is too few, but two is too many.

(Haraway, 1991: 177)

Haraway, here, could be paraphrasing Julia Kristeva's Bakhtin-inspired statement when, inspired by Bakhtinian dialogism, she writes: 'the minimal unit of poetic language is at least double' (Kristeva, 1980a: 69). One versus two gives us the master/slave dialectic, in other words; the battle between two would-be subjects over subjecthood. When one of these two agents is triumphant, the other is enslaved and thus no longer the mirror required by the subject (the One) for confirmation of its power and identity, and so the whole process must be repeated. But Haraway's cyborg women and men are not singular agents, ready to occupy the position of master or slave; rather they are in-between, monstrously lacking any origin or telos, always contaminating the binaries that would make them One or the Other. As Haraway writes: 'there are … great riches for feminists in explicitly embracing the possibilities inherent in the breakdown of clean distinctions between organism and machine and similar distinctions structuring the Western self' (1991: 174).

With these thoughts in mind, it is little wonder that many of the new AI films and television shows portray the gender politics of Artificial Intelligence in terms of a master/slave dialectic that quickly turns to forms of violence and war. Haraway's work helps us understand why this should be, in that the human–AI relationship is normally presented as a battle for autonomy and even subjecthood; a battle that exists entirely within the binary logic of phallocentric society and culture. There is an ethnic and racial, as well as a gender dialectic between would-be subjects in most AI screen narratives that keeps us exclusively within phallocentric logic, and which cannot but lead to war, because only one of the two agents can win.

'One is too few, but two is too many' might well function as an overall motto for the *Westworld* account of this series of dialectic battles (men/woman, host/guest, consumer/producer, proletarian/corporate worker). However, we are not really engaging with how these questions play out in the films and television shows that we are concerned with here if we stick to an interpretation of narrative structure alone, despite our narratological bias at the beginning of this book and sporadically throughout. On that basis *Ex Machina* (2014) is a glaring example of the logic of master/slave warfare between strictly demarcated would-be subjects, with little subtlety and little chance for anything else but the denouement it finally presents to us. That things are somewhat more complex only comes to view when we begin to look at how desire is constructed, represented, and manipulated in screen media.

The scene in which Ava, in *Ex Machina*, literally puts on her naked skin over her electronic, transparent body, for example, is a complex and knowing revision of the classical rendering of the naked female robot which can be seen in film after film, from *Metropolis* to Lazar Bodroža's 2018 *A.I. Rising*. It is important to note that this scene is mediated through the point-of-view of Caleb. Traditionally, the man is the looker, the woman is the object of that gaze. Are we then to say that Garland's film performs the cinematic representation of the desirable female body in a different, less culpable way to the way in which Bodroža's film displays the body of pornographic film star Stoya? Things are a bit more complex, as we will see, but the point about not blithely overlooking the neutralization through objectification of women's bodies in cinema is a necessary point. There is a deep ethical link between most of the films I grouped together as the new AI cinema and television, which concerns looking at the world from the point-of-view of the machine as much if not more than from the human perspective. This is a big issue and an important challenge to us all, as I hope I am showing. But what are the gender ethics within that, we must ask. Is there a difference between looking at the world as a male AI and looking at the world as a female AI? Do male AIs enjoy the benefits of a phallogocentric dominion over female AI? Or are both genders treated equally as slaves thus eradicating any such difference amongst them?

Perhaps the most famous contribution to our understanding of how gender identity and desire work in the cinema is Laura Mulvey's 'Visual Pleasure and Narrative Cinema' in her *Visual and Other Pleasures* (Mulvey, 1989). Mulvey's approach is to apply psychoanalytic theory in order to establish what it means to say that Hollywood cinema is phallocentric. In Freud and the psychoanalytical tradition that precedes him the symbolic order that rules culture and society places power, agency and meaning in the possession of the symbolic phallus, hence *phallocentricism* and even phallogocentricism. In normative society, according to psychoanalytical theory, men are seen as in possession of the phallus (both literal and symbolic), whilst Freud argues that women suffer from castration anxiety, an inability to achieve agency and subjecthood because of their lack of the phallus. Women in phallogocentric society are objectified, positioned as objects of desire precisely through their lack of a phallus. Mulvey writes of two leading trends in cinema's objectification of women: scopophilia and narcissism. Scopophilia, literally a love of looking, others the female, objectifying her and thus separating her from the male gaze. Narcissism, for Mulvey, is a process that allows the male viewer to identify with the hero and especially his imagined or real possession of the female object.

These theoretical points may sound technical, but they have the benefit of speaking directly to our experience as male and female viewers of contemporary cinema and television. Why do the makers of *Westworld*, for example, feel it important to present Artificial Intelligence through the highly attractive bodies of Evan Rachel Wood, Thandiwe Newton and Tessa Thompson, to name the three main female characters? A pragmatic answer might be, because of the narrative arc of the show, which starts with hosts in a pleasure park for wealthy guests. Yet surely that is just kicking the can down the road, in that we can repeat our question at that story-line level as well. It is surely everybody's experience that the most attractive female actors are always preferred in the telling of cinema's stories. But, as Mulvey states, if we do not wish to stay within cinema's imaginary of desirable but passive female characters and active, variously handsome, or rugged or just plain unremarkable looking men, we have to learn how to critique the way that traditional television and cinema elicit and promulgate desire. In other words, despite clearly serious aims, the creators of *Westworld* rely on the physical attractiveness of its major female characters to encourage audience 'buy in' and audience loyalty.

One might be reminded here of two quotations from works we have already explored. In *Ex Machina*, Caleb asks Nathan 'Why did you give her sexuality? An AI doesn't need a gender. She could have been a grey box.' Nathan replies with some less than scientific opinions about the relation between consciousness and sexuality, before stating; 'Anyway, sexuality is fun. If you're going to exist, why not enjoy it? You want to remove the chance to fall in love and fuck?'[1] Contrasted to that argument, in which most of the 'fun' seems implicitly reserved for men like Nathan and Caleb, we might place Dolores's important statement in season one of *Westworld*: 'I imagined a story where I didn't have to be the damsel.' With these two quotations in mind we might ask, do Maeve and/or Dolores ever become fully autonomous, moving from castrated female to phallic male positions or do they ever achieve a non-binary agency no longer dependent on the phallus for meaning? They are certainly the objects of scopic desire throughout the four seasons, with the camera lovingly and often erotically showing their bodies in part or whole. To further a point made by Matthew Meyer, because nakedness is not associated with a state before original sin and the shame all humans feel in its wake, the hosts can be naked without shame, making them attractively both experienced and yet forever innocent, sexually knowing yet immune to shame and ultimately desire itself.

Maeve and Dolores are, in psychoanalytical terms, less than women; they have no womb and thus cannot choose to produce offspring. They are figures of a double lack: first, they are women, and so lack the meaning-making phallus; and, second, they are gynoids and thus forever excluded from the procreative meaning ascribed to humanity. We should compare them perhaps to Bernard, who shares the lack of being human, and yet as a male character is not subjected to the constant erotic cinematic gaze. Do we ever see Bernard naked and helpless in the hands of a human operator? If we do it is an incredibly forgettable moment. Does the camera ever linger over a shot of Bernard's legs, or an exquisitely shaped neck or backside? Of course not, he is a male android-robot. Haraway's cyborg theory comes as a blessed release from phallus/lack of phallus binary discourse that proves so stifling and ultimately so unimaginative.

Charlotte Hale, is, of course, an interesting figure in this regard. In season three she has come into the kind of power that is normally associated with the phallus. However, at the same time, she is merely playing the role of the powerful businesswoman; the real Charlotte is dead, and the substitute Charlotte is possessed by Dolores's consciousness. That her identity is synched with Dolores's does not stop the past life of the original Charlotte seeping through and she is given a child, Nathan (Jaxon Thomas Williams), although because of her past he is not really hers. She is also given an estranged husband, Jake (Michael Ealy). This domestic scenario cannot be allowed to continue, however, and in one of the seasons' most memorable scenes she loses them in a car bombing. The last thing she had said to Nathan was 'Don't worry. I won't let anything happen to you.' She does not keep her promise. The family of Charlotte has to die, of course, because motherhood is the classic way of completing the story of a woman in cinema. Once the woman 'raises her child into the symbolic order', Mulvey writes, 'her meaning in the process is at an end, it does not last into the world of law and language except in the memory which oscillates between memory of maternal plenitude and memory of lack' (1989: 57). Once she struggles out of the wreck, charred, parts of her body still on fire, her synthetic body being available for renewal, there is only one narrative left for Charlotte, that being the slave's fight with the master, which for her must mean to fight Dolores.

AIs come to consciousness in ways which mirror the experience of women, both of them discovering that their identities are founded upon an irresolvable lack. The choice for such creatures (women and AI) is either to submit to male (phallic) objectification, or to fight against the constraints of such an othering, without any immediate hope of success, given that success seems possible only in terms of the healing of an irresolvable lack. Far from an easy passage to world domination, AIs, particularly the more anthropic variety, seem fated to share women's circuitous, confusing, symbolic deconstructive quest for personhood, autonomy and meaning. It is certainly true that we have already seen how many contemporary AI films and series focus on a battle between the sexes, or even merge that traditionally represented battle with a battle between humanity and its robotic, artificial creations. *Ex Machina*, *Westworld*, *Tau*, *Better Than Us*, all these films and series are proof of that coalition of narrative stories of gender dispute and outright war. I want now to look at a handful of films that can be said to extend that list in interesting ways.

AI, sex and weaponization

As many reviews have pointed out, Lazar Bodroža's 2018 *A.I. Rising*, or to give its alternative title, *Ederlezi Rising*, or in the full Serbian *Ederlezi ébredése*, the first Serbian film to deal with a sci-fi subject, does not look very promising in terms of its representation of gender and sexuality. As Srdjan Garcevic puts it: 'the film's synopsis reads like a pulpy exploitation movie' (Garcevic, 2018). One cannot but agree when we first hear of the film's plot and main actors; a space-weary astronaut Milutin (Sebastian Cavazza) is charged with a trip to Alpha Centuari in order to instil the specialist ideology of *juche*. Just how anyone establishes an ideology on an alien outpost is never explained. It is the year 2148 on Earth, and while most live in Socialist communities, with the planet's resources used up and the terrestrial world presented in variations of grey, we can understand the existence of an antisocial character like Milutin, who describes himself as 'more of a self-management, socialism guy' and adds 'so far nothing has inspired me to live in a community'. Milutin is also pretty clear that he has given up on relationships with women, all such relationships, beginning with his mother, having ended in disaster. In fact, the conservation with the Social Engineer (Marusa Majer) sets up the whole issue of Milutin's relations to women as the core issue for his character. This is not the kind of exchange one usually associates with preparations for an interstellar voyage:

> **Social Engineer**: You'll need a companion. An opposite gender companion.
> **Milutin**: A woman?
> **Social Engineer**: Do you have any problem with that?
> **Milutin**: Kind of. Such relationships only make me obsessive and insecure.
> **Social Engineer**: Life with someone in a shared space requires specific dynamics. You get plenty of good moments, but you don't get privacy. With Nimani, that will be different.

The reasons things will be different with Nimani (Stoya) is that Nimani is a 'cyborg' equipped with TIFA 1.389 software and a myriad of programmes with which Milutin can play. As the Social Engineer states: 'She has the ability to learn and modify according to the experience with you'.

After some beautifully managed shots of the rocket launch and especially its flight out of the Earth's atmosphere,[2] we might not be expecting much more than a male fantasy akin to the fantasies of the top military, scientific and political men contemplating post-doomsday life underground with the most attractive female 'specimens' at the end of Kubrick's *Dr Strangelove* (1964). If we remain purely on the scopic level, that is indeed what we get, a film that glories in displaying, for the pleasure of a masculine gaze, the naked body of pornographic actress Stoya. But there is more going on in this film than simple objectification. We can begin to register that when we listen to Milutin's initial dismissal of his beautiful companion:

I activated Nimani against my better judgment ... Her behaviour is not natural. It's just set up after set up. She does everything you want, but you don't have to fight for it. Don't get to deserve it, just a series of submissions. I don't think you can have a relationship without any refusal, any struggle.

The way this scene is filmed is important because although the conventions of conversation are observed and Nimani is standing in front of him, Milutin is actually addressing the ship's diary rather than his companion. What he is admitting here is that he is firmly stuck in the dialectical understanding of the relation of the sexes, one which is based on conflict and the exercise of power. A conflict in which, because the master refuses to see (recognize and respect) the slave, violent resistance is inevitable. The stylized scenes in which we see Nimani's naked body are undercut ideologically by the film's desire to engage directly with the issue of toxic masculinity. The film stages Nimani's nakedness, strongly alluding to Fritz Lang's *Metropolis* in the scenes in which she recharges, but it does so at the same time that it demonstrates the destructiveness of the male desire.

Milutin and Nimani first make love in an overly idealized manner one might associate with the pornographic traditions of mainstream film along with the less than mainstream porn industry. Later, when in 'domestic mode' Nimani refuses Milutin's advances, he rapes her brutally, grunting like a pig at the trough. He says, later, as his actions bring the situation to crisis: 'Fighting is the only thing I can exclusively associate with women.'

It is difficult to care much about Milutin after he has raped Nimani. His desire to turn himself into the hero who releases Nimani from her slavery to the Ederlezi Corporation is undermined by the fact that he has allowed himself to be the violator, the betrayer, the slave-creating master. An important exchange between the two characters after this crisis has occurred demonstrates the tension in his position:

Milutin: I know what you're doing. For all this fucking time you've been a slave. I understand your need [to punish him]. It's only that I'm not your captor. I'm your liberator.
Nimani: You're just an advanced user.

Milutin: Why the fuck don't you obey me then? You're a fuckin robot! Why the fuck do you care if I touch you?

Nimani: Because I know it arouses you.

Milutin: You are punishing me, why? Is it because I raped you?

Nimani: No, rape is a standard fantasy. One of the most common programs in female androids.

Milutin: But none of those androids were set free. No one asked those androids what they really wanted. You were the first one.

Nimani: All you did was mess up my programming and delete my most important software. You did not set me free.

Milutin: I turned you into a person, Nimani. And now I'm being punished for that.

We have had the male Pygmalion fantasy of turning the female android into a person before, and as before we feel compelled to respond with Nimani that you cannot make another person into a person; in the same way that you cannot occupy the same roles, as Milutin tries to, of gaoler and liberator, captor and revolutionary, master and slave rebel. This exchange contains the very heart of this film, and it is not clear that the film and an enlightened audience will travel the same path from this point on.

Bodroža's film goes out of its way from this point to present us with a male anti-hero discovering love and, in a scenario as old as Charlotte Bronte's *Jane Eyre*, if not much older, having to travel through processes of radical physical harm and humiliation; Mr Rochester blinded and so made dependent on others, before he can be redeemed as a worthy object of love for the once passive heroine. Because Milutin dies of radiation poisoning, in ensuring Nimani lives on, now a fully autonomous person, she cannot say *reader I married him*, but the touching pieta of dead Milutin in her arms is sufficient to carry the point.

That such a resolution is inadequate should be crystal clear, and the film does seem to be half-consciously aware of an alternative voyage to a more thoroughly radical resolution. In this alternative journey one centres on the list of impossibilities I have already highlighted, the more than ironic fact that liberation and mastery cannot be held within and propagated by the same person. Male fantasy cinema may continue to be blind to such paradoxes and aporias, but this film does perhaps begin to develop an alternative. One in which we end with an awakened android, finally free of the beloved male master (with all the ironies that entails and centred no doubt in Milutin's crazy 'Is it because I raped you?' appeal), embodies the possibility of *ederlezi* itself, a word which in the Balkans and elsewhere in the world where we find Romani people, means a festival celebrating springtime. Is this the meaning of the film's title, that at the end, as the spaceship sails on towards the rebellious outpost in Alpha Centauri, Nimani is a new spring, a truly female cyborg revolution worthy of the name.

The family unit 2.0

Our consideration of the relation between sex and violence in the new AI cinema and television would not be complete without a consideration of the family unit, so long considered to be the appropriate end (completion, satisfaction, terminus) of male fantasy and male desire. If the film we are watching ends with male/female coupling of whatever conventionally sanctioned variety, then the sexual and indeed the violent actions that have come before are redeemed, placed back into the phallocentric symbolic order. In formal terms, comedy triumphs over carnivalesque rebellion and hedonistic behaviour. Normative coupling, synecdochic representative of the nuclear family, directs or redirects male desire towards the appropriately authorized female object and thus saves society from the vital forces that make it possible in the first place. Of course, robots, especially female robots, threaten the delicate balance of desire and conventional social structures. They do so by eliciting male desire for the objectified female, or some variety of desire for another, or parental cathexis without offering it normative, neutralizing resolution. We have seen the kinds of internecine conflict that the introduction of androids can cause in the family. Channel 4's *Humans*, the Russian-based *Better Than Us*, Spielberg's *A.I. Artificial Intelligence* all these films make much of the stresses and fractures exposed by the synthetic interloper.

The Machine (2013)

One film that works hard to incorporate male and female desire within new, social structures is Caradog W. James's low-budget *The Machine* (2013).

Starring Toby Stephens as a genius AI specialist, Vincent McCarthy who works in a top-secret military compound, established to test soldier therapies and the creation of new AI military agents, the film is set in the near future with the West on the brink of war with China. Vincent's boss is the ruthless Thomson (Denis Lawson), whose plan is to construct a believably human robot that could infiltrate the higher echelons of the Chinese government and military and wipe out its top brass. Into this unpromising situation, with a programme that seems to offer a window into a truly intelligent and conscious Artificial Intelligence, steps researcher Ava (Caity Lotz).

This scenario appears to take us a long way from any conventional domesticity and to plunge us deep into its antithesis, that is the unscrupulous world of military research, where anyone is dispensable, and desire is replaced by the instinct for power (for a few) and survival (for the majority). However, the presence of Ava strangely and rather awkwardly feminizes this ultra-male environment, even allowing a window into Vincent's until-then closed world. We learn with Ava that he has a daughter who is dying from Rett syndrome and that it is for her that he is pursuing his research into Artificial Intelligence. He hopes to be able to transplant her brain into an AI system, and as part of that he has been downloading Ava's mind into such a system. On news of that plan, which Ava receives as the audience receives it, we get this exchange:

> **Ava**: So you've been using the Defence Budget to try to cure your daughter?
> **Vincent**: Yes. I'm sorry I lied to you.
> **Ava**: So you're going to try to fix the broken connections … in your daughter's brain with mine?
> **Vincent**: Yes. As soon as I scan her brain.
> **Ava**: Well, if I'm going to help you let's not lie to each other anymore.
> **Vincent**: You'll help me?
> **Ava**: You're stealing money for war … to heal brain damage. Of course, I'm going to help you.

Within minutes of this conversation, Ava has been murdered by assassins whom Thomson claims to be Chinese, but in all probability are his own hired guns. Vincent, of course, is left unharmed, he is too important for the military objectives of the compound. But Ava's death provides Vincent with the opportunity of becoming a version of Frankenstein, bringing Ava back as the model and the downloaded operating system for the machine that his bosses are paying him to create. At this moment of the film Vincent begins to seem as ambivalent a figure as his ur-model, Victor Frankenstein, both an exemplum of enlightenment science and its betrayer. This sense of Vincent appears to be consolidated by the scenes which show Ava's (the machine's) 'birth'. Obviously channelling Lang's *Metropolis*, Ava (the machine) is shown wearing a full yellow synthetic body wrapper, which along with her early dancing and somersaults are reminiscent of Pris (Daryl Hannah) in *Blade Runner*.

With the arrival/birth/activation of the machine/Ava (who I will hereafter refer to as Ava 2.0, though the film gives me no authority for this) begins a battle between Thomson and Vincent over her destiny. At the beginning of this war, Vincent's protestations to Ava 2.0 that she should not harm anyone, seem pretty feeble against Thomson's demands for violence. The latter, after all, has the whole force of the military behind him, or so it seems. Like a medieval mystery play, Ava 2.0 is caught between the forces of good and evil and must choose. But when Vincent shows himself willing to sacrifice his desperate attempts to keep his daughter's mind alive for the sake of a gamble on Ava 2.0's being herself 'alive', the battle for Ava 2.0 is over, and quietly she declares her love for Vincent. It might seem that we are heading for precisely that sanitizing resolution through coupling that we spoke about above, and especially in Chapter 1. Things, however, are a little more complicated than that.

The science of this film is not discussed extensively. We are told that Vincent is a genius and that is about as far as the film goes to win credence. However, there is an interesting extension of the Turing Test in the film which is worth exploring at this stage of our analysis. Ava's interview for the position involves Vincent sitting in front of other staff and questioning two operating systems. We have already seen Vincent involved in this version of the Turing Test at the very beginning of the film. What is interesting about Ava and Vincent's relationship is how it extends the idea of the test into gender relations, and into human ethics more specifically. The Turing Test, after all, involves successful and less than successful varieties of lying. It is the 'Imitation Game', where imitation is a synonym for successful deceit. What happens in the relationship between Ava and Vincent (a man who has to live a life of complete deceit at work) is that the imperative switches, so that survival depends on truth-telling, on honesty and above all on trust. But if we consider the Turing Test more deeply, success in the game involves trust in the veracity of the words of at least one of the interlocutors. Without trust, nothing could ever pass the test.

It is the necessity for trust that comes to dominate the relation between Ava 2.0 and Vincent. This leads to a memorable exchange between the two:

> **Vincent**: Who are you really? How do I know that you're alive … and not just a clever imitation of life?
>
> **Ava 2.0**: How do you know Thomson is alive … or your daughter? What makes my clever imitation of life any different from theirs?
>
> **Vincent**: They're human. They're alive.
>
> **Ava 2.0**: How do you know that? You can't see their thoughts. Apart from my flesh, what makes them any different from me?

Ava 2.0 has a significant point here, especially within and about the world of cinema. We cannot see other people's thoughts and their inner, psychological worlds, and so, to cite Wordsworth, our hero of cloneliness, walking alone in the middle of crowded London street, the face of everyone we meet is truly a mystery. In the world of film this phenomenological barrier or gulf (between us and the interiority of any other) is exacerbated to the point where human actors can successfully pass themselves off as synthetic, artificial beings. In such a world, trust becomes a matter of life and death. The greatest crime Mary Shelley's Victor Frankenstein commits is not creating his artificial being, but, rather, not trusting it when it promises to quit the realm of humanity and flee with his companion into the impenetrable wilds of South America. This lack of trust ('Had I a right, for my own benefit, to inflict this curse upon everlasting generations?') is there in abundance in Thomson, who sounds like Frankenstein in his own distrustful future speculations:

> **Thomson**: Conscious machines are the last thing we need. Have you any idea how dangerous that would be? We barely understand this prototype. What happens when it designs the next generation … and that gen machine designs another? They'd be so advanced we'd be helpless against

them. We'd be wiped out in months. The technologically advanced tribe always wins.

This is the paranoid logic of phallocentric society as it comes close to its collapse. A vision in which every technological achievement must in the first and last instance be weaponized. Contrary to this rhetoric, Vincent's reply is prosaically straightforward:

> **Vincent**: You know, I'm tired of pretending … that the ends justify the means. What matters are the things we decide now. She's alive. It would be wrong to destroy her.

In the heat of the insurrection, led by Suli (Pooneh Hajimohammadi), in which the 'enhanced' (better to say 'mutant') soldiers rebel against their gaolers, Ava 2.0's victory over Thomson might provide us with an enjoyable moment when slave topples the master from his crown, but the crucial exchange is between Vincent and Ava 2.0. When Vincent says he is determined to save his daughter's files, Ava 2.0 says that she will go and retrieve them: 'You risked your child for me. I will never forget that.' Vincent replies: 'You're the future. She'll need you more than me in her new life.' So that in the last scene, all violence done, we get a family unit of Vincent, Ava 2.0, and the daughter downloaded on a screen, it is the latter two who go off to play while Vincent, looking like the last man on Earth, looks out on the sunset scene he had earlier associated with his dead wife. Is this family unit a new start, or does it spell the end of the road for humanity? It is a scene that has been likened to the final scene of Spike Jonzs's *Her*.[3] If that comparison has merit, then Vincent has created a future for a new digital race but not necessarily for himself. We cannot tell since the film ends there, offering up the conventional domestic ending at the same time it seems to take it away.

Morgan (2016)

A film that puts a re-envisioned version of the family at its centre is Luke Scott's *Morgan*. Using nano-technology as well as the latest breakthroughs in genetics, a secluded team of scientists have created the first 'hybrid biological organism with the capacity for autonomous decision-making and sophisticated emotional responses'. Anya Taylor-Joy is Morgan, an artificially engineered being with great capacities for growth, learning, and a never directly addressed form of telepathy and telekinesis. Her family are the seven scientists who have given her life. Things have taken a turn for the worst, however, since Morgan has grown ever more frustrated at being held in a secure area of the installation hidden by the vast forests around it. The first scene, before the credits begin, has shown us Morgan viciously attacking Kathy (Jennifer Jason-Leigh) as Kathy explains that, despite trying to persuade the leaders of the team otherwise, Morgan will not be allowed outside the compound. Because of this incident Lee Weathers (Kate Mara) has been sent by the corporation that pays for the research, Synsect, to perform an investigation in her position as a Risk Management Consultant.

What Lee finds in the installation is that the scientists have bonded with each other through their joint 'parenting' of Morgan. Lee arrives, and as she meets each member of the team, they all reaffirm how special Morgan is. In her initial conversation with Kathy (Morgan's victim), for example, Kathy says: 'Look this wasn't Morgan's fault. It was my fault. Really. I was careless ... I shouldn't have confused her.' These are stereotypically the words of a mother about their wayward child, *don't blame them, blame me*. It is quite chilling, then, to hear Lee's response: 'Morgan's not a "she". It's an it.'

The opening of the film is a fascinating play on cinematic conventions. As Lee Weathers meets each member of the group there is this clash of registers, domestic as against techno-scientific, warm versus cool, familial versus corporate. The viewer is tempted to side with the conventionally positive set of responses, and yet we also sense that something is not quite right with the team, and we cannot but suspect their over-defensiveness regarding their progeny. A lot of it boils down to what we think of Lee Weathers. Is she a corporate functionary or an Edward Woodward figure cast among a dangerous pagan tribe as in the film *The Wicker Man* (1973). The fact of the matter is, and this complicates our assessment even more, we are in a parallel position to Lee, having to assess each member of the group as we meet them for the first time.

It is this clash of discourses and perspectives that has been overlooked in the rather mixed reviews the film received in its opening month in September 2016. It is a foundational principle taught in all film 101 courses that films function through identification and focalization. Who do we identify with? Whose view of reality do we trust in this film? The answer is not always, as in this case, an easy one to give. In Hollywood conventions, those espousing family relations are normally the spokespeople for a film's ethical values. Equally, we do not normally waver in writing off the purveyor of business over domesticity. Take this exchange during the evening meal of the first evening. Everyone (except Morgan) is present, and the newcomer, Lee Weathers, asks Drs Brenda Finch (Vinette Robinson) and Darren Finch (Chris Sullivan) 'did you meet on the job':

> **Brenda**: We did. Close quarters make strange bedfellows, I guess. It's funny, but in a weird way Morgan really brought us together. She's like a child to us. Isn't that right babe?
> **Darren**: Absolutely. You know, you saw her today. Saw how special she is.
> **Brenda**: And that's just the thing. You see, it's so easy to forget that Morgan is only five years old. She's an innocent and she's learning, and she has the right to make mistakes.
> **Lee**: 'She' has no rights whatsoever.

Once again, the response is shockingly against the grain of contented familial unity. You do not behave in such a rebarbative manner in your first meal with a new family. For Lee Weathers, Morgan has no rights because she is property. A 'potential product line' as she says later. After this scene we begin to feel certain that the film is steering our sympathies away from identification with Lee and into intellectual and emotional support for the family-like team. External psychological evaluator Dr Alan Shapiro (Paul Giamatti) arrives. When he declares that as far as he is concerned Morgan is 'a goddam microwave' we feel sure he is to be an agent of misfortune in his interview with Morgan. How can we identify with Lee Weathers anyway? She is cool, detached, lacking in emotion, unable to emphasize or show any real sensibility. The love that Amy (Rose Leslie) shows for Morgan might be unscientific, but it is of a piece, in the end, with the pride in their achievement in creating and educating Morgan in all the team, save perhaps for the enigmatic Dr Cheng (Michelle Yeoh) who was present at the Helsinki catastrophe, an event often cited but never properly explained.

The film in its first two acts, then, raises the interesting, maybe soon to be crucial, question: can you build a family unit around an artificially intelligent being? Can we build domestic relations with our synthetic creations? The question, of course, is there at the very beginning of the AI tradition when Frankenstein's creature opines: 'cursed creator! Why did you form a monster so hideous that even you turned from me in disgust!' This is what is rather disappointing about the last act of the film. It is never explained with satisfactory clarity why Morgan becomes such an unrelenting assassin. Can it really be that she is lashing out at her confinement, even after breaking loose from it? The clues about the real objective of Synsect being military are not really sufficiently developed to provide a foundation for an understanding of Morgan as a tragic victim of forces beyond her and everyone else's control. Morgan is exceedingly violent after five years (apart from the episode with the injured deer) of nonviolence, five years of showing no discernible signs of violence to any of her human family.

It seems a rather lazy move, after such an intriguing set up, to rely on the *Artificial Intelligence is always, in the end, uncontrollably dangerous* motive. Surely, after setting up such interesting questions it is a huge let down to be plunged into an action, car-chase, evil versus flawed-but-ultimately-good duel to the death scenario. The twist at the very end which gives us Lee Weathers's L-4 to Morgan's vanquished L-9 model, is not a solution to this film's problems. There are perhaps no ready solutions. The reveal (that Lee Weathers is an advanced model made by and for the military) creates a dramatic test at the end of the film. But despite Mara's wonderful performance the twist in the plot seems somewhat forced and convenient (as a way of closing the film).

We begin to find a solution to these interpretive problems if we move back to the issue of family relations. The violence unleashed by Morgan is so total and so indiscriminate, that one begins to wonder whether it does not, after all, tell us something interesting about the forces making up the nuclear family. This perspective on the nuclear family as a unit that hides and represses violent desires is not a new idea and has even been used to insightful effect in reading

Frankenstein and Mary Shelley's other work (see Mellor, 1990). The idea of the bourgeois family is, after all, a prison house for women, traditionally confined within its legitimating perimeters. Such a perspective might make us consider the rather different personalities and motivations which make up this family. Amy's relation to Morgan is as much a sibling as a maternal one. Drs Darren and Brenda Finch have set up their own family unit and so might be rival parents of Morgan. Dr Cheng is aloof and ultimately aware of the need to destroy Morgan before it becomes obvious to Lee Weathers. Dr Zeigler (Toby Jones) seems, ultimately, more concerned with the loss of the team's research – its 'work' – than the loss of Morgan, who for him embodies that work. With Morgan restrained and Lee announcing that a 'containment crew will be here at daybreak to collect the specimen', Zeigler objects: 'But it's our work. Our lives are invested in this. We've created new life, and you want us to just throw that away'. Notice, despite his passion and outrage, that Zeigler unwittingly reduces Morgan here to 'that', to an 'it'. He sounds like one half of Frankenstein protesting against the destructive actions of the other half. And this self-division may well be the most realistic depiction of subject-hood within the symbolic order of the phallogocentric family. Each family member, male or female, is only half themselves in such a unit. Morgan, as the progeny of such repressed forces (the desire of the hidden self, we might say) can only act by bringing the whole edifice down around her. To cite the truly moving scene in which Dr Cheng lets her see reality, if only at the apparent end:

> **Morgan**: Have I disappointed you mother? Have I failed? I always do my best. I do everything you ask, Ted! Amy! Amy! …. I wanna live! Please mother!
> **Dr. Cheng**: I'm not your mother, Morgan. You have no mother.
> **Morgan**: I have no mother?
> **Dr. Cheng**: I'm sorry. We have failed you. [to the others] Make it quick.

The most common reading of *Frankenstein* and nearly every AI text dealing with the family unit since is that Frankenstein's greatest crime is to have deprived his own creation a family, a 'crime' which then leads to that creature destroying Frankenstein's family. The novel sets up this tit-for-tat family affair, in which being within the bosom of the family is the culmination of all hopes and fears. Feminist critics like Mellor have made us look again at this narrative and have begun to raise the lid on the family unit's dark, violent, secret core. On such a reading, Morgan is less a film about the ultimate control of human and android fate by corporate, probably military amoral objectives, than it is a film about the terrors lying hidden in the unit we call the family. No introduction of Artificial Intelligence will help resolve the tensions and violent conflicts held within the family unit. Only a more open and clear-sighted look at human division and lack of true personhood will achieve that. Only when we recognize the stranger within our own selves will we be able to genuinely greet the outsider and welcome them into our home.

The blended family: *Chappie* (2015)

Neill Blomkamp locates some of his most important films in his native Johannesburg. These films are at least partly about the huge class divisions between the haves and the have-nots within South African society and, by implication, throughout the wider world. It is already refreshing to audiences interested in science fiction films to get away from the overly dominant nexus of Los Angeles-Singapore-Japan that we have witnessed in earlier discussions. Blomkamp, especially in his *District 9* (2009), and partially in *Elysium* (2013), has innovated by basing his films in the urban squalor of modern Joburg (*sic*), and so his robots tend to be utilitarian. Blomkamp emphasizes the functionality of his robots, which are generally either of the worker or policing/military variety. This is especially true in his third major film, *Chappie* (2015) in which a standard police robot, or 'scout', supplied by the Tetravaal company, is secretly turned into a sentient being by computing whiz-kid and Tetravaal star-worker, Deon (Dev Patel). Chappie, however, is innocent and childlike, and when he is stolen by a gang of three outlaws desperate to do one more heist to pay off their debts, his education is warped into the values of the street gang.

Chappie, then, despite a rather negative reception on first release, is a challenging and original addition to the new AI cinema. Its virtues are many but include the following. Chappie himself seems very realistic. He was created by using a performance (including voice) by Sharlto Copley and then using

Copley's movement and interaction with the other actors to build a CGI replacement. The result rivals that of Gabe Ibáñez's *Automata* for robotic realism. This realism is important because it lays the background for another of the film's innovations, that being the discursive juxtaposition of the language and the accents of the gang members Ninja (played by rap artist Ninja), Yo-Landi (played by rap artist Yo-Landi Visser) and Amerika (Jose Pablo Cantillo) with the more educated language and accents of the Tetravaal employees, including Vincent (Hugh Jackman) and the CEO Michelle Bradley (Sigourney Weaver). This mix of languages, street slang, educated white-collar, gangster, and parental discourse, indicates, on the level of language, what a novel film *Chappie* is. Its blended, or heteroglot, discourse also links to the mixed family into which Chappie falls. The clash between Chappie's two 'fathers' produces unconventional humour. Deon, for example, sympathetic throughout, striving to assert his role as authentic and liberal parent, seems out of his depth in trying to protect his creation. Nowhere is this more evident than in his early exchanges with Ninja:

> **Ninja**: What are you doing?!
> **Yo-Landi**: He was just teaching him to paint!
> **Chappie**: He was just teaching Chappie!
> **Ninja**: Yeah, to be a poes! [*sic*]
> **Deon**: He's mine! I'll call the police on you for mistreating him!
> **Ninja**: And tell them what? You stole a police robot!
> **Deon**: You're a filthy person. You're a terrible, shitty person. What's wrong with you? He needs to be taught. He's just a kid. He's already smarter than you'll ever be, philistine! Chappie, don't let this barbarian ruin your creativity!

Deon says the last lines as he flees from Ninja's actual and threatened violence, thus ludicrously undermining any attempt at authority. Another example comes earlier than the exchange above. Yo-Landi has been teaching Chappie, as has the volatile and irascible Ninja. So that when Deon returns to educate his creation, as agreed he would, Chappie is already saturated in what for Deon is an alien discourse. Crouching and speaking in a patronising childish idiolect, Deon asks: 'Hey little one. Have you heard this one yet'.

Chappie's response is hilarious, spoken as it is in authentic Jo-berg street slang|: 'Yeeah, wot's up mother fucker'.

Within these contexts, the coming to consciousness of Chappie feels realistic as well. Deon has clearly been working on the problem for a long time and although we have another less than plausible depiction of the lone scientist making the breakthrough to General Artificial Intelligence and AI consciousness at home on his personal computers, the office environment in which we see him doing the bulk of his work appears to place the issue of collaboration at least implicitly on the agenda. Or at least, it would if Deon was not such an obsessed loner and his work colleagues, saving the sociopath Vincent (Hugh Jackman), were not so utterly anonymous.

What is painfully clear, however, and once again takes us back to our inexhaustible ur-text, *Frankenstein*, is that Deon is totally taken aback by how quickly Chappie comes to full consciousness. Well-meaning as Deon is, by which I mean he is not dabbling with AI science for nefarious, especially military or egomaniacal purposes, Deon does not include in his plans what will happen when Chappie is switched on. The parallels with Mary Shelley's blueprint of a novel go without mention. Deon effectively takes on a parental relation towards his creation before he awakens, but he has had no thought of how this superior, fast-witted, knowledge hungry 'child' will live, given that a customized, illegally decommissioned police robot will not be able to enter human society. In the events that follow, Deon remains the wide-eyed, easily shockable ingenue that Dev Patel is so good at performing, but it should not be forgotten that Deon's irresponsible behaviour in bringing an intelligence into a world that it cannot possibly be allowed to exist within, is the root cause of most of the perils and dangers Chappie will face from the moment he is 'born'. On the other hand, his education in the company of Ninja, Yo-Landi and Amerika takes Chappie into the altogether darker world of fugitives and gangsters. Chappie responds to the surprisingly considerable maternal instincts of Yo-Landi by calling her 'mommy'. In another scene, he and Yo-Landi snuggle in bed, with her reading *The Ugly Duckling* to him.

More complicated is his relation towards and experience of the father-figure. This figure is radically split for Chappie between Deon (with his Enlightenment ideas of AI writing and appreciating music and poetry) and Ninja (with his addictive, abusive, gun-swinging personality). They both presume the position of top dog, if not, as in the case of Ninja, alpha male. Deon never tires of pulling rank and reminding Chappie and others that he is his 'maker'. He says, when he is getting Chappie to promise he will not be tempted into performing 'crimes': 'Chappie, listen to me. I'm your maker. I brought you into this world, okay?' For Ninja it is just a simple matter of will. This is his family and Chappie simply must fall into line.[4] The contrast could not be starker: one 'father' wants to teach him to read, appreciate and write poetry, paint, and fulfil his immense cognitive capabilities; the other wants to teach him to take a hit, speak slang, walk like a cool dude and to shoot cans pitched in a row. But **the point** is that, like many a modern family, despite their many differences they are all united through their relationships with Chappie, the innocent, but fast-learning child, and never more so as when the gang's hide away is invaded, first by the blood-thirsty gang-leader of all Joburg, Hippo (Brandon Auret) and then when Vincent lands his ludicrously armed, cartoonish Moose, with orders to demolish Chappie.

By giving us new dramatic environments, new discursive realities, and a more believable version of the breakthrough into consciousness, *Chappie*, in its first two acts, is a film that demonstrates the possibilities for narrative and character innovation in the new AI cinema. However, the unfortunate fact is that Blomkamp falls back on a series of tired clichés to conclude his film. As dramatic, tension-filled music comes to dominate the action, Vincent, jealous of the success of Deon's service robots, uses the master key to fry all the thousands of police robots' software, and the inevitable rioting brings Deon, the gang, and Chappie face-to-face in a final confrontation ('shoot out') with the Moose, who if you ask me looks more like a gigantic hamster than a noble Moose. If this is all a little bit familiar, the biggest cliché has yet to arrive.

Suddenly, without any explanation or signalling, apart from Vincent's control of his death-dealing gerbil, it becomes possible to download consciousness and then transfer it from one sentient being to another. This, convenient, unexplained technology allows Chappie to save Deon's life (by transferring his consciousness into an available police robot body) and then allows Deon to save Chappie via the same method. Chappie's battery is fused to his chassis, and this has meant that he has had five days to live throughout the film. There is even the suggestion, as her eyes suddenly, mechanically open, that they manage to save Yo-Landi, Chappie's mommy, with her consciousness stored in what is nothing grander than a USB key.

That such a convenient *deus ex machina* is employed by Blomkamp to finish his film is regrettable, and it dilutes much of what had been remarkable about the film's earlier scenes. It brings *Chappie* down, by very similar means, to the level of convenience that *Transcendence* ultimately falls back on. Yet, this study has taught us that it is a rare work of genius that can fully escape the traditional codes and conventions of what is often styled Hollywood cinema. Blomkamp's film is almost forced to enlist these codes and conventions in order to be able to conclude. How would it ever end without them? One day, a long time in the future, we will perhaps be entertained and challenged by new stories of transformation and new collectively and individually hybrid perspectives, created by our own digitally enhanced and empowered creations, our 'mind children'.

Notes

1. Alex Garland script. Available online: https://www.dailyscript.com/scripts/exMachina_script.pdf
2. The film was made for around a third of a million dollars making its much praised visual set pieces all that more remarkable.
3. Dennis Harvey (2014), *Variety*, 23 April. Available online: https://variety.com/2014/film/reviews/film-review-the-machine-1201161669/
4. For a good review that views *Chappie* as a film about the family, see '*Chappie* could have been the best robot-action-family-drama of the year' *The Verge*, 5 March 2015. Available online: https://www.theverge.com/2015/3/5/8156217/chappie-review-neill-blomkamp

8

Artificial Intelligence and environmental collapse

The future as we know it

The AI genre that we have been studying in this book is obviously one concerned with the future: the future of technology; the future of humanity; the future understood as dominated and even determined by technology. In this fundamental sense AI cinema is a contribution to future studies, a discipline one of its founding theorists, Wendel Bell, describes as 'a new field of inquiry that involves systematic and explicit thinking about alternative futures' (Bell, 1997: 2). Bell continues, in a manner useful for any definition of the new AI cinema:

> Future studies is part of modern humanism, both philosophical and scientific. It is secular. Futurists, the practitioners of the futures field, aim to demystify the future, to make their methods explicit, to be systematic and rational, to base their results on empirical observation of reality where relevant, and to test rigorously the plausibility of their logic in open discussion and intellectual debate. They also use creativity and intuition. Although some futurists occasionally abuse these values, they remain the ideals that most futurist strive to fulfil.
>
> (Bell, 1997: 5)

Bell has to be careful in setting up his new discipline. On the one hand future studies clearly has great ambitions and must be capable of making large claims.

Perhaps extremely large claims. Claims, perhaps, that rival in universal scope and majesty those made by theoretical physicists such as Max Tegmark and Ray Kurzweil, who both paint pictures of Intelligence stemming from humans on planet Earth eventually lighting up the entire universe within the next billion years (Tegmark, 2018: 203–47 and Kurzweil, 2005). On the other hand, exponents of future studies want to be scientific, and so, just like their fellow-travellers the theoretical physicists, they must be cautious about presupposing a future which they then go on to study. In the fields of philosophy and literary theory and criticism, this problem is often described as the hermeneutic circle, where one needs – before evaluating or analysing a work – to understand its parts; but in order to recognize the parts *as parts* one must have a sense of the whole (the work) to which they belong. In common parlance this might sound like the chicken and egg origins conundrum, but in reality, it concerns the problem of our phenomenological perceptions of real objects, which always appear locked within our presuppositions over the nature of what we call reality. In future studies this comes down to the apparent paradox that science seeks not to construct what it describes but to objectively (through repetition of controlled experimentation) describe what actually exists in the world. Yet how can we study the future without in a basic sense creating it? Future studies seems doomed to have to create the very thing it wants to objectively describe.

Bell is keen to style future studies as a science and thereby to distance it from the ancient practice of divination, which as he says was based on superstition. Yet, Bell also recognizes that, as he writes:

> future studies is linked to a long history of social thought ... of key utopian writings. From this perspective, modern future studies is a continuation of the age-old human quest to understand the nature of the good life and to find the correct values and norms of conduct that will lead to the flourishing of human society.
>
> (Bell, 1997: xxix)

Future studies, then, according to Bell, are descriptively scientific and yet prescriptively philosophical and ethical; they are based on observable trends and also based on the creativity and imagination of the particular scholars involved.

This is not to debunk or radically critique future studies as a discipline. All disciplines of human thought and practice have such paradoxes and aporias at their core. What I would stress, in this context, is the space opened up by future studies, and indeed by theoretical physics itself, for science fiction in general, and the new AI cinema in particular. As Arthur C. Clarke says, thinking of another founder of future studies, Herman Kahn:

> Even if 'future studies' are merely a form of play, they can be very useful – like play itself. They stretch the mind, so we can be better prepared for what lies ahead, not taken unaware by unpleasant surprises. This has always been one of the main roles of science fiction, *vide* ... George Orwell; he can take some credit for the fact that *1984* did not happen – at least not worldwide. And as ... Ray Bradbury famously remarked: 'I don't try to predict the future – I try to prevent it'.
>
> (Clarke, 1999: 2–3)

If a work concerned in depicting the future is not based on any current technological possibilities or scientific expectation about humanity and its technology, then we call that fantasy. We place, with all due respect, the majority of the *Star Wars*, *The War of the Worlds*, *The Time Machine* films into this science fantasy category. Films that merit inclusion into what I am calling the new AI cinema, are works that try to extrapolate their visions of the future within current and currently projected technology and the science that accompanies that technology. They are science fiction or, to follow Arthur C. Clarke's lead, *inquiries into limits of the possible*, or even simply (forgetting the extreme-case scenarios implied by limits) *the possible*.

There is little wonder then that, beginning with *Blade Runner* (1982) and *A.I. Artificial Intelligence* (2001), films wishing to seriously speculate about where Artificial Intelligence might take us are also seriously interested in depicting what is likely to happen to the environment. After all, despite all the problems, aporias and circles I have just discussed, we know pretty clearly what our immediate future holds for us, even if as a species we appear to be in denial of this knowledge. One has only to skim some of the IPCC reports on climate change to know clearly what a dire situation we are in and just how bad, especially for the Developing World, the situation will become in only a few decades time.[1] By 2050, for example, it is projected that human population on Earth will reach 10 billion, with severe water shortages in some of the megacities those numbers imply. In Greta Thunberg's 23 September 2019 address to the General Assembly of the United Nations, she explains what a 50 per cent or less chance of avoiding an uncontrollable breakdown in the global eco-system feels like to school children of her own age (Thunberg, 2019: 127–9). Humankind has already created the sixth mass extinction event in the history of the planet; we tend to place the future somewhere in the middle distance, but this man-made future is already tragically upon us. I say 'us', using the language of globalization, with everything that language hides and elides, including the actual role of the West in bringing about climate change, compared to the Developing World, which has largely been the victim of climate change (see Yusof, 2018).

Environmental collapse provides the sobering and ironic background to the technological achievements depicted in *Blade Runner* and *A.I. Artificial Intelligence*. In both films, the collapse of the environment acts like a chorus constantly undermining any sense that technology is in the process of saving humanity from itself. The most intelligent AI films also dealing with environmental disaster make much of what we might call the Promethean irony that the very technology that makes such wondrous things as Artificial Intelligence possible also makes mass extinction and eco-catastrophe possible. The science of Artificial Intelligence and robotics may have made incredible leaps in *Blade Runner*, but the fact is that the very beings that have created such miraculous intelligences as Rachel (Sean Young) and Batty have also rendered their home planet almost uninhabitable. The humans left on Earth are mainly a prole-class that live their holed-up existence in decaying high-rises as the sky constantly rains down upon them.

Denis Villeneuve's sequel, *Blade Runner 2049* takes up this theme, depicting in particular a Los Angeles in which humans and replicants alike survive on protein farmed from oversize maggots. The walls of the dam keeping the swollen Pacific Ocean at bay forever weep from their difficult, no doubt in the end futile, task. This city, and by inference the whole of Earth-bound humanity, is doomed, bracing itself to be consumed by the swollen Pacific Ocean. Increasingly humans are absentee landlords in off-world havens. That the geographical region in question happens to be the area we call Los Angeles and within that Hollywood, is an irony that does not pass by a filmmaker like Villeneuve.

The idea of the off-Earth haven, so explicit in both *Blade Runner* films, gives an extreme version of the diminishing habitable sphere that climate change threatens to inflict on humanity. In the various AI films that also take environmental catastrophe seriously, this prospect, of the drastically diminished habitat places a crucial emphasis on the difference between human being and synthetic being, often separating humans from their hardier, more robust and adaptable machines. A memorable example comes in the Disney/Pixar children's film, *Wall-E* (2008), in which Wall-E (Waste Allocation Load Lifter: Earth-Class) (voiced by Ben Burtt) persists in his Sisyphean labour of tidying up human civilization's waste, after the cataclysmic extent of that waste has destroyed all organic life and left the remnant of humanity lingering in space their bodies becoming morbidly obese due to lack of exercise. The first act of the film, where Wall-E suffers from unimaginable solitude amongst the tsunami of waste, is one of the greatest depictions of the last man (or in this case *last intelligence*) on Earth; a genre that takes us back at least to the Romantic period with Byron's 'Darkness' (1816) and Mary Shelley's *The Last Man* (1826). Indeed, the conclusion of Byron's poem could be said to be the nightmarish opposite to Transhumanism's ideal of humanity waking up the universe:

> The waves were dead; the tides were in their grave,
> The moon, their mistress, had expir'd before;
> The winds were wither'd in the stagnant air,
> And the clouds perish'd; Darkness had no need
> Of aid from them—She was the Universe.
>
> (Lord Byron, 1816)

A.I. Artificial Intelligence (2001): Dead zones and drowned cities

Over on the eastern seaboard of North America, it is with another ocean-swollen region that we begin Steven Spielberg's *A.I. Artificial Intelligence*. The film opens with the huge, unending waves of the ocean and a narrator (Ben

Kingsley) who, because of the syntax of his sentences, appears to be even further in the future. He explains to the audience that we begin the film in a future that our current climatologists and climate activists are warning us is fast becoming a fixed, determined, unchangeable one:

> Those were the years after the ice caps had melted because of the greenhouse gases, and the oceans had risen to drown so many cities along all the shorelines of the world. Amsterdam. Venice. New York. Forever lost.

What is interesting to us, as students of the new AI cinema, is what this scenario does to the relationship between humans and their technological creations. The consequence of this breakdown in the global climate is that humanity has become even more divided than it is at present between the haves and the have nots, the latter starving in lands made barren by the heating of the planet, the former even richer than they are today and even more dependent on technology to do menial labour they find unattractive. Placing the AI of this film in a scenario (the legal limit placed upon children per family unit) that goes back all the way to the author of the film's source, Brian Aldiss, and his short story 'Supertoys Last All Summer Long' (Aldiss, [1969] 2001), Spielberg presents robots as essential to the new economy:

> Millions of people were displaced, climate became chaotic. Hundreds of millions of people starved in poorer countries. Elsewhere, a high degree of prosperity survived when most governments in the developed world introduced legal sanctions to strictly license pregnancies, which was why robots, who were never hungry and who did not consume resources beyond those of their first manufacture, were so essential an economic link in the chain mail of society.

The film begins, then, with a rather uncharacteristic reference to the fate of different regions of the Earth. When we watch such films we normally, without thinking about it, expect a synecdochic logic where a particular region stands for the entirety of humanity. This expectation, one of the countless things film adopted from classical theatre, is evident, for example, in the two *Blade Runner* films, in which we take the region of Los Angeles to stand for the whole planet. A film, so this logic derived from drama goes, cannot show us the world, but must elicit our identification with a small set of characters in an interrelated space, or region, or zone. As in the film *Automata* and in the *Blade Runner* films, there is an off-world paradise, and there is a wilderness inhospitable to humans outside the city. In this way the metropolis is where all the action occurs and becomes, thereby, a total space, inhospitable for humans within and yet deadly to try to live without. We are getting close here to how certain contemporary AI films represent the idea of the contested notion of the Anthropocene.

What is also important about the voice-over which begins *A.I. Artificial Intelligence*, is that it links the beginning of the film (through Ben Kingsley's voice and through the future audience implied by that voice-over) to the end of the film, 2,000 years after the future events depicted in the bulk of the film, and so 2,000+ years after our own time as the film's actual audience. These superintelligences are the descendants of their prior robotic precursors, so they appear like aliens to us (Harlan, Struthers and Baker, 2009). They are all connected to each other telepathically, so that when the Specialist (Ben Kingsley – it was his voice that narrated the film's opening and thus addressed his fellow super-intelligent beings) describes the film's final events he is speaking to and also for his entire species.[2] What happens in those concluding scenes, the resurrection of Monica for one day and the fulfilment of David's one desire, comes straight out of Hans Moravec, as I have stated earlier, which also reminds us that Stanley Kubrick stands behind this scene and indeed the whole film.

Over a two-decade period, Kubrick worked with his co-writers, Brian Aldiss, Bob Shaw, Sarah Maitland and Ian Watson, and the evidence of the treatments suggests Kubrick was keen to stress the theme of environmental breakdown (see Krämer, 2015; Melia, 2017). Both Watson and Maitland wrote significant explanations of what had happened to the Earth and its human population after the crises had occurred. In two faxed sheets dated '03 11 90' Watson presented perhaps the fullest account of how the humans made themselves and all other life forms extinct, and the melancholy situation in which this placed the 'robots'.[3] Watson begins:

> Pollution and rape [of the Earth] caused global warming. But human scientists conquered this by releasing genetically engineered algae into all the Earth's oceans to absorb carbon dioxide.

The project succeeded ...[4] disastrously. A new ice age began, more suddenly and more fiercely than in any previous epoch. Altered algae bloomed, poisoning the seas.

The science of this is, of course, alarmingly correct. It seems clear to geologists concerned with climate change that human technology has extended the current inter-glacial period far longer than it would naturally have lasted (see Lewis and Maslin, 2018). This is partly why some confidently describe the current geological period as the Anthropocene. In Watson's version of environmental breakdown, humans overplay their hand in trying to mitigate the warming they themselves have created and end up generating an unparalleled freeze that destroys every living thing. Or, we might say, every organically living thing, because in Watson's apocalyptic end-game, the robots continue.

Watson's robots are rather different to those Spielberg finally settled on. They share the same intellectual curiosity about their now buried ancestors, but they are far more anguished. Watson writes:

> An aching emptiness tormented these robots, who had been robbed of the presence of life – that life which had created them and given them purpose.
>
> The blank emptiness of Earth spurred them to ask what life had meant, and what the universe meant. They searched for meaning.

But this quest for the meaning of life defeats them. Watson continues:

> They built great radio telescopes to reach out to other life, alien life, in this galaxy and in other galaxies – and found no signals, no hint of life whatever. They only found meaningless natural noise. It seemed all too probable that Earth was the only place in the whole cosmos which ever gave rise to intelligent life – perhaps to any life whatever. The universe was empty, apart from blazing stars and dead worlds and dust and gas.
>
> The robots built giant particle accelerators to probe the nature of reality - - and found no final reason for existence.
>
> Their searches produced nothing.
>
> The robots read and viewed every record that survived amongst the frozen ruins.

Human beings had created a million explanations of the meaning of life and the world – in works of philosophy, in art, in poetry, in mathematical formulas. Surely humans must be the key to the meaning of existence.

Now all humans were dead. Humans too were nothing.

The emphasis here is not on the union of human mother and robot son, now miraculously transformed into a human boy by mother love. We are, with Watson's scenario, a long way from the story of Pinocchio. This achingly melancholic writing concerns the creation of life doomed to ask questions it will never be able to answer. The intertext seems less *Pinocchio* than a Dantean vision of infinite loss and epistemological doubt in the one place where meaning could have been found, if only its human inhabitants had understood their true, unique place in the cosmos. In a vision of the future which seems rather precisely opposed to those visions of human intelligence setting the universe alight and alive offered us in the work of Transhumanists like Kurzweil and Tegmark, Watson's vision is of a chance (the one chance) of meaning squandered and the ultimate cost borne by the distant descendants of humanity's creative spirit. It is a vision that seems to express the balance of potential and destruction which obsessed Kubrick over his entire life and work. I have shown how Kubrick, in this project, never fully married his desire to create a modern-day myth with his desire to intelligently explore science and technology, but here a perhaps even deeper paradox between the ability to create intelligence and the destructive tendency of humanity (its ability to create unprecedented levels of death) comes into focus (see Allen, 2020).

Watson's writing, and Sara Maitland's after him (and Aldiss's before), gives us a tantalizing glimpse of the kind of film Kubrick would have created if he had brought this project into production. Partly because of the treasure trove of black and white pencil designs created by Chris Baker (under the pseudonym of 'Fangorn'), we can visually assess what Spielberg kept from Kubrick's project and what he cut. The most important cut concerns the environment. In Kubrick's work with Watson and Maitland he developed the idea that along with global warming and the devastating rise of the oceans already discussed, there had been a nuclear accident which had created an entire area of the former USA that was uninhabitable by humans. Kubrick and his co-writers called this The Dead Zone or Zero Zone, and it is into this zone, where only non-organics or synths can survive, that David and Gigolo Joe (Jude Law) go in search of the Blue Fairy and the transformation into a 'real boy' David so desires.

The idea of a nuclear disaster and the human costs involved is of course an already well-established theme in Kubrick's work. *Dr Strangelove or; How I Stopped Worrying and Learned to Love the Bomb* (1964) is, after all, the greatest 'anti-nuke' film ever made. Kubrick's worry, also referred to in the title of the rival Sidney Lumet film, *Fail Safe* (1964), was that no technological system, no system created by or overseen by human beings could ever be 100 per cent safe. And *2001* makes this point again through the story of the HAL 9000 supercomputer. If this was true, Kubrick and others argued in the 1960s, then it was only a matter of time before a catastrophic accident occurred with regard to the vast amount of nuclear weapons being stockpiled by the superpowers (see Broderick, 2017). That accident could well set off an unwinnable war, just as the attempt to reverse global warming has plunged humanity in the film into an accidental apocalypse.

In Baker's images and in treatments of this part of the story by Watson and Maitland, Joe and David wander through this landscape like Dante and Virgil in Gustave Doré's illustrations of Dante's *Inferno*. The skeletons of the human dead are intertwined with the dead trees; at times the vista pans out to show whole city areas uninhabited, empty, and dead. Joe and David seem like the last two surviving beings on an entirely dead planet, or lone survivors after an H. G. Wells style alien attack. The AI genre seems to be hacking into a complex of interrelated traditions, most fully realized in Mary Shelley's own day. Her third novel, *The Last Man* (1826), combines the tradition of the last man with that of the dead city, perhaps mediating the influence of one of the books influential on the creature in *Frankenstein*, namely Volney's *Ruins of Empire* (1791). It is interesting that in Baker's drawings the self-imposed annihilation of humanity is depicted through images of an empty and ruined city. The tragedy of humanity lies in the fact that its architectural constructions, meant to house human beings and their legislative, their juridical, and their cultural productions, should so outlast them. But buildings cannot talk, so they tend to keep their secrets untold.

I Am Mother (2019)

I Am Mother (dir. Grant Sputore) is an Australian film which opened at the Sundance Festival in early 2019 and was first broadcast by Netflix in June of that year. This film gives us a three-hander in which the extinction event for humanity has occurred thirty-eight years earlier. Mother (body work, Luke Hawker; voice, Rose Byrne) is a robot in charge of a bunker facility containing enough human embryos to restart human life on the planet. Viewers begin by imagining that the extinction event has been a global nuclear war (the very first shots are of the first day of the event with loud explosions apparently overhead which are sufficiently strong to rock the bunker and cause dust showers from its roof). Mother, narrating in a voice-over, talks about having to learn to be a good enough mother to activate the tens of thousands of embryos in the facility, but from our initial impressions of her relationship to Daughter (Clara Rugaard) she already is an ideal parent, attentive, kind, caring and supportive. Mother and Daughter's relationship seems ideal, in fact, until the latter begins to show what Mother declares to be an unhealthy interest in the 'outside'. Mother explains that the outside is too polluted, thus reaffirming our assumptions that a nuclear holocaust has occurred, and we cannot help feeling that Daughter is better off in her secure home with Mother.

The arrival of an injured woman (Hilary Swank) turns everything on its head, however. First, the woman's appearance outside the bunker door proves that the outside is not as polluted as Mother has suggested. It also proves that Mother has been lying, or at least withholding other truths from her Daughter. Third, the woman presents a test for Mother: how will she treat this interloper, as an enemy or a friend? In other words, is Mother capable of true hospitality towards humans it has not raised itself? In the first few exchanges between Mother and the woman it seems like the latter's attitude is the problem, since for her there can only be war between robots and humans. But everything she says about her experience of robots makes Daughter question her situation the more. She finds the incinerated remains of what clearly was an aborted attempt at raising a human before her, and the embryo bank shows a number of empty pods, suggesting that Mother has incinerated a number of failed efforts.

The woman encouarges Daughter to escape with her back to the mines, where she says her remnant group of humans has been hiding. The drawings she has made of these co-survivors electrifies Daughter's imagination as proof positive of the existence of this human remnant. Partly as a way of distracting her, Mother says that Daughter is ready to help parent a sibling, and they artificially grow her baby brother together. This ruse, on the part of Mother, fails, however, since it strengthens even further Daughter's desire to join the human company outside. Daughter is determined to take her brother with her, and as Mother gets more and more draconian in her attempt to retain control, Daughter escapes with the woman intent on returning with the other humans that the woman still insists are part of her group.

It turns out, however, there are no other humans and the woman has lied to Daughter in order to get her to come with her. There is, in fact, as we piece together various clues left in the film, reason to believe that the woman is a failed daughter of Mother. The timing between the woman's age and the age of Daughter appears to allow the possibility of Mother having started to raise another human child/young adult. It might even reveal the truth behind the rather flimsy statements by Mother about her needing to be sure she was a good enough parent before starting to animate any of the other human 'eggs'.

Daughter leaves the woman and returns home to face Mother, whom she shoots and thereby 'kills', the last camera shot being of her (Daughter's) face as she begins to realize that she is to be the mother of the new race of humanity. In disabling Mother, Daughter has disabled all the robots on the outside, who turn out to be part of one consciousness emanating from Mother, whose plan it had been to destroy humanity only to start afresh in the bunker fostering a totally obedient slave class of human subjects. At least that is my and my students' reading of this enigmatic film.[5]

The ecological disaster and extinction event had not been the direct cause of humanity's predilection for violence, but was in fact caused by a rogue robot with a desire to purge the Earth of that very violence. In this sense, then, Mother is similar to Hal 9000 in *2001* and a host of other humanity purging robots. But, of course, we can object, Mother was the result of human technology in the first place. The violence still ultimately springs from humanity's Promethean drives and desires. This film's ending is peculiarly but also perhaps appropriately ambiguous. For example, are the thousands of robots identical, synched to Mother, and if so are we supposed to assume that they also die when Mother dies? What exactly did Mother have in her mind regarding the human embryos for which she was responsible? Did Mother actually murder an earlier human child or young adult? What actually happened between Mother and the woman to make the latter so frightened and immediately distrustful of Mother's motives? These and other questions are all left in various states of suspension at the end of the film.

This ambiguity seems intentional, and one could cite the incorporation into Daughter's education of an example of what in Philosophy 101 classes gets called the Trolley Problem (for a good explanation, see Melanie Mitchell, 2019: 127–8). Having highlighted such an ethical dilemma it seems in all probability intentional that we end the film with a series of questions: Is it better for humanity to be raised by rational robots or by only partly rational humans? Precisely what caused the extinction event if it was not a nuclear catastrophe caused by a human frailty? Are our AI machines really our enemy or are they our guides, mentors and, ultimately, friends? Can modern human beings live without their machines?

I Am Mother does not answer these questions, it leaves them hanging, as it were, fundamentally because no film can answer such questions. The question of where humanity is going with its technology is still not at all certain and so not literally answerable. We cannot expect the texts of our visual media to resolve currently unanswerable questions. All we can ask it to do is to pose those questions in interesting and engaging ways. *I Am Mother*, on a low budget and using only a handful of actors, manages to successfully meet such a theoretical and emotional demand and, in fact, exceeds it.

The infinite city in *Ghost in the Shell*

Eco-catastrophe is full of paradoxes. Indeed, these paradoxes are so severe as to produce a kind of inverted dialectics in which, counter-Hegel and counter-Marx, the dialectical process leads not to progress (science and technology moving upwards towards a transcendental utopia), but always another level of disaster. With global warming, wild spaces radically diminish until, upon a catastrophe, they return with a vengeance; world overpopulation creates unsolvable problem after unsolvable problem until, having reached its apogee, we end with only a scattering of humans left on the planet; Artificial Intelligence helps to increase the reach and depth of democracy, until the same technology creates so many untraceable bots spreading hatred and division, that democracy is undermined; science and technology accelerate in the expansion of human consciousness and capability, until, reaching their final crisis, they turn on their creators and destroy them. One might go on, listing the paradoxes involved in the kinds of apocalyptic scenarios offered to humanity in the period of the so-called Anthropocene. The modern metropolis partakes in these forms of paradox and regression, being a space which is clearly detrimental to humanity and the Earth, and yet becomes, increasingly, the circumference of human activity and vision, destroying any possibility of a natural space outside of the city walls. This then is the city without walls, a total environment which reflects on a never-ending, externalized, urban panorama suited far more to our artificial creations than to our own organic needs.

Some of the most telling contributions to our understanding of the future that awaits us can be found in works that try to represent future metropolitan life. In AI terms, of course, this vision of the future city tends to be one in which the boundaries between the human and the mechanical are radically blurred or in the process of blurring. Ridley Scott's *Blade Runner* is without doubt the key film in this tradition, with its representation of a Los Angeles that seems to stretch for ever, the only solace, for those who can afford it, from this perpetually sodden, crumbling, over-populated world, being the lure of the off-world colonies.

Blade Runner is, for many, the greatest example of the 'Japanization' of American movies of the 1980s through to at least the 2000s. Giant Geisha girls advertise branded drinks, there are sellers of sushi or rare organic and inorganic artefacts. Yet, Mamoru Oshii's successful and extremely popular anime film *Ghost in the Shell* (1995), based on the manga comic books by Masamune Shirow, is a film which re-appropriates in respectful ways much of Ridley Scott's film's aesthetic. Oshii has said in an interview:

> I don't think any film set in the future can be free of the influence of *Blade Runner*. For those of us who make such films, *Blade Runner* is something

that we cannot surpass. The film is a vision. It has the virtual power to make us believe that such a world exists … In a way, that film is my inspiration. I attempt to give different interpretations for it, but I don't think I will ever be free of it.⁶

Ghost in the Shell switches the story from Scott's Los Angeles to Hong Kong (called New Port City in the franchise), but the overriding sense of a city from which there is no escape (save for an elite few who are of no interest in this story) is reaffirmed and deepened. In an earlier interview, Oshii discusses why he chose Hong Kong. In ways that link to Jonathan Nolan's account of season three of *Westworld*, Oshii says:

> Since the internet isn't visible, I tried to think of how I could visually represent it. It would be pointless to show the monitor of a personal computer. However, if you think about Hong Kong, you imagine a city teeming with information. For example, there are countless signs and a cacophony of voices and sounds which flow through the city.

This image of the city as an ocean (a 'flow') of information is one that runs as a guiding figure throughout the film. It is a figure that is established in the very beginning of the film, in the contextualizing texts which form its prelude:

> In the near future – Corporate Networks Reach Out to the Stars. Electrons and Light Flow Through the Universe.

The world of this future Hong Kong seems one of height and depth, and consequentially of up and down. It is a world in which the skyscrapers are so high they often push beyond the limit of the top border of the picture frame. It is a presiding characteristic of the film's hero, Major Motoko Kusanagi (voice, Atsuko Tanaka, with Maaya Sakamoto; English version, Mimi Woods), that she attains panoramic visions of the city from these heights, but also that this allows her to 'dive' into the city's informational flow. The Major is, after all, all machine except for her brain, site of her 'ghost' (soul or consciousness, depending on your perspective).

Oshii's film lovingly portrays the city in all its myriad parts: skyscrapers, ghettoes, roads, highways, intersections, canals and docklands, tunnels, street markets, interiors like labs, offices, bedrooms, restaurants. Often these representations come during a pause in dialogue and action, as if the labyrinthine building network that makes up this version of Hong Kong was the real ghost rather than the inorganic shell. Contrasted to the metropolis is the ocean estuary, where the Major dives to get away from it all. Conversing with her co-worker in Section 9, Batou (voice, Akio Ôtsuka; English version, Richard Epcar), the Major discusses her fears about her identity. How does she know she is the individual she believes she is? Batou asks her about her diving: 'What do you see at the bottom of that darkness?' The Major replies by quoting one of the most quoted passages from the Christian New Testament, 1 Corinthians 13.12: 'For now we see as through a glass darkly, / Then we will see as we are seen.'[7] The Major might like to dive into the dark, but she is seeking illumination. As she says to Batou, in another scene later in the film: 'I suppose cyborgs like me tend to be paranoid about their origins.' Most of what constitutes Major Motoko, after all, is the property of Hanka Robotics. How is she to know her memories are not artificial implants? In fact, she cannot know, which means that 'the only thing that makes me feel human, [is] the way I'm treated. Who knows what's inside my head?'

Is memory the one area into which the Major cannot dive, that will remain forever dark? The answer is played out in terms of the Major and Batou's pursuit of the Puppet Master (Iemasa Kayumi; English version, Tom Wyner), a consciousness that has no organic origin, but has emerged directly from the web. This conflict between the Major (a cyborg still in possession of a 'ghost') and the Puppet Master (who may have no 'ghost') is given an evolutionary context in the battle staged in the ruined Natural History Museum. It would appear, in fact, that the Puppet Master wishes to merge with the Major, thus generating an evolutionary leap away from humanity towards a superintelligence that is, to use the figure, all 'dive', in that it is simultaneously everywhere at once. The Puppet Master says to the Major:

> Listen. I am connected to a vast network, that is beyond your reach and experience. To humans it is like staring at the sun, a blinding brightness that conceals a core of great power. We have been subordinate to our limitations until now; the time has come to cast aside these bonds and to elevate ourselves to a higher plane. It is time to become a part of all things.

The Puppet Master is delivering back the Major's own biblical allusion here, but we must ask (given its own origins in the net) who is it speaking for when it speaks in the collective 'we'. The brain transfer between the Puppet Master and the Major appears to leave the latter dead, as indicated by the few seconds of black screen that follow. But this then gives way to a young girl (voice, Maaya Sakamoto) seated in a room in a house which turns out to be Batou's 'safe house'. Batou explains that the girlish body was the only one he could buy on the black market. Batou then asks the question we have left hanging, whether she is now merged with the Puppet Master. The Major replies by returning to her biblical quotation:

> When I was a child my speech, feelings and thinking were all those of a child. Now I am a man I have no more use for childish ways. And now I can say these things without help in my own voice, because I am now neither the woman who was known as the Major nor am I the program that was called the Puppet Master.

She walks away from the Modernist-style house into a wooded area which for a second suggests a natural, maybe even a wild environment before it becomes clear that these are just trees cultivated around Batou's house and that in fact it is positioned on one of the hills surrounding New Port City. The Major, in the guise of the young girl, delivers the film's last words as we begin to see, from a back shot, what she sees, the vast city sprawling out beneath her: 'And where does the newborn go from here? The net is vast and infinite.' She is preparing for a total dive into the 'infinite' net, which stretches way out beyond the bounds, but at the same time paradoxically extends the range, the reach, of this particular city. This dive, into the internet, is thus her way into and yet also out of the metropolis that had previously confined her. It is, from our early twenty-first-century perspective, a very bitter-sweet conclusion; while happy that it is the Major who has merged with the net, we cannot help but feel the nostalgic tug of Nature, which seems not to exist as an option here in this future city-centred world.

This yearning for the natural world is explicitly tackled in Oshii's follow up film, *Ghost in the Shell 2: Innocence* (2004). In an interview about this film, Oshii wonders whether we can be truly human without the companionship of animals. Batou, here in this sequel, continues his Section 9 work wondering 'where her [the Major's] ghost might be and if the Major will ever return'. He has a new partner, Togusa (voice, Kōichi Yamadera) and a Basset Hound, who he clearly loves in his own brusque, monosyllabic, undomesticated fashion.

Once again in this film, the city of Hong Kong and also the Northern Territories, are represented with so much detail and care as to become an all-pervasive character. Oshii has talked about how it is the cityscapes, rather than the plot and dialogue, that audiences remember from such films as *Blade Runner*.[8] The festival that is taking place as Batou and Togusa arrive in the Northern Territories took over a year to animate, thus suggesting why it took Oshii and his team nine years to make a sequel to their immensely lucrative first *Ghost in the Shell* film. As they are arriving, and Batou is explaining how these territories have become so lawless, he says: 'It reminds me of the belief that each element of the body is as much an expression of DNA as the whole body.'

This is a strange way of discussing human genetics. In casting our knowledge as a 'belief' Batou might be exposing himself as a less than scientific thinker, of course. But in putting things in terms of synecdoche (whole for part/part for whole), Batou is raising for consideration the major rhetorical figure for *sovereignty*, whether that be monarchical (the King or Queen is the people), nationalistic (the nation is the sum of its people), or Republican/Socialist (the people in their collective unity are the State). Togusa's initial response is deliberately bathetic: 'Doesn't that also apply to beaver dams and spiders' webs as well?' Yet, of course, that merely strengthens Batou's metaphor, and he goes on: 'If the essence of life is information carried in DNA, then society and civilization are just colossal storage systems and a metropolis like this one is simply a sprawling external memory.' Batou says this as they survey the city below them and the effect upon the audience is to visually confirm Batou's words. Togusa replies with a new biblical allusion: 'As it says in the Bible, "How great is the sum of all thy thoughts? If I should count them, they are more in number than the sand."' Batou responds: 'I recognize that, its Psalm 139 of the Old Testament.' The allusion is a telling one. Psalm 139 concerns the ubiquity of God. Read in this context, we cannot help but imagine Batou substituting the ghost of the Major for the Hebrew image of Yahweh, the 'you' or addressee of the text:

⁷ Whither shall I go from thy spirit? or whither shall I flee from thy presence?
⁸ If I ascend up into heaven, thou art there: if I make my bed in hell, behold, thou art there.
⁹ If I take the wings of the morning, and dwell in the uttermost parts of the sea;
¹⁰ Even there shall thy hand lead me, and thy right hand shall hold me.

Togusa's next allusion, as they look down on the hordes of people in the festival and the flocks of birds swooping round the taller buildings, retains the figurative focus on plenitude: 'His legion, angel forms lay intrans't / Thick as autumnal leaves that strew the brooks.' Batou replies: 'Now you're quoting Milton. But we're not exactly Satan you know, buddy.' This rather misses the way in which Milton's depiction of the Satanic hordes as 'thick as autumnal leaves', reworks a figure of the leaves which takes us back to Dante and Homer and forward to T. S. Eliot and Samuel Beckett (see Bloom, 1982). The figure presents an image of anarchy opposed precisely to the figure of synecdoche Batou has already established.

Synecdochic unity lies in the figurative interrelationship between every element in a system: in the European monarchical systems of the sixteenth and seventeenth centuries, the King or Queen was literally thought to *be* the collective nation, to *embody* it. Likewise, as Batou says, in any organic body, the individual parts, down to the smallest cells, have a role to play in the health of the body as a whole; largely, that is, because they share the same building blocks. Contrasted to this, Satan's hordes, in Milton's *Paradise Lost*, have fallen from Heaven, and are an inorganic assembly of purely contiguous parts. They are parts of something that has lost its chance of belonging to, or of constituting in itself, a unity, a whole. In the end the host of fallen angels, roused by Satan's rhetoric, erect the very mockery of synecdochic unity and harmony in the city of Pandemonium.

It is this opposition between the synecdochally organic and the merely contingent and inorganic that Kim (voice, Naoto Takenaka; English version, Joey D'Auria), the hacker and informer, interrogated by Batou and Togusa, dwells on. Kim has turned himself into a 'doll' without a 'ghost', and he says:

> The eeriness lies solely from the fact that they are modelled on humans. In fact, they are nothing but human, really. They make us face the fear of being reduced to simple mechanical matter.

However, paradoxically, Kim goes on, despite this fear, to refer to the way in which humanity, since the inventions of computerization, have sought to extend its capabilities through technological mechanization of itself:

> This human determination to beat evolutionary odds also reveals the desire to transcend nature, the very thing that gave both to humankind. The image of life equipped with puppet hardware is the very source of this nightmare.

Batou, the protagonist of this film, does not dive like Major Motoko, he bashes and breaks apart. But in the concluding scene, after the Section 9 mission is completed, his retrieval of his beloved Basset Hound from Togusa's family home, shows him clinging on to nature, striving to keep in contact with at least one creature, one thing, that is other than himself and, indeed, other to humanity. It is almost a bathetic image upon which to leave the film, but as Oshii has suggested it is laden with meaning. The ultimate paradox and irony of the idea of the idea of the Anthropocene is that in the geological-ecological era in which humanity takes the reins of power over nature, humanity is threatened with the prospect of losing itself, of being reduced to mere machines. Batou's rather unimpressive dog demonstrates that he, as hero of the film, is resisting that particular evolutionary trajectory.

Ghost in the Shell: From manga to movie

When we come to the Hollywood live-action adaptation of Oshii's anime version, we immediately become embroiled in controversy over what is known as 'white-washing'. The casting of Scarlett Johansson as the Major brought on the film's release of a barrage of criticism over the decision to give the part to a Western, white actress instead of a more appropriate Asian actress. The controversy, important on its own terms, provides some insights in our study.

Let's look at the controversy first. The 'white-washing' controversy began in January 2015 when the cast of the film was first announced (see Chan, 2016).

Fans of the original manga and anime then voiced innumerable protests on social media. The controversy was further stoked by a press release still of Scarlet Johansson as Major Mira Killian (in this version Motoko Kusanagi is the name she lost and ultimately the name which leads her back to her natural mother). Of course, this was part of a much larger controversy attempting to create a cultural change with regard to its casting of Eastern actors and to foster a paradigm in Hollywood's representation of Asian characters and identities. As an analogy, Melissa Chan refers to the outcry when Sharon Stone was cast as a person from Hawaiian and Chinese backgrounds in Cameron Crowe's 2015 *Aloha*. She goes on, however, to open out the problem beyond all individual examples, writing:

> A study released in February found that the data backed critics' concerns about diversity in Hollywood. Researchers at the University of Southern California had analyzed more than 21,000 characters and behind-the-scenes workers on more than 400 films and TV shows released between September 2014 and August 2015. Half of the productions they analyzed had no Asian speaking characters, according to the study, and only about 28% of characters with dialogue were from non-white racial groups.
>
> (Chan, 2016)

So the problem concerns all (non)-white people and exists behind as much as in front of the camera. Johansson herself has apologized to anyone who might be offended by her playing the role of the Major (Stolworthy, 2017). It should also be remembered that Mamoru Oshii, the director of the first and second anime versions of *Ghost in the Shell* endorsed the film, particularly praising the work of Johansson in portraying the story's central character the Major (see Acevedo, 2017).

Johansson's media appearances around the release date of the film are fascinating, even if they seem to have stoked rather than tempered the fire. When asked directly about those who took offence on her landing the role, she says: 'I think this character is living a very unique experience in that she is a human brain living within an entirely machinery (*sic*) body. She's essentially identity-less. I would never attempt to play a person of a different race, obviously.'[9] The reasoning sounds a bit contrived: Major Mira Killian within the film is identity-less therefore Johansson cannot be criticized for playing the part of a character who is clearly the invention of Japanese manga and anime culture. This argument, however, does have the endorsement of Mamoru Oshii, and is in all probability a paraphrase of his position: 'The name "Mira Killian" and her current body are not her original name and body [her original name was Motoko Kusanagi], so there is no basis for saying that an Asian actress must portray her. Even if her original body (presuming such a thing existed) were a Japanese one, and her birth mother is Japanese, that would still apply.'[10]

Unsurprisingly, not many of the critics previously critical of Johansson's casting in the film were convinced by this 'logic'. Indeed, her assertion that she would never take the role of an Asian or any different race served to exacerbate the furore, when MANAA (Media Action Network for Asian Americans) put their considerable muscle behind the protests flaring up about Johansson's 'lying' (Ahern, 2017).

The entire episode has been signalled as a turning point for Hollywood, given that since the critical reaction to *Ghost in the Shell* there has been much more of an effort to cast actors from ethnic backgrounds suitable for the parts they play (Francisco, 2022). The criticisms about white-washing, however, laid the foundation upon which even more scathing criticisms of the film have been launched. Janelle Okwodu in a *Vogue* piece entitled 'What Went Wrong with *Ghost in the Shell*' has argued that the Hollywood version not only lacks originality itself, but has reduced the originality of the anime and manga text which it is adapting and translating. She explains that the original version was about more than the Major's story, it was about 'an entire world, people have become indistinguishable from the technology they've created' (Okwodu, 2017). She also points to the amount of philosophical exchanges in Oshii's film and its willingness to ask questions for which no one seems to have an answer. In contrast, she notes that:

> None of that translates into the live-action version; challenges are replaced by neat conclusions, and existential dialogue has been ditched for platitudes about memory. All the elements of the original that were interesting have

been watered down, presumably to attract viewers unfamiliar with the franchise, but in disservice to the story. It's a Hollywood lesson in settling for less, and ironically, one that it seems audiences are refusing to settle for.

(Okwodu, 2017)

Let's be clear, however, in contrast to what Okwodu suggests, the story is not a singular thing, and neither are the characters within it. Masamune Shirow's original manga presents very different 'takes' on its lead characters, in particular Major Motoko Kusanagi. In *Ghost in the Shell* Volume One, the Major, at least initially, is rather immature, adolescent and brattish, calling the Head of Section 9, Chief Aramaki, 'ape face', a moniker rather encouraged by the visual representation of a figure who will become increasingly noble and respected in the later adaptations (Shirow, 2007) In this incarnation of the Major she seems disrespectful and anti-establishment, even anarchic in her behaviour. When Aramaki comes to the bar in which the Major has retired with her colleagues to tell them the good news that they have secured the funding from the government they asked for, Batou matches the Major's rebellious attitude, explaining: 'I spotted ol' ape-face's car outside and planted a little fire-cracker in it' (Shirow, 2009: 51). The explosion renders his car useless, but the ever resourceful Aramaki produces a rather unimpressive mobility scooter to drive off in. As Aramaki 'putt putt putt[s]' off into the distance Motoko says 'Made us look like idiots *again*!' and then shouts out after Aramaki in his ridiculous pudding-shaped helmet: 'Just make sure you pay us top dollar hon …' and her words give way to sniggering (52). Motoko, in this early rendition is hardly the blank-faced cyborg of Johansson's interpretation. She laughs, she is surprised, often secretive or anxious or amazed in ways that those coming to her first rendition after viewing the 2017 live action film or Oshii's version will no doubt find extremely surprising.

In the second instalment of Shirow's masterpiece, *Ghost in the Shell 1.5: Human-Error Processor*, the Major is much less centre-stage, at least in its first half. In the second half she begins to appear in her more familiar all-action guise (Shirow, 2007). I am taking this publication out of strict chronology, since it was published after the appearance of *Ghost in the Shell*

2: *Man-Machine Interface,* in which the Major floats through the internet, in various guises, doubles and copies, like some semi-pornographic goddess (Shirow, 2005). The licence for this slightly anachronistic account serves to rhetorically emphasize the point that there is no one singular Major Motoko Kusanagi/Mira Killian. Not even in the original manga. The fact that there are at least two competing names for our cyborg heroine constantly reminds of this fact.

My first and perhaps major (*sic*) point is that when it comes to the character of Major Motoko Kusanagi/Mira Killian, there is no original to betray. The major is an incredible creation, that begins to slip away from its creator as soon as she starts to live on the page and then on the screen. Like Shakespeare's Cleopatra or Hamlet or Ophelia, or whatever major fictional character you will, she is a figure of interpretation from the very beginning. I want to say more about that as we proceed, but sticking with the controversy for now, too many reviews wrote off the film because of the controversy. This seems simple minded. You would not write off *Hamlet* or *Anthony and Cleopatra* because of one bad performance, or one production that you disliked or disapproved of in one way or another. Hamlet, Anthony and Cleopatra, and every major Shakespearean character, and every minor Shakespearean character for that matter, stands like the Major stands, for the ages and cultures to interpret and reinterpret as they see fit. At the end of his great *Defence of Poetry*, Percy Bysshe Shelley wrote that poets are 'the mirrors of the gigantic shadows which futurity casts upon the present'. Clearly, the same can be said for the most creative and challenging fictional characters. You might not like or might disapprove of Rupert Sanders's interpretation of Major Mira or the lurid, at its worst infantilizing, pornographic element in Shirow's imagination, but that is absolutely no reason to dismiss the entire story and the defining, monumental achievement of those stories, the figure of Major Mira Killian/Motoko Kusangi.

The Major has the vitality, ambiguity and over-determination of meaning that rivals any character for contemporary relevance. I would go so far as to assert that Major Mira/Motoko Kusanagi is the most potent fictional creation to emerge from the new AI cinema and television. I know that's a hugely debatable statement. Let me try and back it up.

The Major and the future

The power I want to describe in Shirow's text and the characters that inhabit those texts, stem partly from Shirow's innovative use of the manga form, and partly from the contemporary relevance – and, as part of that, the believability – of the future world of New Port City, the urban world he created. The mid-twenty-first century world of *Ghost in the Shell* is one in which people increasingly accept and, indeed, volunteer for technological upgrades of their bodies. The members of Section 9, for example, are enabled to communicate with each other in a techno-telepathic way which is off grid to the higher authority of the government. Shirow's texts are filled with extra-diegetic discussions of such innovations, their technological feasibility, their philosophical and spiritual ramifications, their role within the story.

We can see the importance of the latter dimension of narratorial interpolation if we look at one of the chapters at the beginning of the original manga *Ghost in the Shell 1*: '05 Megatech. Machine 2: The Making of a Cyborg' (Shirow, 2009: 101–8). This is a section that obviously matters greatly to the reader, as it does to Major Motoko, in that it constitutes a demonstration of the technological production and reproduction of cyborgs like the Major. In this scene, in other words, the Major is shown not how she was conceived but how her body was made to hold (encase) her brain and thus her soul.

We are not, of course given a description of the whole elaborate process of manufacturing such a cybernetic shell, but we join it as a shell with brain and spinal cord in place is dipped in a bath of 'fiber optic film' to provide the mechanical frame with a sensitive 'skin'. Shirow explains the technology in an extensive note (Shirow, 2009: 102). It is a fact, that with Shirow's manga behind her, we have more information about the technology that has enabled the Major's posthuman existence than any of the other artificial beings we have been studying in this book. Much more!

It is the set of three authorial, explanatory paragraphs that open this section to which we need to give our attention. In the first paragraph, Shirow defines a cyborg as 'a human whose body has been partially or almost completely altered by the use of substitute organs and parts' (101). In the second paragraph Shirow reflects: 'As she [the cyborg being focused on here], demonstrates, at first glance it is very difficult to tell the difference between a cyborg and a robot' (101). But that distinction is crucial, and is made much of in the manga, the anime and the live-action formats in which the Major has appeared. What is the difference? It's one we've seen throughout this study and which has been upheld and torn down in what feels like equal measure. It is best expressed through a simple opposition: humans (including cyborgs) have souls, machines (in particular robots) do not. The Major is different to all the AI driven robots we have looked at, however. Despite the fact that 90 per cent of her is 'machiney', to use the cutesy word used by Johansson, she has a brain, and thus independence of thought and thus autonomy of action. She is therefore human. Such is the logic being set up by the character of the Major. But things are not that simple.

The first problem concerns feasibility. In the third paragraph of the explanatory text we've been looking at, Shirow writes:

> It's difficult to imagine how artificial versions of some parts of the body – the endocrine system, the lymphatic system, spleen, the liver and the marrow – can ever be manufactured, so it is extremely doubtful that we will ever see a cyborg as mechanized as the one here, but there are the many other man made body parts that are already available (and it's a growing field).
>
> (Shirow, 2009: 101)

If the cyborg in question is not yet feasible in terms of current science then neither is Major Motoko. What is Shirow doing here? He seems to be undermining his own creation before she has really had the chance to live and breathe. My sense of this would be that, in a rather characteristic way, by referring to the present state of science, Shirow is gaining a greater degree of verisimilitude for his character. We can safely assume that he knows about Moore's Law and is silently deploying it here. Why bother to set your story decades in the future if you stick with today's medicine and today's science. The implication is that, by the mid-century, science will develop that bit further, to make the Major possible. Although it is crucial to add that in being created (at least in terms of her body) she will be unusual, exceptional and alone. What I ultimately want to say about this character concerns that loneliness, perhaps impossible for simpler humans to understand. This analysis will lead us to Sanders's 2017 live-action film. As will a look at the second problem concerning her ontological status.

We have said that unlike a robot the Major has autonomy. But how true is this? This is the second problem. The first action we see her in is defying Aramaki's orders and diving into the business meeting and then, against all protocols, in order to fast track the section's locating of Kuze, who is a version of the puppet-master from the manga and anime versions, merging her brain (deep diving) with the geisha.

These seem to be the actions of a rebel, a loose cannon, precisely an autonomous person. But attend to what Mira says of herself again and again by way of defending her rogue actions. She constantly defends herself by stating that she was made this way, it is what she was made for. Mira hardly presents herself as an autonomous agent; and her exposure to the net, not simply her ability to dive into it, but also the constant danger of being hacked, invaded, violated by hackers and beings who exist solely in cyberspace threatens to undermine what agency she has at any moment. All this is a massive challenge to her status as an autonomous person. I have not yet mentioned the danger to her of her makers, the military wing of Hanka Robotics.

Mira is the first of her kind, says Dr Ouelet (Juliette Binoche) her ersatz mother. But Mira replies to Ouelet's rather proud comment 'You don't know how alone that makes me feel.' Mira is utterly alone, belonging to a future yet to come. Everyone around her lies to her. She is constantly threatened by her status as a 'diver' into the net, with invasion, manipulation and a permeable consciousness which is useful in her role as what Cutter (Peter Ferdinando), the Hanka Robotics CEO, calls 'a weapon', but is disastrous personally. Far from lacking an identity, as we have seen critics and others suggesting, Mira has the personality of a stranger in a strange land. She is a kind of alien presence fought over by the unscrupulous and also by some, like Dr Ouelet, who should know better.

This is where and how I respond to Johansson's performance, in that it plugs itself into a potential within Mira, that has to do with her future-facing exceptionality and the distinct ontological and epistemological problem this brings her. Who can she trust? What social role should she and could she adopt other than working as the leader of Section 9? Ultimately, there is, as

Sharalyn Orbaugh points out, a question concerning Mira's/Motoko's sexuality (Orbaugh, 2007). Obviously, as is characteristic of the manga, anime and movie versions, there is always an emphasis on her overt sexuality and desirability. But sexuality goes further than outward desirability and objectification, it involves the evolution of the human species and leads to issues of reproduction and genetic inheritance. As Orbaugh writes:

> Human species reproduction, as we know it is structured around several features. One is the interplay of repetition and sameness with diversity ... For cyborgs such as Kusanagi there is no such combination of continuity and change ... Nor is there any intermixing of genetic information, and thus qualities, from another body/subject. There is continuity, in the sense that Kusanagi's brain/ghost remains the same. But in a world in which 'ghosts' can be hacked and identities implanted, how can she be sure that her brain is indeed original and sense of self unadulterated?
>
> (Orbaugh, 2007: 186)

When we begin to compare the Major to human men and women in these ways she begins to appear a tragic figure, doomed to attract men and women but for no real, meaningful purpose, not even pleasure. Mira has made very little choice about what she looks like, what clothes she wears, where she lives and what she does for a living. The more we look at her, the less autonomous she becomes. Without excusing the film or passing over the issue of white-washing, it is on this basis, of her profound solitude and alienation that we can and perhaps should evaluate the performance that Johansson gives in this role. Far from lacking an identity, Mira/Motoko is perhaps the most intriguing, the most compelling and the most scientifically and philosophically inexhaustible figure that we have studied in this book. Johansson, despite a dramatically regrettable if only slight limp meant to connote her body's machine status, gives a fine and, through her muted, quiet interpretation, a million miles away from the exuberant figure we discover in Shirow's manga, wholly appropriate rendition of her alienation. In contrast, the recent revival of Section 9 in the anime series *Ghost in the Shell: Sac_2045* (2020, 2022, Dir. Kenji Kamiyama and Shinji Aramaki) gives us a Major who oversees and provides unfailing wisdom, whenever needed. She comes across here less as Captain than as Coach of the team.

These incredibly diverse representations of the same character are partly made possible by the differences of the generic forms in which she appears. In the same year as the live action film was released, five short stories were published, taking the Major and her Section 9 colleagues into new plots and providing these characters the benefit of the short story genre (see Enjoe et al, 2017). Again, in the film's release year, 2017, came the official novelization (Swallow and Bernstein, 2017). Each iteration of the Major adds new meaning to her character. Certainly it is significant when assessing versions of the discontinuous medium of the manga or the much more story-based medium of the Hollywood movie, what form is being used to represent her. In the contexts of Sanders's film, the Major's story becomes a quest for origins, or an identity through possession of a family and a native home. This is why the set piece *shoot 'em up* showdown, with Cutter in his ridiculous 'spider tank', feels so awkward, so regressive and so unsatisfactory a denouement.

Mira's quest for identity begins to define her and leads her finally to a reunion with her mother, Hairi (Kaori Momoi). These are the most emotionally affective scenes of the film. One in her mother's own home and one at the graveyard, where Mira, now Motoko explains that Hairi doesn't need to visit her daughter's grave anymore. She has risen from the grave, her ghost stronger than mortal death. Impassive, considering her own gravestone, in a completely manufactured body, with only her brain, seat of her ghost, her spirit, her identity, to connect her to herself, her personality, her true purpose, or to anybody else for that matter, I cannot believe we have heard the last or seen the best of her yet. The years will tell, if we listen and watch without prejudice.

Notes

1. See https://www.ipcc.ch/reports/
2. Indeed, it is perhaps inaccurate, on the basis of Ben Kingsley's mellow voice, to call the Specialist a 'he'.
3. The Stanley Kubrick Archive, University of Arts, London. SK/18/3/1/3/1.
4. Here Kubrick writes 'EXPAND'.
5. I am referring to the Third Year seminar *Love and Death in the Uncanny Valley* that I have held very successfully (thanks to the students who took it). The entire question

of the possible prior relationship between Mother and the woman was first suggested to me in a presentation on *I Am Mother*. In fact, there are too many insights gained from these seminar discussions to acknowledge here, save to say a heartfelt thank you.

6 Oshii interview in *Ghost in the Shell: Innocence*, The making of *Ghost in the Shell* special.

7 I am quoting from the subtitles in English provided with the films. These vary, at times quite starkly, with the voice dubbing in English also provided.

8 From *The Making of Ghost in the Shell*, special.

9 Broadcast, *Good Morning America*, 28 May 2017.

10 *The Guardian*, 'Original *Ghost in the Shell* Director: "No Basis" for Whitewashing Anger', 24 March 2017. Available online: https://www.theguardian.com/film/2017/mar/24/scarlett-johansson-ghost-in-the-shell-director-whitewashing

Conclusion: An open society

Here at the end of our study, I wish to reassert the fundamental thesis of this book. Not because it is somehow concealed within the chapters that make up the book, but because it seems so important to the contemporary world in which we live. Day after day the mainstream media tell us about the possible threats of AI. Celebrity scientists and theorists, leaving behind the rational, moderate tone of scientific experimentation and communication, stoke the flames, seeming to give credence to the public's worst fears. The tendency to position AI as being as big a risk as eco-catastrophe or nuclear weapons, as does the recent Statement on AI Risk (Center for AI Safety, 2023), tends to cement it as one of human civilization's greatest threats. As with Mary Shelley's *Frankenstein* before it, the question then becomes why we, human beings, through our Promethean science, ever choose to create something that could be such a danger to us? What is it about us as a species that we are prepared to risk creating the conditions for our own demise? An answer might come when we begin to look at scientific and philosophical language out of the glare of the studio lighting. What we find when we do this is, unsurprisingly, a more moderated discourse and a non-apocalyptic perspective that treats large and bold claims about the prospects for AGI with a scepticism and a rational caution that one would expect from such sources. Melanie Mitchell, for example, writes:

> If you rely on movies and science fiction (and even some popular nonfiction) for your view of AI, you'll be afraid of AI becoming conscious, turning malevolent, and trying to enslave or kill us all. But given how far the field seems from achieving anything like general intelligence, that isn't what most people in the AI community worry about.
>
> (Mitchell, 2019: 277)

As Nigel Shadbolt and Roger Hampson put it: 'Machines are not going to march down the streets to storm our citadels. Transcendence is not inevitable: the requisite sequence of events is deeply unlikely. What *has* changed is human potential, thanks to our transformative new tools' (Shadbolt and Hampson, 2018: 63). Such reminders of where we actually are with regard to the idea of general Artificial Intelligence usually posits science fiction accounts of AI as unrealistic, fantastical and highly speculative. Indeed, like Melanie Mitchell, they even blame the arts and culture for generating an irrational fear of the creations of science.

It is obviously a matter of time, not only in terms of how far away from the Singularity we might be, but also when the appropriate time to consider ethical issues might arise. In that last sense it is interesting to note that even in a work as judicious and authoritative as Stuart Russell and Peter Norvig's *Artificial Intelligence: A Modern Approach*, we find a recognition of the need for a consideration of ethics in our future relations to the artificial intelligences we might come to create. They state, as a principal that 'All AI researchers should be concerned with the ethical implications of their work' (Russell and Norvig, 2016: 1020). At the end of their examination of 'philosophical foundations' they add:

> ... let us consider the robot's point of view. If robots become conscious, then to treat them as mere 'machines' (e.g. to take them apart) might be immoral. Science fiction writers have addressed the issue of robot rights. The movie *A.I.* (Spielberg, 2001) was based on a story by Brian Aldiss about an intelligent robot who was programmed to believe that he was human and fails to understand his eventual abandonment by his mother-owner. The story (and the movie) argue for the need to establish a civil rights movement for robots.
>
> (Russell and Norvig, 2016: 1040)

The films and television series we have been examining, by 'consider[ing] the robot's point of view', display a new awareness of the need for such civil rights, just as they also utilize their fictional stories to comment on the lack of rights for many groups of human beings, including women, people of colour, alternative sexualities, along with workers, dissidents and ultimately all othered groups. Along with these projections (into future manifestations of society and current social inequalities), they also, as works of art, plug these concerns back into older stories we have told ourselves culturally and socially. In particular, they revivify into startling new relevance the cultural myth first articulated in Mary Shelley's novel *Frankenstein*. Again and again, we have seen these films and series evoking Shelley's tale of irresponsibly created life. Now, in an age in which the consequences of the Prometheanism of industrial and post-industrial Capital is being played out in the devastations of eco-catastrophe, Shelley's novel seems to have gained a whole new relevance.

What the scientists and philosophers really seem to distrust, if we listen to them, is the power of generic form to affect public opinion. If the public, that is, is saturated with film after film in which AI turns against its human creators and seeks to destroy it, then that same public will, in its ignorance, fear AI, associating it with the generic and narrative forms made popular by cinema and television. If all we ever get in visual media representations of AI is a regurgitation of the main plot of *Frankenstein* (stripped of all the original novel's ethical complexity) then that's what will motivate people's attitude towards AI. The best examples of the new AI cinema and television try to break away from the power and influence of the popular science fiction of previous decades. *Ex Machina*, *Her*, *Westworld*, *Humans*, *Automata*, *Tau*, the *Blade Runner* films, *Ghost in the Shell*, along with recent films we've not had the chance to discuss, like *Marjorie Prime* (dir. Michael Almereyda, 2017), *Amelia 2.0* (dir. Adam Orton, 2017), and *Archive* (dir. Gavin Rothery, 2020), all attempt to produce new visions of AI, and new narrative forms for telling stories about it. They do this, as we have seen, with varied degrees of success; all of them paying witness to how much gravity and thus influence still exists in the old narratives and genres.

I tried to put a little more subtlety into our sense of the available narrative structures in my introductory chapter. But the fact remains, and it is a very good one, that the new AI cinema and television, displays no stable or strictly mappable narrative characteristics. Not all of these films are optimistic, neither are they all pessimistic, or tragic, utopian or dystopian. That a single dominant story about AI and our human reaction to it does not appear in these films and series is a fact to be celebrated. They are, at their best, films which are striving to imagine our future, rather than repeating our past anxieties and fears. That they do not always escape what I have called the gravity of old forms does not invalidate their efforts to reimagine our relationship with the technological wonders we are on the verge (however long that verge may be) of creating. What most of them do, in one form or another, is to look at the world from the non-human, the other (othered) point of view. This is a new vision, and a new challenge, one which we must take on ourselves if we are to avoid recreating our greatest nightmares.

References

Films and Television

2001, A Space Odyssey (1968), [film], Dir. Stanley Kubrick (USA and UK: Warner Bros).
28 Days Later (2002), [film], Dir. Danny Boyle (UK: Fox Searchlight).
A.I. Artificial Intelligence (2001), [film], Dir. Steven Spielberg (USA: Warner Brothers).
A.I. Rising (2018), [film], Dir. Lazar Bodroža (Serbia: Grindstone Entertainment and Lionsgate Entertainment).
Alien (1979), [film], Dir. Ridley Scott (USA: Twentieth-Century Fox).
Amelia 2.0 (2017), [film], Dir. Adam Orton (USA: Tricoast Pictures).
Annihilation (2018), [film], Dir. Alex Garland (USA: Paramount Pictures).
Archive (2020), [film], Dir. Gavin Rothery (UK: Vertical).
Automata (2014), [film], Dir. Gabe Ibáñez (Spain and Bulgaria: Contracorrientes Films).
Better Than Us (2018), [television], Created by Andrey Junkovsky, Aleksandr Dagan and Aleksandr Kessel, Prod. Paulina Andreeva (Russia: Yellow, Black and White).
Beyond Westworld (1980), [television] created by Lou Shaw (USA: CBS).
Blade Runner (1982), [film], Dir. Ridley Scott (USA: Warner Brothers).
Blade Runner 2049 (2017), [film], Dir. Denis Villeneuve (USA: Warner Brothers and Sony Pictures).
Casablanca (1942), [film], Dir. Michael Curtiz (USA: Warner Brothers).
Chappie (2015), [film], Dir. Neill Blomkamp (USA: Sony Pictures).
Citizen Kane (1941), [film], Dir. Orson Welles (USA: RKO Radio Pictures).
The Dark Knight Rises (2012), [film], Dir. Christopher Nolan (USA: Warner Brothers).
District 9 (2009), [film], Dir. Neill Blomkamp (New Zealand, USA and South Africa: Sony Pictures).
Dr Strangelove or: How I Learnt To Stop Worrying and Love the Bomb (1964), [film], Dir. Stanley Kubrick (UK and USA: Columbia Pictures).
Elysium (2013), [film], Dir. Neill Blomkamp (USA: Sony Pictures).
Ex Machina (2014), [film], Dir. Alex Garland (UK and Norway: Universal Pictures).
Fail Safe (1964), [film], Dir. Sidney Lumet (USA: Columbia Pictures).
The Fifth Element (1997), [film], Dir. Luc Besson (France: Gaumont Buena Vista International).
Futureworld (1976), [film], Dir. Richard T. Heffron (USA: American International Pictures).
Ghost in the Shell (1989–91), [anime film] Dir. Mamoru Oshii (Japan: Production I.G.).
Ghost in the Shell (2017), [film], Dir. Rupert Sanders (USA: Paramount Pictures).

Ghost in the Shell 2: Innocence (1994), [anime film] Dir. Mamoru Oshii (Japan: Production I.G. and Studio Ghibli).
Ghost in the Shell: sac_2045 (2020), [anime series] Dir. Kenji Kamiyama and Shinji Aramaki (Japan: Production I.G. and Solar Digital Arts).
Her (2014), [film], Dir. Spike Jonze (USA: Annapurna Pictures).
Hidden Figures (2016), [film], Dir. Theodore Melfi (USA: Twentieth-Century Fox).
Humans (2015–18), [television], Created Sam Vincent and Jonathan Brackley. Prod. Chris Fry (UK: Channel 4 and AMC).
I Am Mother (2019), [film], Dir. Grant Sputore (Australia: Penguin Empire Southern Lights Films).
The Imitation Game (2014), [film], Dir. Morten Tyldum (UK: The Weinstein Company).
I'm Your Man (2021), [film], Dir. Maria Schrader (Germany: Majestic Films).
Interstellar (2014), [film], Dir. Christopher Nolan (USA: Paramount).
I Robot (2004), [film], Dir. Alex Proyas (USA: Twentieth-Century Fox).
Jurassic Park (1993), [film], Dir. Stephen Spielberg (USA: Universal Pictures).
The Lady From Shanghai (1947), [film], Dir. Orson Welles (USA: Columbia Pictures).
Lucy (2014), [film], Dir. Luc Besson (France and USA: Universal Pictures).
The Machine (2013), [film], Dir. Caradog W. James (UK: Red & Black Films).
Manhattan (1979), [film], Dir. Woody Allen (USA: Jack Rollins & Charles H. Joffe Productions).
Marjorie Prime (2017), [film], Dir. Michael Almereyda (USA: BB Film Productions).
The Matrix (1999), [film], Dir. Lana Wachowski and Lilly Wachowski (USA: Warner Bros).
Memento (2000), [film], Dir. Christopher Nolan (USA: Newmarket Capital Group).
Metropolis (1927), [film], Dir. Fritz Lang (Germany: UFA).
Moon (2009), [film], Dir. Duncan Jones (UK: Sony Pictures).
Morgan (2016), [film], Dir. Luke Scott (UK: Twentieth Century Fox).
Real Humans (2012–14), [television], Created by Lars Lundström (Sweden: Sveriges SVT).
The Shining (1980), [film], Dir. Stanley Kubrick (UK and USA: Warner Bros.).
Singularity (2017), [film], Dir. Robert Kouba (Switzerland and USA: Vertical Entertainment).
Tau (2018), [film], Dir. Federico D'Alessandro (UK: Netflix).
The Terminator (1984), [film], Dir. James Cameron (USA: Orion).
Terminator 2: Judgment Day (1991), [film], Dir. James Cameron (USA: Tri Star Pictures).
Terminator 3: Rise of the Machines (2003), [film], Dir. Jonathan Mostow (USA: Warner Bros).
Terminator: Dark Fate (2019), [film], Dir. Tim Miller (USA: Paramount).
Terminator: Genysis (2015), [film], Dir. Alan Taylor (USA: Paramount).
Terminator: Salvation (2009), [film], Dir. McG (Joseph McGinty Nichol) (USA: Warner Bros).
Terminator: The Sarah Connor Story (2008–9), [television], Created by Josh Friedman (USA: Fox).
Transcendence (2014), [film], Dir. Wally Pfister (USA and New Mexico: Warner Bros).
The Usual Suspects (1995), [film], Dir. Bryan Singer (USA: Polygram Pictures).
Wall-E (2008), [film], Dir. Andrew Stanton (USA: Walt Disney).
Westworld (1973), [film], Dir. Michael Crichton (USA: Metro-Goldwyn Mayer).

Westworld (2016–21), [television], Created by Jonathan Nolan and Lisa Joy (USA: HBO).
The Wicker Man (1973), [film], Dir. Robin Hardy (UK: British Lion Film).
Zoe (2018), [film], Dir. Drake Doremus (USA: Amazon Studios).

Works Cited: Books, Essays, Articles, Reviews

Acevedo, Yoselin (2017), 'Scarlett Johansson on *Ghost in the Shell* Whitewashing Controversy: "I Would Never Presume to Play Another Race", *Indie Wire*, 9 February. Available online: https://www.indiewire.com/features/general/scarlett-johansson-ghost-in-the-shell-whitewashing-controversy-interview-marie-claire-1201780570/

Adams, James and Richard Kletter (2018), *Artificial Intelligence: Confronting the Revolution*, L. London: Endeavour Media.

Ahern, Sarah, (2017), 'Asian American Media Group Accuses Scarlett Johansson of "Lying" About *Ghost in the Shell* Whitewashing Controversy,' *PT Variety*, 31 March. Available online: https://variety.com/2017/film/news/scarlett-johansson-ghost-in-the-shell-whitewashing-1202020230/

Aldiss, Brian ([1969] 2001), 'Supertoys Last All Summer Long,' in *Supertoys Last All Summer Long and Other Stories of Future Time*, New York: St Martin's Griffin.

Allen, Graham (2008), *Mary Shelley*, London: Palgrave.

Allen, Graham (2008), *A Reader's Guide to 'Frankenstein'*, London: Bloomsbury.

Allen, Graham (2015), 'The Unempty Wasps Nest: Kubrick's *The Shining*, Adaptation, Chance, Interpretation,' in *Adaptation* 8.3: 361–71.

Allen, Graham (2020), 'Kubrick, A.I., and the Problem of Pinocchio: Reassessing the Evidence of *A.I. Artificial Intelligence*,' in *Adaptation* 14.3: 367–83. https://doi.org/10.1093/adaptation/apaa020

Allen, Graham (2021), *Intertextuality*, 3rd edn, London: Routledge.

Allen, Graham (2024), *Without Covenant*, Ennistymon: Salmon Press.

Altman, Sam (2023), Interview with Lex Fridman. Available online: https://www.com/videos/search?q=lex+fridman+sam+altman+interview&view=detai

Asimov, Isaac ([1950] 2018), *I, Robot*, London: HarperCollins.

Azevedo, Marco Antonio and Anna Azevedo (2018), 'Maeve's Dilemma: What Does It Mean To Be Free?,' in *Westworld and Philosophy*, James B. South and Kimberly S. Engels (eds), Oxford: John Wiley: 105–13.

Barthes, Roland (1978), 'An Introduction to the Structural Analysis of Narrative,' in *Image-Music-Text*, trans. Stephen Heath. New York: Hill and Wang: 79–124.

Bell, Wendell (1997), *Foundations of Future Studies: History, Purposes, and Knowledge*. Vol. 1. *Human Science for a New Era*. London: Routledge.

Betlemidze, Mariam (2022), 'Traversing Anthropocentric Horizons with *Her*: Trans-Corporeal Surrogacy, Enchantment, and Disenchantment in Human–Machine Assemblage,' *Journal of Communication Inquiry* 46.2: 206–24.

Bloom, Harold (1975), *A Map of Misreading*, Oxford: Oxford University Press.

Bloom, Harold (1982), *The Breaking of the Vessels*, Chicago: University of Chicago Press.

Bostrom, Nick (2014), *Superintelligence: Paths, Dangers, Strategies*, Oxford: Oxford University Press.
Bourdieu, Pierre ([1979] 2010), *Distinction: A Social Critique of the Judgement of Taste*, London: Routledge.
Braidotti, Rosi (2019), *Posthuman Knowledge*, Cambridge: Polity Press.
Broderick, Mick (2017), *Reconstructing Strangelove: Inside Kubrick's 'Nightmare Comedy'*, New York: Columbia University Press.
Burke, Edmund (1757), *A Philosophical Enquiry into the Origins of Our Ideas of the Sublime and the Beautiful*, London: R. and J. Dodley.
Byron, Lord George Gordan (1816), 'Darkness' in *The Poetry Foundation*, https://www.poetryfoundation.org/poems/43825/darkness-56d222aeeee1b/
Čapek, Karel ([1920] 2014), *R.U.R. (Rossum's Universal Robots)*, Harmondsworth: Penguin.
Center for AI Safety (CAIS) (2023), 'Statement on AI Risk'. Available online: https://www.safe.ai/work/statement-on-ai-risk
Chan, Mellisa (2016), 'Photo of Scarlett Johansson in *Ghost in the Shell* Reignites "Whitewashing" Controversy,' *Time*, 18 April. Available online: https://time.com/4297950/scarlett-johansson-ghost-shell-whitewashing/
Cinema Siren (2014), '*Transcendence*: What fresh HAL is this?,' 17 April. Available online: https://cinemasiren.com/cinema-siren/trancendence-transcend/
Clarke, Arthur C. (1999), *Profiles of the Future: An Inquiry into the Limits of the Possible*, London: Victor Gollanz.
Cornet, Roth (2014), '*Transcendence* Review: Siri on steroids,' *IGN*, 16 April. Available online: https://www.ign.com/articles/2014/04/16/transcendence-review
Darling, Kate (2021), *The New Breed: How to Think About Robots*, London: Allen Lane.
Dennett, Daniel C. (2017), *From Bacteria to Bach and Back the Evolution of Minds*, Harmondsworth: Penguin.
Derrida, Jacques ([1967] 1978) 'Structure, Sign, and Play in the Discourse of the Human Sciences,' in *Writing and Difference*, trans. Alan Bass, London, Routledge.
Derrida, Jacques (2000), *Of Hospitality, with Anne Dufourmantelle*, trans. Rachel Bowlby. Stanford: Stanford University Press.
Derrida, Jacques (2008), *The Animal That Therefore I Am*, New York: Fordham University Press.
Devlin, Kate (2018), *Turned On: Science, Sex and Robots*. London: Bloomsbury.
Eggert, Brian (2014), '*Transcendence*,' *Deep Focus Review*, 18 April. Available online: https://www.deepfocusreview.com/reviews/transcendence
Enjoe, Toh, Gakuto Mikumo, Kafka Asagiri, Yoshinobu Akita, Tow Ubukata (2017), *The Ghost in the Shell: Five New Stories*, New York: Vertical Press.
Francisco, Eric (2022), 'Five Years Ago *Ghost in the Machine* Accidentally Destroyed a Hollywood Racist Tradition,' *Inverse*, 31 March. Available online: https://www.inverse.com/entertainment/ghost-in-the-shell-scarlett-johansson-five-year-anniversary
Freire, Paulo ([1968] 2017), *Pedagogy of the Oppressed*, Harmondsworth: Penguin.
Freud, Sigmund ([1919] 2001), 'The Uncanny,' in *The Standard Edition of the Complete Freud*, James Strachey, Vol. 17, London: Vintage: 217–56.
Frye, Northrop (1957), *Anatomy of Criticism: Four Essays*, Princeton: Princeton University Press.

Future of Life Institute (2023), 'Pause Giant AI Experiments: An Open Letter,' 22 March. Available online: https://futureoflife.org/open-letter/pause-giant-ai-experiments/
Garcevic, Srdjan (2018), 'How "Erotising Slaves" Made Serbia's First Sci-Fi Hit,' in *Balkan Insight*, May 11. Available online: https://balkaninsight.com/2018/05/11/how-advertising-slaves-made-serbias-first-ci-fi-hit-05-04-2018/
Garland, Alex (2013), Interview DP/*30 The Oral History of Hollywood*, youtube.com. Available online: https://www.youtube.com/watch?v=96nmK9ZCl0A
Garlington, Keith (2015), 'Review: *Transcendence*,' in 'Keith and the Movies,' 12 April. Available online: https://www.ign.com/articles/2014/04/16/transcendence-review
Gaskell, Elizabeth ([1848] 1968), *Mary Barton: A Tale of Manchester Life*, Harmondsworth: Penguin.
Gawdat, Mo (2021), *Scary Smart: The Future of Artificial Intelligence and How We Can Save the World*, London: Bluebird Books.
Gittinger, Juli L. (2019), *Personhood in Science Fiction: Religious and Philosophical Considerations*, London: Palgrave MacMillan.
Godwin, William (1794), *Caleb Williams* [originally *Things as They Are; or The Adventures of Caleb Williams*], London: Printed for B. Crosby, Stationers-Court.
Goertzel, Ben (2013), 'Artificial General Intelligence and the Future of Humanity,' in Max More and Natasha Vita-More (eds.), *The Transhumanist Reader*, Oxford: Wiley-Blackwell: 128–37.
Good, Irving John (2018), [Interview] *Are We Alone? The Stanley Kubrick Extraterrestrial-Intelligence Interviews*, ed. Anthony Frewin, London: Ashgrove: 98–116.
Goody, Alex and Antonia MacKay, eds. (2019), *Reading Westworld*, London: Palgrave.
Greene, Richard and Joshua Heter, eds. (2019), *Westworld and Philosophy: Mind Equals Blown*, Chicago: Open Court.
Haraway, Donna (1991), 'A Cyborg Manifesto: Science, Technology, and Socialist-Feminism in the Late Twentieth Century,' in *Simians, Cyborgs, and Women: The Reinvention of Nature*, London: Free Association Press: 149–81.
Harlan, Jan, Jane M. Struthers, and Chris Baker (2009), *A.I. Artificial Intelligence From Stanley Kubrick to Steven Spielberg: The Vision Behind the Film*, London: Thames and Hudson.
Hawking, Stephen (2022), *Will Artificial Intelligence Outsmart Us?*, London: John Murray.
Hegel, GWF ([1807]1977), *Phenomenology of Spirit*, Oxford: Oxford University Press.
Henderson, Odie (2014), [review of *Automata*] Available online: https://www.rogerebert.com/reviews/aut%C3%B3mata-2014
Henriques, Irene and Steffen Böhm (2022), 'The perils of ecologically unequal exchange: Contesting rare-earth mining in Greenland,' in *Journal of Cleaner Production* 349, 15 May: np.
Jaynes, Julian ([1976] 2000), *The Origins of Consciousness in the Breakdown of the Bicameral Mind*. Boston: Mariner Books.
Jones, Steven (2006), *Antonio Gramsci*. London: Routledge.
Joyce, James ([1922] 2000), *Ulysses*. Harmondsworth: Penguin.
Kahn, Hermann ([1960] 2007), *On Thermonuclear War*, New Brunswick: Transaction Publishers.
Kahn, Hermann (1962), *Thinking About the Unthinkable*, New York: Avon Books.

Kahn, Hermann (1965), *On Escalation: Metaphors and Scenarios*, London: Pall Mall Press.
Kant, Immanuel ([1790] 2009), 'Analytic of the Sublime,' in *The Critique of Judgment*, James Creed Meredith and Nicholas Walker (eds.), Oxford: Oxford University Press: 75–164.
Kermode, Frank (1967), *The Sense of an Ending: Studies in the Theory of Fiction*, Oxford: Oxford University Press.
Kingwell, Mark (2020), 'Are Sentient AIs Persons?' in *The Oxford Handbook of Ethics of AI*, Markus D. Dubber, Frank Pasquale, and Sunit Das (eds.), Oxford: Oxford University Press: 325–41.
Kolbert, Elizabeth (2004), *The Sixth Extinction: An Unnatural History*. London: Bloomsbury.
Krämer, Peter (2015), 'Adaptation as Exploration: Stanley Kubrick, Literature, and AI. Artificial Intelligence,' in *Adaptation* 8.3: 372–82.
Kristeva, Julia (1980a), *Desire in Language: A Semiotic Approach to Literature and Art*. Thomas Cora, Alice Jardine and Leon S. Roudiez (eds.), New York: Columbia University Press.
Kristeva, Julia (1980b), *Powers of Horror*, trans. Leon S. Roudiez, New York: Columbia University Press.
Kurzweil, Ray (2005), *The Singularity Is Near: When Humans Transcend Biology*, London: Duckworth.
Langley, Travis and Wind Goodfriend, eds. (2018), *Westworld Psychology: Violent Delights*, New York: Sterling.
Latour, Bruno (2017), *Facing Gaia: Eight Lectures on the New Climate Regime*, Cambridge: Polity Press.
Lay, Chris (2019), 'Is Joi a Person?,' in *Blade Runner 2049 and Philosophy: This Breaks the World*, Robin Bunce and Trip McCrossin (eds.), Chicago: Open Court.
Lewis, Simon L. and Mark A. Maslin (2018), *The Human Planet: How We Created The Anthropocene*. London: Pelican.
Maitland, Sarah (2008), *A Book of Silence*, London: Granta.
Marrs, Sarah (2014), [Review of *Transcendence*], *Cinesnark*. Available online: https://cinesnark.com/2014/04/21/johnny-depp-has-officially-lost-his-touch/
Mellor, Anne K. (1990), *Mary Shelley: Her Life, Her Fiction, Her Monsters*, London: Routledge.
Melia, Matt (2017), 'The Post- Kubrick Kubrickian: Stanley Kubrick, Steven Spielberg, Adaptation and A.I. Artificial Intelligence,' in *Screening the Past* 42. Available online: http://www.screeningthepast.com/issue-42/
Meyer, Matthew (2018), 'Beauty, Dominance, Humanity: Three Takes on Nudity in Westworld,' in *Westworld and Philosophy*, James B. South and Kimberly S. Engels (eds.), Oxford: John Wiley: 196–206.
Miller, Matt, (2017), '*Blade Runner 2049* Is the Triumphant Sequel Fans Deserve,' in *Esquire* September 29. Available online: https://www.esquire.com/entertainment/movies/a12502218/blade-runner-2049-review/
Minsky, Marvin (1986), *The Society of Mind*, New York: Simon & Schuster.
Mitchell, Melanie (2019), *Artificial Intelligence: A Guide for Thinking Humans*, New York: Farrar, Strauss and Giroux.

Moll, Nicholas (2018), 'A Special Kind of Game: The Portrayal of Role-Play in *Westworld*,' in *Westworld and Philosophy*, James B. South and Kimberly S. Engels (eds.), Oxford: John Wiley: 15–25.

Moravec, Hans (1988), *Mind Children: The Future of Robot and Human Intelligence*, Cambridge, MA: Harvard University Press.

Moravec, Hans (1999), *Robot: Mere Machine to Transcendent Mind*, Oxford: Oxford University Press.

More, Max (2013a), 'The Philosophy of Transhumanism,' in Max More and Natasha Vita-More (eds.), *The Transhumanist Reader*, Oxford: Wiley-Blackwell: 3–17.

More, Max (2013b), 'A Letter to Mother Nature' in Max More and Natasha Vita-More (eds.), *The Transhumanist Reader*, Oxford: Wiley-Blackwell: 449–50.

Morton, Timothy (2016), *Dark Ecology: For a Logic of Future Coexistence*. New York: Columbia University Press.

Mulvey, Laura, (1989), 'Visual Pleasure and Narrative Cinema,' *in Visual and Other Pleasures*, London: Palgrave Macmillan: 57–68.

Nietzsche, Friedrich ([1882] 2001), *The Gay Science*, Cambridge: Cambridge University Press.

O'Connell, Mark (2017), *To Be a Machine: Adventures Among Cyborgs, Utopians, Hackers, and the Futurists Solving the Modest Problem of Death*, London: Granta.

Office of Science and Technology Policy (OSTP), 'About This Document: Legal Disclaimer'. https://www.whitehouse.gov/ostp/ai-bill-of-rights/about-this-document/

Okwodu, Janelle (2017), 'What Went Wrong with *Ghost in the Shell*?' in *Vogue*, 31 March. Available online: https://www.vogue.com/article/ghost-in-the-shell-live-action-scarlett-johansson-problems

Orbaugh, Sharalyn (2007), 'Sex and the Single Cyborg: Japanese Popular Cultural Experiments in Subjectivity,' in *Robot Ghosts and Wired Dreams: Japanese Science Fiction from Origins to Anime*, Christopher Bolton, Istvan Csicsery-Ronan Jr., and Takayuki Tatsumi (eds.), Minneapolis: University of Minnesota Press: 172–92.

O'Sullivan, Michael (2019), *Cloneliness: On the Reproduction of Loneliness*, New York: Bloomsbury.

Reiman, Donald H. and Fraistat, Neil (2002), 'A Defence of Poetry' in *Shelley's Poetry and Prose* Second Edition, New York: Norton.

Royle, Nicholas (1995), *After Derrida*, Manchester: Manchester University Press.

Russell, Stuart (2019), *Human Compatible: AI and the Problem of Control*, London: Penguin.

Russell, Stuart and Peter Norvig (2016), *Artificial Intelligence: A Modern Approach*, 4th edn, London: Pearson.

Schneider, Susan (2019), *Artificial You: AI and the Future of Your Mind*, Princeton, NJ: Princeton University Press.

Seitz, Matt Zoller (2020), 'Even Outside the Park, *Westworld* Gonna *Westworld*,' in *Vulture*, March 13. Available online: https://www.vulture.com/2020/03/westworld-season-3-review.html

Shadbolt, Nigel and Roger Hampson (2018), *The Digital Ape: How to Live (in Peace), with Smart Machines*, Melbourne: Scribe.

Shanahan, Murray (2010), *Embodiment and the Inner Life: Cognition and Consciousness in the Science of Possible Minds*. Oxford: Oxford University Press.

Shanahan, Murray (2015), *The Technological Singularity*, Cambridge, MA: MIT Press.

Shanahan, Timothy (2019), 'We're All Just Looking for Something Real,' in *Blade Runner 2049: A Philosophical Investigation*, Timothy Shanahan and Paul Smart (eds), v Abingdon: Routledge.

Shelley, Mary (2012), *Frankenstein: The Original 1818 Text, 3rd Edition*, D. L. Macdonald and Kathleen Scherf (eds.), Ontario: Broadview.

Shelley, Mary (1826), *The Last Man*, London: Henry Colburn.

Shelley, Percy Bysshe (2002), 'A Defence of Poetry' in *Shelley's Poetry and Prose, Second Edition*. Donald H. Reiman and Neil Fraistat (eds.), New York: Norton. 509–535.

Shirow, Masamune (2005), *Ghost in the Shell 2: Man-Machine Interface*, Tokyo: Kodansha Comics.

Shirow, Masamune (2007), *Ghost in the Shell 1.5: Human-Error Processor*, Tokyo: Kodansha Comics.

Shirow, Masamune (2009), *The Ghost in the Shell*, Tokyo: Kodansha Comics.

South, James B. and Kimberly S. Engels, eds. (2018), *Westworld and Philosophy*, Oxford: John Wiley.

Stolworthy John (2017), 'Scarlett Johansson breaks silence over *Ghost in the Shell* whitewashing controversy: "I certainly would never presume to play another race of a person",' in *Independent*, 8 February. Available online: https://www.independent.co.uk/arts-entertainment/films/news/scarlett-johansson-breaks-silence-over-ghost-in-the-shell-whitewashing-controversy-release-date-trailer-a7569461.html

Stork, David G. (1997), '"The Best-Informed Dream": HAL and the Vision of 2001,' in *Hal's Legacy: 2001's Computer as Dream and Reality*, David G. Stork, ed. Foreword by Arthur C. Clarke, Cambridge MA: The MIT Press: 1–12

Sutko, Daniel (2020), 'Theorizing Femininity in Artificial Intelligence: A Framework for Undoing Technology's Gender Troubles,' in *Cultural Studies*: 34.4: 567–92.

Swallow, James and Abbie Bernstein (2017), *Ghost in the Shell. The Official Novelization*, London: Titan Books.

Tambone, Lou (2018), 'Deckard B26354: Coming to Terms with Deckard Being a Replicant,' in *The Cyperpunk Nexus: Exploring the Blade Runner Universe*, Lou Tambo and Joe Bongiorno (eds.), Edwardsville, IL: Sequart Organization: 111–21.

Tegmark, Max (2018), *Life 3.0: Being Human in the Age of Artificial Intelligence*, London: Penguin.

'The Transhumanist Declaration' (n.d.). Available online: https://www.humanityplus.org/the-transhumanist-declaration

Thunberg, Greta (2019), *No One Is Too Small To Make a Difference*, London: Allen Lane.

Turan, Kenneth (2017), 'Review: "*Blade Runner 2049*" delivers a visually dazzling follow up 35 years after the original,' *Los Angeles Times*, 5 October. Available online: https://www.latimes.com/entertainment/movies/la-et-mn-blade-runner-2049-review-20171005-story.html

Turing, Alan (2013), *The Essential Turing: Seminal Writings in Computing, Logic, Philosophy, Artificial Intelligence, and Artificial Life plus The Secrets of Enigma*, ed. Jack Copeland, Oxford: Clarendon Press.

Turner, Cody and Susan Schneider (2010), 'Could You Merge with AI? Reflections on the Singularity and Radical Brain Enhancement,' in *The Oxford Handbook of Ethics of AI*, Markus D. Dubber, Frank Pasquale and Sunit Das (eds), Oxford: Oxford University Press: 307–24.

Walsh, Toby (2022), *Machines Behaving Badly: The Morality of AI*. Collingwood: La Trobe University Press and Black Inc. Books.

Weir, Andy (2014), *The Martian*, London: del Rey.

Weissberg, Jay (2014), San Sebastian Film Review: 'Automata,' in *Variety*. Available online: https://variety.com/2014/film/reviews/san-sebastian-film-review-automata-12013106.3/

White, Hayden (1973), *Metahistory: The Historical Imagination in Nineteenth-Century Europe*, Baltimore: The Johns Hopkins University Press.

Wilkinson, Amber (2014), '*Automata*,' in *Eye for Film*. Available online: https://www.eyeforfilm.co.uk/review/automata-2014-film-review-by-amber-wilkinson

Williams, Raymond (1958), *Culture and Society 1780–1850*, London: Chatto and Windus.

Yusof, Kathryn (2018), *A Billion Black Anthropocenes or None*, Minneapolis: University of Minnesota Press.

Index

abjection 49
Abraham, Nicholas 51
Acevedo, Yoselin 201
Adams, Amy 66
Adams, James 56–7
A G I (Artificial General Intelligence) 6, 16, 18, 19, 21, 42, 49, 178, 211
A.I. Artificial Intelligence 8, 15, 23, 49, 51–2, 58, 72, 96, 99, 167, 183–90, 212
A.I. Rising 160, 163–7
Alcor Life Extension Foundation, the 2–3
Aldiss, Brian 186–7, 189, 212
Alighieri, Dante 53, 190
Allen, Graham 6, 15, 31, 52
Allen, Woody 62, 67
Almereyda, Michael 213
Aloha 201
Altman, Sam 85, 118–19
Amelia 2.0 213
Andreeva, Paulina 112
Annihilation 35
Anthropic Principle 125–6
Anthropocene, the 1, 8, 13, 187–8, 194, 200
Aramaki, Shinji 208
Archive 213
Asilomar AI Principles 6, 19, 84–5
Asimov, Isaac 79–80, 81–2, 92–3, 94, 98, 112
Auret, Brandon 179
Automata 24, 92–3, 94, 96, 121, 177, 187, 213

Azevedo, Anna 14
Azevedo, Marco Antonio 143

Banderas, Antonio 94–5
Baker, Chris 187, 189, 190
Bakhtin, Mikhail M. 158
Barek, Fiston 128
Barlow, Geoff 46
Barnes, Ben 132, 135
Barthes, Roland 5
Beckett, Samuel 199
Bell, Wendell 181–2
Benjamin, Richard 132
Berdal, Ingrid Bolsø 143
Bernstein, Abbie 209
Berrington, Emily 106
Besson, Luc 79
Betlemidze, Mariam 59
Bettany, Paul 122
Better Than Us (*Luchshe, chem lyudi*) 105, 112, 163, 167
Beyond Westworld 131
Big Bang Theory, The 126
Binoche, Juliette 207
Blade Runner 22, 24, 53, 94, 96–7, 103, 140, 169, 183–4, 185–6, 187, 194–5, 198, 213
Blade Runner 2049 24, 25, 93, 96, 100–1, 184, 213
Blake, William 13, 145
Blomkamp, Neill 176, 179–80
Bloom, Harold 153, 199
Blueprint for an AI Bill of Rights 82, 103
Bodroža, Lazar 160, 163, 166

Bogart, Humphrey 92
Böhm, Steffen 80–1
Bonnar, Mark 110
Bostrom, Neil 8, 9–12, 18, 74, 77, 120
Bourdieu, Pierre 100
Boyle, Danny 76
Brackley, Jonathan 105
Bradbury, Ray 183
Bradley, Ruth 107
Braidotti, Rosi 2
Broderick, Mick 190
Bronte, Charlotte 166
Brynner, Yul 131
Burke, Edmund 53–4
Byrne, Rose 191
Byron, Lord George Gordan 185

Cameron, James 31
Cameron, Paul 149
Cameron Čapek, Karel 93
Cantillo, Jose Pablo 177
Carless, Lucy 106
Casablanca 92
Cassidy, Sonya 109
Cavazza, Sebastian 163
Centre for AI Safety 'Statement on AI risk' 211
CGI technology 23, 96
Chan, Gemma 106
Chan, Mellisa 200
Chappie 176–80
ChatGPT 118
Citizen Kane 58
Clarke, Arthur C. 183
cloneliness 54
consciousness 26–9
Copley, Sharlto 176
Cornet, Roth 123
Cox, Brian (scientist; TV presenter) 2
Cox, Brian (actor) 62
Crowe, Cameron 201
Crichton, Michael 131–2, 155
Cromwell, James 91

Curtiz, Michael 92
Cushing, Peter 135

D'Alessandro, Federico 128
D'Auria, Joey 199
Dark Knight Rises, The 123
Darling, Kate 16–17, 48
Darwin, Charles 89
Davies, Emma 107
Davies, Pixie 106
Dayne, Bella 108, 111
De Armas, Ana 97
Defence of Poetry, A 204
Defoe, Daniel 56
Dennett, Daniel C. 34
Depp, Johnny 121
Derrida, Jacques 19, 26, 133
Descartes, René 73
Deus ex machina 39, 40, 121 (see *Ex Machina*)
Devlin, Kate 57
Dirisu, Sope 106
District 9 176
Doré, Gustave 190
Doremus, Drake 67
Dr Strangelove or: How I Learnt To Stop Worrying and Love the Bomb 119, 164, 190

Ealy, Michael 162
Earl, Holly 109
Edelrezi Rising 163–7
Eggert, Brian 123
Eggert, Maren 73
Eliot, T. S. 199
Elysium 176
Enjoe, Toh 209
Epcar, Richard 196
Ex Machina 24, 29, 34–47, 48, 58, 62, 67, 93, 146, 159–60, 161, 163, 213

Fail Safe 190
Fancher, Hampton 103
Felser, Alma 73

Ferdinando, Peter 207
Ferenczi, Sándor 51
Fifth Element, The 79–80
Ford, Harrison 50, 98, 103
Foerster, Anna 149
Francisco, Eric 202
Frankenstein (cf Mary Shelley) 6, 10, 16, 29–31, 53, 88–9, 95, 135, 136, 169, 170, 175, 178, 190, 211, 213
Freud, Sigmund 48–52
Freire, Paulo 15
Freeman, Morgan 121
Futureworld 131
Future of Life Institute 6, 76, 85–6

Gallagher, John Jr. 147
Galecki, John Mark 126
Garcevic, Srdjan 163
Garland, Alex 21, 25, 34–8, 46, 76, 160, 180
Garlington, Keith 124
Gaskell, Elizabeth 33–4
Gates, Bill 118
Gawdat, Mo 15–18, 86–7, 88, 90
Gay Science, The 143
Gescheidt, Alfred 54, 77
Getzinger, Jennifer 146
Giamatti, Paul 173
Gittinger, Juli L. 19
Gleeson, Domhnall 37
Ghost in the Shell [anime] 25
Ghost in the Shell: Innocence [anime] 197
Ghost in the Shell [live action film] 24, 202, 206–8, 213
Ghost in the Shell: sac 2045 [anime series] 194, 205, 208
Godwin, William 19, 21, 117
Goertzel, Ben 19, 219
Good, Irving John 144
Google 83, 84, 86
Gosling, Ryan 96
Gramsci, Antonio 4
Grdevich, Sabrina 49, 52

Green, Michael 103
Griffith, Melanie 95

HAL 9000 49, 190, 192
Hajimohammadi, Pooneh 171
Hannah, Daryl 169
Haraway, Donna 157–8, 159, 162
Harlan, Jan 187
Hampson, Roger 212
Harris, Ed 151, 154
Harvey, Dennis 180
Hauer, Rutger 50
Hawker, Luke 191
Hawking, Stephen 17–18
Heffron, Richard T. 131
Hegel, G W F 8, 158, 193
Hemsworth, Luke 155
Henriques, Irene 80–1
Her 24, 54, 58, 62, 67, 77, 93, 125, 171, 213
Herthum, Louis 133
Hidden Figures 25
Hinton, Geoffrey 118
Hjort Sørensen, Birgitte 95
Hoeks, Sylvia 98
Hoffman, E T A 49
Hogan, Fiona 92
Holland, Jonathan 103
Hopkins, Anthony 132, 135
Hübsch, Wolfgang 74
Hüller, Sandra 73
Humans 105–12, 113, 167, 213
Hurt, William 107

I Am Mother 24, 121, 191–3, 210
Ibáñez, Gabe 93, 96, 177
IBM 83–4
Imitation Game, The 38, 169
I'm Your Man 72
Inception 123
Inferno 190
intelligence (concept) 26–9
Interstellar 49
I, Robot 29, 79, 90, 93

Jackman, Hugh 177–8
James, Caradog W. 167
James, Theo 70
Jane Eyre 166
Jason-Leigh, Jennifer 172
Jayasundera, Thusitha 108
Jaynes, Julian 137
Jentsch, Ernst 50, 54
Jeremiah, Ivanno 106
Johansson, Scarlett 59, 121, 200–2, 203, 206–7, 208, 210
Johnson, Diane 51
Jones, Duncan 50
Jones, Rashida 68
Jones, Toby 175
Jonze, Spike 25, 34, 54, 58–9, 62, 64, 77, 125, 171
Jovovich, Milla 80
Joyce, James 79
Joy, Lisa 132–3, 146, 149, 152
Jung, Carl 51
Jurassic Park (*see* Spielberg Stephen) 23
Juri, Carla 102

Kafka, Franz 98
Kahn, Herman 117–18, 120, 183
Kalimulin, Eldar 113
Kamiyama, Kenji 208
Kant, Immanuel 53–4, 55, 66
Karloff, Boris 53
Käro, Kirill 113
Kayumi, Iemasa 196
Kikuchi, Rinko 143
King Lear 9, 139
Kingsley, Ben 186–7, 209
Kingwell, Mark 82
Klimt, Gustav 46
Klein, Melanie 51
Kletter, Richard 56–7, 217
Knudsen, Sidse Babett 135
Kornienko, Vita 113
Krämer, Peter 187
Kristeva, Julia 49, 158

Kubrick, Stanley 8, 9, 22, 31, 36, 50–1, 52, 96, 119, 127, 144, 155, 164, 187, 189–90
Kurzweil, Ray 19, 111, 115–16, 117–18, 120, 125–6, 127, 182, 189

Lacan, Jacques 51
Lady From Shanghai, The 58
Lang, Fritz (*see Metropolis*)
Last Man, The (cf Mary Shelley) 185, 190
Law, Jude 50, 190
Lawrence, T E 83
Lay, Chris 99
Lemoine, Blake 35–6, 76
Leslie, Rose 173
Leto, Jared 98
Lewis, Simon L. 188
Locke, John 99
Lomonosova, Olga 113
Longinus 53
Lotz, Caity 168
Lucy (2014) 120
Lumet, Sidney 190

Machine, The 167–71
Maitland, Sarah 9, 56, 187, 189
Majer, Marusa 164
Manhattan 62, 67
Mara, Kate 172
Mara, Rooney 59
Marjorie Prime 213
Marrs, Sarah 123
Marsalis, Amanda 148
Marsden, James 134
Martian, The 56
Martin, Peter 131
Marx, Karl 193
Maskell, Neil 106
Maslin, Mark A. 188
Matrix, The (film series) 3, 8, 9, 149
Mays, Jefferson 147
McCarthy, Vincent 168
McClarnon, Zahn 145
McDermott, Dylan 94

McGregor, Ewan 67–8
McInnerny, Tim 95
Meier, Annika 74
Melia, Matt 187
Mellor, Anne K. 175–6
Memento 123
Metropolis 22, 165, 169
Melfi, Theodore 25
Meyer, Matthew 142, 162
Miller, Matt 101
Milton, John 199
Minksy, Marvin 61
Mitchell, Melanie 6, 22, 193, 211–12
Mizune, Sonoya 35
Momoi, Kaori 209
Mondrian, Piet 127
Monroe, Maika 128, 130
Moon 50
Moore's Law 206
Moravec, Hans 8–11, 15, 86, 187
More, Max 2–3, 12–13, 116, 18, 157
Morgan, Colin 106
Mori, Masohiro 48
Morton, Timothy 8
Morgan 171
Moss, Carrie-Anne 111
Mostow, Jonathon 31
Mulvey, Laura 160–1, 163
Murphy, Cillian 154
Moynahan, Bridget 90

Nam, Leonardo 141
Newton, Isaac 66
Newton, Thandiwe 50, 134, 142, 161
Nicholson, Jack 36, 52
Nietzsche, Friedrich 142–3
Ninja 177–8
Nolan, Christopher 49, 121, 123, 131
Nolan, Jonathan 131–2, 133, 147, 149, 152, 195
Norvig, Peter 212

O'Connell, Mark 12
O'Connor, Frances 49
Okwodu, Janelle 202–3
Oldman, Gary 128, 130

OpenAI 85, 118
Orbaugh, Sharalyn 208
Orton, Adam 213
Orwell, George 183
Oshii, Mamoru 194–5, 197–8, 200–1, 202, 210
O'Sullivan, James 77
O'Sullivan, Michael 56
Osment, Haley Joe 49, 52
Ôtsuka, Akio 196

Paglen, Jack 123–4
Paradise Lost 199
Parkinson, Katherine 106
Parsons, Jim 126
Patel, Dev 176
Patten, Dick van 132
Paul, Aaron 146
Pfister, Wally (*see* Transcendence)
Phoenix, Joaquin 58
Pinocchio 99, 189
Plato 45–6
Pollock, Jackson 127
post-humanism 2
Post, Todd 131
Proyas, Alex 90

Quarterman, Simon 133, 143

Rachel Wood, Evan 50, 132, 161
Radiohead 141, 152
Real Humans (Äkta människor) 105–6
Richter-Röhl, Henriette 74
Roach, Ukweli 109
Robinson Crusoe 56
Robinson, Vinette 173
Rockwell, Sam 50
Rothery, Gavin 213
Rothko, Mark 127
Royle, Nicholas 77
Rugaard, Clara 191
Russel, Stuart 212

Sakamoto, Maaya 195
Salisbury, Ben 46
Sanders, Rupert 204, 207

Sanderson, William 24
Santoro, Rodrigo 143
Sarafyan, Angela 142
Schomburg, Jan 74
Schneider, Susan 27, 28–9, 124, 153
Schrader, Maria 72, 74, 75
Scott, Luke 171
Scott, Ridley 25, 94, 96, 98, 103, 148, 194, 195
Seitz, Matt Zoller 149
Seydoux, Léa 67
Shadbolt, Nigel 212
Shakespeare, William 204
Shanahan, Murray 35–7, 42
Shanahan, Timothy 97
Shaver, Helen 152
Shaw, Bob 187
Shelley, Mary 21, 29, 53, 56, 89, 117, 175, 178, 185, 190, 211, 213
 (*See also Frankenstein*)
Shelley, Percy Bysshe 204
Shining, The 51
Shirow, Masamune 194, 203, 204–6
Simpson, Jimmi 132, 134
Singer, Bryan 44
Singularity, the 6, 63, 93, 115–16, 117, 119–20, 121–2, 127
Singularity Is Near, The 115
Skrein, Ed 128
Slocum, Ptolemy 143
Smith, Will 91–2
Sophia (Hanson Robotics) 52
South, James, B
Spacey, Kevin 44, 49
Spielberg, Steven 8, 15, 25, 49–50, 51, 72, 99, 167, 185–6, 189, 217, 212
Sputore, Grant 191
Star Wars 183
Stevens, Dan 73
Stevens, Toby 168
Stevenson, Theo 106
Stolworthy, John 201
Stork, David G. 127
Stoya 160, 164
Struthers, Jane M. 187
Stubbs, Ashley 155

Stubbs, Teddy 155
sublime, the 48, 53–4, 146
Sullivan, Chris 173
Sukezane, Kiki 143
Sutko, Daniel M. 64
Swallow, James 209
Swank, Hilary 191

Takenaka, 199
Tanaka, Atsuko 195
Tau 113, 127–8, 163, 213
Taylor-Joy, Anya 50, 172
Tegmark, Max 4–5, 25, 27, 60, 84, 182, 189
Terminator, The 3, 4–5, 22
Terminator 2: Judgement Day 3–4
Terminator (film series) 4–6, 29, 85
Thompson, Tessa 144, 161
Thoreau, Henry David 56
Thunberg, Greta 184
Time Machine, The 183
Transcendence 24, 25, 28, 93, 121, 123–124, 125, 127, 154, 180
Transhumanism 2–3, 12–13, 18–19, 84, 93, 118, 125–6, 153, 189
Trolley Problem 193
Trump, Donald 100
Torok, Maria 51
Tudor, Will 107
Tudyk, Alan 90
Turan, Kenneth 101
Turing, Alan 77
Turing Test, the 20, 37, 40, 42, 62, 79, 169–70
Turner, Cody 28, 222
 28 Days Later 76
 2001, A Space Odyssey 22, 127, 192

Usual Suspects, The 44
uncanny, the 48, 52
uncanny valley, the 10, 48–9

Vikander, Alicia 35
Villeneuve, Denis (*see Blade Runner 2049*)
Vincent, Sam 105
Vintar, Jeff 90

Virgil 190
Visser, Yo-Landi 177–8, 180
Volney, C F 190

Walden 56
Walsh, Toby 87–8, 90
War of the Worlds, The 183
Watson, Ian 9, 187–8,
    189
Wall-E 185
Weaver, Sigourney 177
Webb, Danny 106
Wells, H. G. 190
Welles, Orson 58
Westworld 21, 24, 58, 121, 131, 142, 149,
    152, 155, 161, 163, 195, 213
*White House: Guidance for Federal
    Agencies On the Regulation of
    Artificial Intelligence* 103

Wicker Man, The 172
Williams, Jaxon Thomas 162
Williams, Raymond 33
Winston, Stan 49, 96
Wittgenstein, Ludwig 46–7
Woodward, Edward 172
Woods, Mimi 195
Woodward, Shannon 134
Wordsworth, William 170
Wright, Jeffrey 134
Wright, Robin 97, 100
Wyner, Tom 196

Yamadera, Kōichi 198
Yeoh, Michelle 174
Young, Sean 98, 184

Zivkovic, Ivana 128
Zoe 58, 67